Other Books by James Montgomery Boice

Witness and Revelation in the Gospel of John
Philippians: An Expositional Commentary
The Sermon on the Mount
How To Really Live It Up
The Last and Future World
How God Can Use Nobodies
The Gospel of John: An Expositional Commentary (5 vols.)
"Galatians" in the *Expositor's Bible Commentary*
Can You Run Away From God?
Our Sovereign God, editor
The Sovereign God (Volume I of this series)
God the Redeemer (Volume II of this series)
Awakening to God (Volume III of this series)
The Foundation of Biblical Authority, editor
Making God's Word Plain, editor
Epistles of John

Foundations of the Christian Faith
VOLUME IV

GOD
& HISTORY

James Montgomery Boice

InterVarsity Press
Downers Grove
Illinois 60515

InterVarsity Press is the book-publishing division of Inter-Varsity Christian Fellowship, a student movement active on campus at hundreds of universities, colleges and schools of nursing. For information about local and regional activities, write IVCF, 233 Langdon St., Madison, WI 53703.

Distributed in Canada through InterVarsity Press, 1875 Leslie St., Unit 10, Don Mills, Ontario M3B 2M5, Canada.

Acknowledgment is made to the following for permission to reprint copyrighted material: unless otherwise indicated, the Scripture quotations in this publication are from the Revised Standard Version of the Bible, copyrighted 1946, 1952, © 1971, 1973 by the Division of Christian Education of the National Council of the Churches of Christ in the U.S.A.
From Body Life by Ray C. Stedman. © Copyright 1972. Regal Books, Ventura, CA 93006.
From "Seven Stanzas at Easter": Copyright © 1961 by John Updike. Reprinted from Telephone Poles and Other Poems, by John Updike, by permission of Alfred A. Knopf, Inc., and by permission of Andre Deutsch Limited.
From "Deacons, the Neglected Ministry," The Presbyterian Journal, 8 Nov. 1978, p. 9. Used by permission of the author, George C. Fuller, dean of faculty, Westminster Theological Seminary.

ISBN 0-87784-746-0

Printed in the United States of America

Library of Congress Cataloging in Publication Data

Boice, James Montgomery, 1938-
    God and history.

      (His Foundations of the Christian faith; v. 4)
      Includes bibliographical references and indexes.
      1. History (Theology) 2. Church. 3. Eschatology.
I. Title. II. Series.
BR115.H5B55   230'.51   80-24457
ISBN 0-87784-746-0

18	17	16	15	14	13	12	11	10	9	8	7	6	5	4	3	2	1
95	94	93	92	91	90	89	88	87	86	85	84	83	82	81			

*To him
who sits upon the throne
and to the Lamb*

PART I TIME AND HISTORY

1 What's Wrong with *Me*? *15*

2 The March of Time *27*

3 Christ, the Focal Point of History *45*

PART II THE CHURCH OF GOD

4 Christ's Church *59*

5 The Marks of the Church *73*

6 How to Worship God *87*

7 Salvation's Signs and Seals *99*

8 Spiritual Gifts *115*

9 Equipping the Saints *137*

10 Church Government *149*

11 Body Life *165*

12 The Great Commission *177*

PART III A TALE OF TWO CITIES

13 The Secular City *189*

14 The Secular Church *201*

15 God's City *213*

16 Church and State *229*

PART IV THE END OF HISTORY

17 How Will It All End? *247*

18 Home at Last *261*

Notes *273*

Subject Index *281*

Scripture Index *286*

Preface

In the preface to the third volume in this series, I referred to America's current preoccupation with the self. That volume dealt with the application of salvation to the self by the Holy Spirit. We were already looking beyond the self, of course; it meant viewing the self in relationship to God. In this volume we want to look at the individual in light of two other relationships: to other believers and to history.

The trouble with our current preoccupation with self is not that the self in unimportant. The individual is important because God has made us in his image. That means we possess intrinsic value and are able to enter into a personal and productive relationship with him. But when we concentrate on the self alone—*my* spiritual progress, *my* spiritual experience, *my* personal fulfillment—we are doomed to frustration because *we* are not the end or the center of the universe (however much we sometimes wish we were). God has put us in a context. He has placed us spatially, making us members of a specific, geographically located body of his people on earth.

He has placed us in time; we are members of that particular body of believers in these decades of this century, for example, and not another. Those two dimensions, space and time, are the warp and woof of our existence.

For the Christian, life is filled with meaning. The believer has entered a fellowship that is meaningful in itself and has been placed in history in such a way that what he or she does, whether for good or evil, matters eternally.

These four volumes have paralleled the structure developed by John Calvin in his *Institutes of the Christian Religion*. Volume one corresponds roughly to Calvin's Book I, in which he discussed the doctrine of God the Father. Volume two corresponds to his Book II, in which he discussed doctrines associated with the Lord Jesus Christ as Redeemer. Volume three corresponds to Calvin's Book III, in which the work of the Holy Spirit in the application of salvation is dominant. This volume deals with the church, the fourth of Calvin's sections. My studies, however, have ranged over matters not discussed by Calvin and have neglected matters important to him. Those deviations are nowhere more apparent than in this final study. Calvin was carrying on a polemic against sixteenth-century Roman Catholicism, which is of little interest to me. He had almost no concern for developing a Christian view of history, which I consider to be of paramount importance for the well-being of twentieth-century Christians.

In my discussion of the doctrine of the church, I have been helped immeasurably by others who have been exploring the nature of the church and its ministry in recent days: Ray C. Stedman, Gene A. Getz, John R. W. Stott, Elton Trueblood, Keith Miller and others. I have also been helped by older thinkers such as James Bannerman, a Scottish preacher and thinker of the nineteenth century, and, of course, John Calvin. It has been harder to find good contemporary Christian works on history, but I have read and drawn upon works by Reinhold Niebuhr, Oscar Cullmann, R. G. Collingwood,

Herbert Butterfield and others. The debt to these men shows up in the writing. In places I have drawn upon material already published by myself in other volumes. This is indicated in the notes.

I wish to express appreciation to Miss Caecilie M. Foelster, my secretary, who assists in the production of all my books. She carries the heavy burden of typing, proofreading and preparing the indexes. I am also thankful to the congregation of Tenth Presbyterian Church in Philadelphia, to whom these chapters were first preached in sermon form and who responded with many helpful comments and suggestions.

Each of these volumes bears a biblical dedication to God in terms appropriate to the subject matter of the volume. This one is "to him who sits upon the throne," as Lord and Judge of history, "and to the Lamb," who has redeemed us by specific acts within history's flow. May he be honored in the sale and use of this book and may many find him to be Lord of their personal history because of it.

PART I
TIME AND HISTORY

That which we have seen and heard
we proclaim also to you, so that you may have
fellowship with us; and our
fellowship is with the Father and with
his Son Jesus Christ.
(1 Jn. 1:3)

"Our Father who art in heaven,
Hallowed be thy name. Thy kingdom come,
Thy will be done, on earth as it is in heaven."
(Mt. 6:9-10)

But when the time had fully come, God
sent forth his Son, born of woman,
born under the law, to redeem those who were
under the law, so that we might
receive adoption as sons.
(Gal. 4:4-5)

1 WHAT'S WRONG WITH *ME?*

Margaret Halsey is an author whose work has appeared in *Newsweek* magazine. I mention her because an article she wrote, "What's Wrong With Me, Me, Me," is an excellent reference point with which to begin this book. As Halsey pointed out, ours has rightly been termed the "me" generation and our recent past the decade of the new narcissism. The outlook on life to which those designations point is based on the idea that "inside every human being, however unprepossessing, there is a glorious, talented and overwhelmingly attractive personality [which] will be revealed in all its splendor if the individual just forgets about courtesy, cooperativeness and consideration for others and proceeds to do exactly what he or she feels like doing."[1]

With such a philosophy, however narrow or even wrong it may be, one would expect that people would at least have the best of all chances for fulfilling themselves. But it does not work that way. In spite of almost unlimited indulgence and uninhibited expression, the cult of *self* has left thousands dissatisfied.

There are many disadvantages to the self-absorbed world view. One is the tendency of the individual to manipulate others for his or her own gratification—a disadvantage to the other person as well as to the manipulator. The typical male egoist lauded by the *Playboy* philosophy is an example. He uses women much as he uses cars, stereo sets or clothes: to enhance his self-image and increase his pleasure. A tendency to manipulation can also be seen in some segments of the women's liberation movement, even though in theory it rejects the *Playboy* attitude. Writing in *Harper's,* contributing editor Sally Helgesen speaks of the view that a woman's goal should be to "eat, sleep, make love, watch television, listen to music, go out, come in, read, use the telephone, write, type, talk, work, sing —when you want to," noting that such a goal is in reality no different from the *Playboy* world view and therefore is equally subject to commercial exploitation. "This imaginative creed, wherein the tenets of a timeless hedonism are harnessed to serve the ends of a consumer culture, is attended by all kinds of clever justifications, which assure the adherent that, by thinking of his own needs first, he will somehow benefit mankind in the long run."[2]

Frustration is a second disadvantage to the cult of self. Fulfillment does not come from unlimited self-expression or indulgence. If people think it should, they are inevitably frustrated or even angered when things do not work out as they anticipate. A warping of the personality or an unreasonable tendency to blame others—husband or wife, politics, the state, the environment or God—is the result.

Search for Answers

In her article Halsey suggests a number of flaws in the self-absorbed world view. She argues first that the basic theory "that inside every human being ... there is a glorious, talented and overwhelmingly attractive personality" is false. Although there may be attractive elements in everyone, the reality of human nature is that "a mess of unruly primitive impulses" spoils our "self-discovery." When people say, "I don't know who I am," what they actually mean is that they are not satisfied with what they know themselves to be. Since they do not know how to be delivered from themselves or change themselves, they turn their backs on the unpleasant facets of their being. Second, Halsey argues that "a search for identity is predestined to fail" for the simple reason that identity is not something _found_ but rather something _made_ through choices, hard work and commitments to others.

Here Christianity is in hearty support of Halsey's thesis, although it would state it in even stronger terms. It would agree that within the heart of the individual there is "a mess of unruly primitive impulses." But the situation is worse. The heart is "dull" (Mt. 13:15), "proud" (Lk. 1:51), "hard and impenitent" (Rom. 2:5) and filled with "lusts" (Rom. 1:24). Above all, it is set rebelliously against God (Mt. 15:8). Jesus taught that the largest part of the world's evil comes out of such a heart (Mt. 15:18-19). The individual needs a new heart —forgiveness—and a new life through the work of God's Son.

Christianity also stresses that identity is something to be developed. True, it speaks of an identity that is given to us by revelation and redemption. We are creatures of God who are brought into the family of God by Christ's work. But Christianity speaks of a developing sense of identity—as those who have been saved by Christ enter increasingly into an experiential knowledge of Jesus and his character through the work of the Spirit of God in their hearts. That is what Christian theology calls sanctification.[3]

Yet Christianity shines out against any merely secular analysis. It goes on to speak of the church and history as a further and fuller answer to the human dilemma. The human being has many needs: to know God, for salvation, of a power able to overcome the sinful and debilitating tendencies of his or her nature. But in addition there is a need for relationships on the highest level and a sense of purpose and belonging within history.

The contemporary pursuit of the self erupts in two main agonies: isolation (with its accompanying sense of cosmic loneliness) and meaninglessness. According to the Bible, God has dealt with the first through creation of the church, to which a believer in Christ automatically belongs, and with the second by the incorporation of the Christian into the meaningful flow of biblical history.

The People of God

Roman Catholics have an expression—"No one has God for his Father who does not also have the Church for his Mother" —which, although it is sometimes used wrongly to maintain that there is no salvation outside the Roman Catholic Church, nevertheless has an element of truth. Fellowship with God inevitably brings fellowship with other Christians within the body of the church. The apostle John indicated this in the opening verses of his first letter: "That which we have seen and heard we proclaim also to you, so that you may have fellowship with us; and our fellowship is with the Father and with his Son Jesus Christ" (1 Jn. 1:3). Here are two fellowships: with God and with other Christians. Yet nothing in this verse indicates that either one of them can be had without the other. Rather, they are one fellowship. To have fellowship with other Christians is to enter into fellowship with the Father. To have fellowship with the Father is to have fellowship with those for whom Christ also died. It is to be a part of God's family.

People today and in every age need to understand this. When God created a companion for Adam he explained his action by saying, "It is not good that the man should be alone" (Gen. 2:18). That expresses God's reasons for marriage, but also refers to the whole of life. Isolation is not good. People need fellowship, and it is God's will that they should have it.

Lacking the true and fulfilling fellowship that God means for them to have, many people go about establishing an empty kind of "fellowship" based more on proximity than on true relationships. The camaraderie of the social club is one example. So is the frenzied interaction of the discotheque. These groupings of people have been popular because they substitute proximity for true community and thereby help people to forget the fundamental and tragic loss of personal identity that drives them there.

Four kinds of loss of identity are common today: loss of family identity, national identity, religious identity and personal identity. Each is supplied in the church, even though the other supportive institutions which we should ideally enjoy—an understanding and stable family and a country of which one can be proud—may be lacking.

The church was established on earth for several purposes: worship, service, organized dissemination of the gospel. In addition to these obvious purposes, another chief end of the church is the union of Christ's followers into one visible fellowship and the substitution of a social for a "privatized" Christianity. Nothing that rightly pertains to the relationship of an individual to God is set aside by that fact. On the contrary, one's relationship to God is actually to be developed and expanded by relationships with other believers.

James Bannerman, who wrote a study of the church as an outgrowth of his lectures to theological students in Scotland in the nineteenth century, declared,

> There is something in the very nature of man that makes union and fellowship with other men essentially necessary to develop the whole faculties and powers of his being; and this characteristic of man's nature has been taken advantage of in the economy of grace; so that, under the power of association, believers are not merely or only units in the dispensation of God, but brethren also in the enjoyment of communion with each other collectively, as well as in the enjoyment of communion individually, each one with

his Savior. According to the arrangement of God, the Christian is more of a Christian in society than alone, and more in the enjoyment of privileges of a spiritual kind when he shares them with others, than when he possesses them apart. . . . Such, for example, is the blessing promised to "two or three" when "gathered together in the name of Christ," over and above what is promised to the solitary worshipper; and such is the more abundant and gracious answer that will be returned to prayer, when men, even a few, "shall agree together to ask anything of God," rather than when they ask separately and alone. . . .

The Christian Church was established in the world, to realize the superior advantages of a social over an individual Christianity, and to set up and maintain the communion of saints. In his union to Christ the Head, the individual believer becomes ingrafted into the same body, and partakes of the same privileges with other believers. He is one with them in the same Spirit, in the same faith, in the same baptism, in the same hopes, in the same grace, in the same salvation. The bonds of that spiritual union go to strengthen his own individual Christianity, the sympathy of it to call forth his own individual affections, and the incitement of it to enlarge his own personal faith and hope; so that, in the fellowship of the Church, and within the magic circle of its influences, the believer is in a more eminent sense a believer, than apart from them.[4]

Warp and Woof

God's answer to human isolation and meaninglessness is not only the church, through which the individual enters into fellowship with others of like mind. Entering into the church also brings the Christian into the flow of biblical history, which makes one's own life meaningful. The church locates believers spatially. They belong to the church of God at Jerusalem or Rome or New York or London, to use the New Testament method of referring to churches. History locates believers in time—in the twentieth century, for example, rather than in the period of the early church or the age of the Reformation.

Biblical religion is historical and the God of the Bible is pre-eminently the God of history. That factor more than any other sets Judaism and Christianity off from the religions among which they flourished. In Old Testament times virtually all the religions of the peoples surrounding the Hebrews were nature religions. They identified the most high god or gods with the sun, winds, rains, seasons. In some cases, as in the religion of Baal, which was a constant threat to Israel through much of its history, those identifications produced a fertility religion. At particularly low periods even the human reproductive organs were worshiped. The same was true in Egypt. In all cases, the flow of the religion was cyclical—from one moon to the next or from one harvest to the next—and history as such had no meaning.

The religion of the Old and New Testaments is different. Note how God called Abraham: "Go from your country and your kindred and your father's house to the land that I will show you. And I will make of you a great nation, and I will bless you, and make your name great, so that you will be a blessing. I will bless those who bless you, and him who curses you I will curse; and by you all the families of the earth shall bless themselves [or, will be blessed]" (Gen. 12:1-3). Two features of this call stand out. First, the call was in the nature of a promise or covenant made by God to Abraham—it was unsolicited by Abraham. Second, it was made in and is to be fulfilled in history. As we read the biblical history that follows, we realize that this historical fulfillment unfolded over a considerable period of time. Abraham did leave his own land, and God did bring him to a new land. But the nation that was to descend from him did not come into existence during Abraham's lifetime, in fact not until several generations later. Nor did the full measure of the blessing come until the appearance of the Messiah at the start of the Christian era.

Another milestone in the historical religion of the Old Testament was the deliverance of the descendants of Abraham, by then a large nation, from Egypt. In that deliverance, God altered the normal behavior of the elements, animal life and heavenly bodies to bring judgments on Pharaoh and force him to let the people go (Ex. 5:1). Because of that deliverance, Israel was to worship the Lord and obey the ethical commandments he gave them (Ex. 20:1-17). The covenant made with Abraham was reiterated but this time with a balance of blessings and curses depending on the people's obedience or disobedience (Deut. 11, 27, 28).

During David's reign a promise was given of One who would govern Israel forever (2 Sam. 7:12-16).

In each of these milestones in God's dealings with his people the historical element is dominant. God intervenes and guides in history so that the promises he has made to his people might be fulfilled. History is going someplace, according to this system of thought, and because it is going someplace it has meaning to the individuals who by God's grace are caught up in it.

The appearance of Jesus of Nazareth brought this period of promise and expectation to a climax, but it also launched a new period of history which flows from his work of redemption. The appearance of Jesus was the *decisive* intervention of God in history. It gave the conclusive meaning to history as well as the basis for judgment upon it.

The Greek language has many words for time: *hēmera* (day), *hōra* (hour), *kairos* (season), *chronos* (time), *aiōn* (age) and others. The most important word is *kairos,* which is used repeatedly of the coming of Christ and of his death and resurrection as the key moments or events in that coming. The impact of this word is best seen by contrasting it with *chronos.* Both *kairos* and *chronos* refer to time and are frequently translated *time* in our Bibles. But *chronos* refers to the flow of time, the following of one event upon another. We have this idea in our word *chronology*. *Kairos* refers to a moment in time that is especially significant or favorable. It can be used secularly as in the words of King Felix to Paul, "When I have an *opportunity* I will summon you" (Acts 24:25). But *kairos* is especially appropriate in referring to the appearance of Christ. Thus, Peter wrote of the Old Testament prophets' inquiry about "what person or *time* was indicated by the Spirit of Christ within them when predicting the sufferings of Christ and the subsequent glory" (1 Pet. 1:11). Jesus referred to his Passion as his *kairos:* "My *time* is at hand" (Mt. 26:18). In John's Gospel the same effect is achieved by Christ's reference to the *hour* of his death and glorification (Jn. 2:4; 7:30; 8:20; 12:23; 13:1; 16:32; 17:1).

Jesus was a figure of history whose life and teachings may be investigated by normal academic techniques. Whenever that truth is lost, Christianity itself is lost, for it is and must be historical. Yet the life of Christ is even more than this— it is *historic*. The meaning of all history is disclosed in the history of the Lord Jesus Christ, and a choice between commitment to him or rejection of him and his history determines our destiny.

That line of thought brings us back sharply to the dilemma of contemporary men and women. We have seen that the two felt needs of our age, a need for identity and a need for significance or meaning, are met by incorporation into the church and into biblical history. But here we must say that only through faith in Christ and commitment to Christ does that incorporation take place. True, the church is the answer to loneliness on the deepest level. But it is Christ's church. It is his body (1 Cor. 12:27; Eph. 1:23; Col. 1:18), and he is the door through whom alone we are enabled to enter into its fellowship (Jn. 10:7-10).

The answer to meaninglessness is to enter into the flow of meaningful history. It is Christ's history, and the way into it is through him.

One Minute to Twelve

Without the church we are left with a religion of pure individualism in which each person does what is right in his or her own eyes. Without a biblical view of history we are left with a religion of nebulous love and sentimental fellowship. Both are needed. Only then are we part of a company on the move, a company seeking to carry out the directives of God for our time and place—knowing that the results will be significant.

Some years after the end of World War 2 an English historian, Herbert Butterfield, wrote a book on the Christian view of history. In it he tried to set the events of the recent past in perspective and to rally believers to significant and ethical behavior. He wrote,

> *It has always been realized in the main tradition of Christianity that if the Word was made flesh, matter can never be regarded as evil in itself. In a similar way, if one moment of time could hold so much as this, then you cannot brush time away and say that any moment of it is mere vanity. Every instant of time becomes more momentous than ever—every instant is "eschatological," or, as one person has put it, like the point in the fairy-story where the clock is just about to strike twelve. On this view there can be no case of an absentee God leaving mankind at the mercy of chance in a universe blind, stark and bleak. And a real drama—not a madman's nightmare or a tissue of flimsy dreams—is being enacted on the stage of human history. A real conflict between good and evil is taking place, events do matter, and something is being achieved irrespective of our apparent success or failure.*[5]

That insight is one that every Christian, and not just a Christian historian, should share.

I conclude this chapter with one more biblical word for time, the word *now (nun)*. It shows us that the *kairos* in which we live is of eternal importance: "Once you were no people but *now* you are God's people; once you had not received mercy but *now* you have received mercy" (1 Pet. 2:10); "Blessed are you that hunger *now*, for you shall be satisfied. Blessed are you that weep *now,* for you shall laugh" (Lk. 6:21); "Behold, *now* is the acceptable time; behold, *now* is the day of salvation" (2 Cor. 6:2).

If Christ's life counted in the flow of history, then by God's grace and by union with Christ our lives can count too. Our *now* matters.

2 THE MARCH OF TIME

During World War 2 and for a number of years before and after, a series of popular newsreels was shown weekly in most American movie theaters. The series, produced by the Time/Life corporation, was called *The March of Time*. Stirring march music, the voice of an enthusiastic and assured announcer, a sequence of scenes from around the world impressed the viewer with all that seemed to be happening in this "modern," fast-paced age. The title of the series said it all. Time really did seem to be marching along, perhaps even racing. It was an age of progress. So, although there was often bad news—about military reverses, for example—few doubted that time would eventually take care of things and that progress would be inevitable.

How times have changed! Today people are not at all sure that progress is inevitable (though they often speak as if that were the case). Progress requires planned or directed motion, and that requires both a Planner and a plan. Today people are not so sure that either a Planner or a plan exists. The optimistic, progressive view of history of an earlier age has given way to a view that sees history as just possibly a series of unrelated and uncontrolled motions. And that is frightening.

Does history march? If it does, to what drummer? The only way to answer these questions is to go back to the beginning and ask where the modern view of historical progress came from and on what grounds it was believed. We have to begin with the ancient view of history which the modern view replaced.

Round She Goes

Although the Greeks epitomize the ancient view of history, it is sometimes said that they were not interested in history. That is not an entirely fair comment on a race that produced such historians as Herodotus, who chronicled the rise of Greece, and Thucydides, who recorded its decline. But there is more than an element of truth in that negative statement, despite those two eminent figures.

The Greeks' interest in history, insofar as it existed (and it was not universal), was directed to where their own race and its unique outlook on life had come from. But while they undoubtedly considered themselves to be a giant step beyond and above the barbarism which preceded them, they did not think of that as a stage in some unending upward movement of the race. Rather it was a peak that would inevitably give way to poorer times again. The Greek view of time was circular. That is, there was undoubtedly change in history, but it was change that constantly returned upon itself, just as the planets or seasons do. Nations had risen to power in the past and had then declined. They would do so again. The citizens of those nations did not "get anywhere" by their rise, nor did others "advance" by their fall. The only meaning was in the circle itself, and the only salvation for a person caught up in such a circle was to escape from it. As far as history was concerned, the Greeks would have had no trouble applying the carnival barker's description of his wheel of fortune: "Round and round and round she goes, and where she stops nobody knows."

The classical view of the Greeks involved five propositions:

1. The Greeks had no interest in the past, in the sense of studying it to seek reasons for why things are as they are. It may be true, R. G. Collingwood maintains,[1] that Herodotus was an exception at this point, but the dominant view was that if the past had interest at all it was only as an illustration of those characteristics of human thought and behavior that were also observable in the present.

2. They had no real interest in the future.

3. Nothing new was to be expected in history. Epicurus said, "Nothing new happens in the universe, if you consider the infinite time past."[2] Marcus Aurelius, a later Roman Stoic philosopher, said the same thing:

The rational soul ... traverses the whole universe, and the surrounding vacuum, and surveys its form, and it extends itself into the infinity of time, and embraces and comprehends the periodical renovation of all things, and it comprehends that those who come after us will see nothing new, nor have those before us seen more, but in a manner he who is forty years old, if he has any understanding at all, has seen by virtue of the uniformity that prevails all things that have been and all that will be.[3]

4. Human bondage to time through bodily existence is a curse.

5. Salvation is deliverance from that eternal circular course and therefore from time itself. Plato gave a classic expression to that thought: "The soul ... is ... dragged by the body into the region of the changeable, and wanders and is confused; the world spins round her, and she is like a drunkard when under their influence.... But when returning into herself she reflects; then she passes into the realm of purity, and eternity, and immortality, and unchangeableness, which are her kindred, and with them she ever lives ... and being in

communion with the unchanging is unchanging."[4]

We may summarize by saying that for the Greeks the events of history were cyclical and that salvation consisted in being freed from history through rational thought.

Inevitable Progress

It would be difficult to show, even in a very long essay, how and at what point the classical view of history passed over into the modern notion of historical progress. It is enough to say that Christianity had a major if not exclusive role in that transformation.

Christianity brought to the picture its doctrine of a God who revealed himself in history, the point made in the last chapter. God was neither the futile, half-human, half-divine gods and goddesses of the Greek pantheon nor the unchanging and unchangeable First Mover of the Greek philosophers. This God loved his people, grieved for his people and moved heaven and earth, as it were, for their deliverance. Another element that Christianity brought into the picture was its view of the human being, not as a divine soul imprisoned in a perishable and evil body (as the Greeks thought), but as a union of body, soul and spirit all created in God's image. Each part of the human being was important and valuable. Salvation was to be conceived, therefore, not as salvation of the soul or spirit alone but of the body as well, through a final historical resurrection. Finally, Christianity introduced a heightened moral consciousness which required a final balancing out of rewards and punishments at the last judgment.

Those doctrines slowly worked their way into history. During the Middle Ages, Christianity mingled with Platonism and Aristotelianism to produce an otherworldliness that often obscured Christianity's historical interests. But in the late sixteenth and seventeenth centuries—first through the budding scientism of Francis Bacon (1561-1626) and then through the philosophy of such thinkers as René Descartes

(1596-1650) and Baruch Spinoza (1632-77)—the value of knowledge, perceived by the Greeks, and the idea of a flow of history, derived from Christianity, were combined into a faith in inevitable scientific and social progress. That view flowered in the eighteenth-century rise of science and the nineteenth-century rise of industry—the Industrial Revolution. At the end of that period, when Charles Darwin (1809-82) introduced the idea of an evolutionary progression among living things, the victory of the new outlook seemed complete.

Gordon H. Clark summarizes the matter by showing that this final, mature view of history as progress involved three cardinal doctrines and was based upon three supposedly adequate causes.

1. Progress is a natural process and must always have been in operation.

2. Progress must occur in all spheres. There must be social, moral and philosophical improvement as well as scientific advance.

3. If progress is conceived of as a natural law, then it must be necessary and inevitable.

These points gave the nineteenth and early twentieth centuries their optimism. It was believed that, although there are sometimes setbacks in history through mistakes in judgment, it is nevertheless the nature of the human will to seek progress, and that innate desire, like any other "natural" law, will win out ultimately. The causes of such progress are the accumulation of _knowledge,_ political and social _planning_ and biological _evolution._[5]

Each of these three causes is today increasingly seen to be inadequate to sustain such optimism. The advance of scientific knowledge is obviously inadequate for the reason that nothing in the scientific enterprise in itself determines how the discoveries of science are to be used. Science can produce atomic energy, but the energy can then be used to produce nuclear weapons as well as to provide for peacetime nuclear power stations—and even those stations are not unambiguously a step forward. Science can produce a seemingly infinite variety of things for the hyped-up consumer market. But it is questionable whether such multiplication is progress, or whether it is not rather a case of the soul being suffocated beneath its possessions.

Again, there is faith in social planning, but what does that amount to? It is questionable whether political and social planning really work, to begin with. In our day most major problems seem to be beyond the solutions proposed for dealing with them—inflation, international unrest, crime, irrational violence, to name just a few. But even if it were true that such planning could be effective, there is still no guarantee that the planning would be put to truly "progressive" ends. In the hands of evil rulers, for example, such planning could be used to debase and enslave a people.

Finally, as far as evolution is concerned, the arrogance of those who assume the human race to be the epitome of biological advance seems ludicrous in view of our ability to blow ourselves off the face of the planet.

In his treatment of these themes, Clark makes one other sly observation, asking if a philosophy of progress does not itself ultimately require its own rejection. He asks,

> *If progress is the law of history, if our moral and intellectual baggage is superior to that of antiquity; and if our society and our ideas are to grow into something better and vastly different; if our imagination is to evolve to a degree not now imaginable; if all the old concepts which served their time well are to be replaced by new and better concepts, does it not follow that the theory of progress will be discarded as an eighteenth and nineteenth century notion, which no doubt served its age well, but which will then be antiquated and untrue? Could it be that the best contemporary evidence of progress is a growing disbelief in "progress"?* [6]

No doubt the values of these arguments vary, but their accumulated weight is such that the optimistic view of history as progress which dominated the nineteenth century can now be said to be shattered. It has been shattered by two world wars, numerous small wars and their accompanying atrocities. One war might be termed an aberration, a war "to make the world safe for ... whatever." But a sequence of wars and other horrors demands a more rigorous explanation.

Are we to say that the modern view of historical progress is entirely mistaken? Shall we conclude that history contains no meaning after all? Must we return to the historical escapism of the Greeks and other ancient peoples? That is not necessary. What is necessary is a return to the biblical view of history in which God, not human beings, is in control. His will, rather than human will or some abstract historical principle, is done. Christians express confidence in this and desire for it when they pray, "Thy kingdom come, Thy will be done, On earth as it is in heaven" (Mt. 6:9-10).

A Christian View of History

Those sentences from the Lord's Prayer illustrate several components of a Christian view of history: a goal (God's kingdom), a struggle (the recognition that God's kingdom does not naturally come, nor is his will naturally done, without opposition), human responsibility (to pray for and work toward the realization of that kingdom). But a better way of tracing a Christian view of history is inherent in the unique biblical doctrines that bear upon it: creation, providence, revelation, redemption and judgment. When applied to history those doctrines teach that there is a comprehensive and universal history of the human race; that God controls history; that because of this, history has a pattern or goal; that God acts redemptively in history; and that men and women are responsible for what they do or do not do within history's flow.

1. The first teaching is the biblical _doctrine of creation:_ the

world is not eternal but came into being as an expression of God's will and through his explicit acts. The natural world is viewed as the backdrop for the world of men and women (Gen. 1). That is, the human race is not one minor or accidental part of an eternal order of things but rather a specific and valuable part of creation, for which the other parts were brought into existence. The entire human race descended from one original pair, Adam and Eve, and is therefore one, despite subsequent division into national or ethnic groups. The purpose of history must involve all these groups and not merely Western or other "favored" ones.

The ancient world had no philosophy like this anywhere, nor is any like it today except through borrowings from Christianity. The Greeks had no concept of creation; for them matter was eternal. Nor did they have anything like a universal outlook in which all human beings from all races were part of one grand picture or design.

The need for a universal scope for history has been stressed only recently by secular historians. One thinks of the histories of Oswald Spengler and Arnold J. Toynbee. What is unique about these authors is their explicit desire to write a universal history of the race. Spengler in his two-volume *Decline of the West*[7] is critical of his predecessors at this point. He says they have been provincial in thinking that Europe is the all-important center of history simply because they happened to live there. They have neglected other people and areas. More serious than their provincialism, however, is the error of interpretation to which such provincialism leads. By restricting one's concern to Europe it may be possible to devise the kind of progressive view of history the historians of recent centuries have provided. But when one looks beyond Europe to Asia and other previously neglected areas of the world one sees at once that history is not an upward linear process but rather a phenomenon in which cultures are born, grow strong, deteriorate and die. On the basis of that analogy Spengler predicted the West's decline (hence the title of his book). That prediction gained him instant recognition.

Toynbee is more optimistic than Spengler and also less pretentious. His work is called _A Study of History,_[8] that is, he regarded it as merely one interpretation among many and not as _the_ interpretation of history for all time. Although different in approach, Toynbee's object is the same as Spengler's, namely, to bring all history within one overall framework. In doing that he has isolated thirty-four civilizations, including thirteen "independent" civilizations, fifteen "satellite" civilizations and six "abortive" civilizations. Each is characterized by a dominant motif.

Here is the interesting thing. Although both Spengler and Toynbee seem alert to the fact that the human race is one and that the history of the race should therefore be a universal history, their histories are remarkably different. It is striking how little overlap there is between them. What is wrong? Does this mean that desire for a universal history is misplaced, that no one history exists after all? Not necessarily. But significant divergence between such great historians as Spengler and Toynbee does point out how difficult it is for one human mind to grasp a subject of such proportions. That point can be put even more strongly. Since the writing of history involves a selection and interpretation of facts and since selection is always made at least in part on the basis of the subjective experience and judgment of the interpreter, it is impossible to write a purely objective history. Historical interpretations of this scope, or even of a more limited scope, will always differ. The only way out of the problem is for us to receive an interpretation of history from outside history, as it were, from a Being who perfectly understands history but who is above and beyond it and is therefore not affected by the distortions and prejudices that living and working in history introduce. The only way to have an objective and universal view of history is for God, the God of history, to provide it.

Christianity maintains that God has done that. When we talk of a doctrine of creation and its implications for a universal view of history, we do so only because God has first revealed these things to us through the holy Scriptures.

2. Such reasoning leads naturally into the Christian doctrine of revelation, but before considering that point, it is necessary to look at the *doctrine of providence* which also follows naturally the doctrine of creation. The Bible reveals that having created the world God did not then abandon it, as if it were a large mechanical clock which he had wound up and was then allowing to run down. On the contrary, God guides the development of history through his eternal decrees and sometimes intervenes supernaturally both in nature and history to accomplish them.

The doctrine of divine providence puts a Christian view of history into categories entirely different from those of naturalism. The naturalist believes that there are certain unalterable laws to history according to which it is possible to predict what is coming. Spengler is an example of that view; he has used laws of birth, growth, decline and death to predict the fall of Western civilization. An even better example is Karl Marx (1818-83), who reduced the laws of history to materialistic or economic factors. Marx was influenced by Hegel's dialectic, but he boasted that he had stood the dialectic on its head. What he meant was that Hegel had made the spirit of rationality the determining factor in the eternal flow from thesis to antithesis to synthesis, whereas he, by contrast, had based even those rational forces on nature. Marx's view was that of Ludwig Feuerbach (1804-72), who taught by use of a pun in the German language that *der Mensch ist was er isst* (man is what he eats). According to his view, materialistic or economic factors are everything—with the result that class struggle, revolutionary action and eventually the classless society are the inevitable products of them.

Christians are not locked into such determinism. According to the Bible, God does have a plan in history and history is following out that plan. But that does not mean that the outworking of this plan is mechanical. Here, of course, we get into one of the great mysteries of the Christian faith: the relationship between the eternal decrees or will of God and contrary human wills. We cannot always say precisely how that relationship works, but we can say that each is real and that the flow of history is therefore wrapped up at least partially in human obedience to or rebellion against God. The most important consequences of that human factor in regard to God's plan in history is that his plan therefore does not unfold with what we would regard as mathematical regularity. By contrast, it comes in fits and starts. There are periods of fast-moving spiritual events. There are periods in which God's promises seem delayed. The deliverance of Israel under Moses contrasted with the previous four hundred years of captivity, for example. As individuals, God seems at times to be moving quickly in our lives. At other times we see little progress.

With our twentieth-century penchant for tight schedules and regular progress that kind of ambiguity usually seems frustrating. But it makes sense when we realize that God's purpose in history is not to build buildings (even churches) faster than anyone else or run the trains or planes according to a tighter schedule, but rather to develop godly character and conduct in his people. This must have happened with Abraham during the twenty-five years he waited in the Promised Land for the birth of Isaac, the son of promise. He was seventy-five years old when God first appeared to him and gave him the promise, but he was one hundred years old when the child was born. Likewise, Joseph spent many years in slavery and later in prison before he was raised to the position of second-in-command in Egypt. Moses was forty years old when he made his choice to identify with his people rather than with Egypt's elite. But he had to flee Egypt, and it was another forty years before he was finally called by God to return with God's command to Pharaoh: "Let my people go." In each case God used the difficult years to develop the kind of character he needed in one later to be called to great responsibility.

Moreover, since such conduct and character can come only from association with himself, God has arranged things so that we will inevitably be drawn to him in prayer and other forms of fellowship. Thus, we pray for the coming of God's kingdom, and we ask for a revelation of his will where our individual lives are concerned.

3. Another teaching that has major bearing on a Christian view of history is the *doctrine of revelation.* This doctrine has relation to the first two. We know that this world has been created by God and is guided by God according to his own perfect plan only by the revelation of these things to us.

Revelation has both a general or objective character and a personal or subjective one. That is, there is a revelation of God's overall plan in Scripture beginning with the creation of the race and continuing through the Fall, the calling out of a special people through whom a Redeemer would come, the appearance and work of Christ, the establishing of the church and the promise of Christ's eventual return. All that is the objective framework for a Christian view of history. But the revelation also has a subjective character. As we read the Bible, God also speaks to us to call us personally into that framework through faith in and obedience to Christ. Christ is the focal point of history. We become a part of God's work in history and serve his plan for history only as we come into a relationship to that One who stands at the center of his workings.

The most important biblical idea at this point is the kingdom of God, which was discussed at some length in volume two of this series.[9] The kingdom of God has three dimensions, each of which bears on a Christian view of what is happening in history. One dimension is what we would call God's general or sovereign rule. "The Most High God rules the kingdom of men, and sets over it whom he will" (Dan. 5:21). "His dominion is an everlasting dominion, and his kingdom endures from generation to generation; all the inhabitants of the earth are accounted as nothing; and he does according to his will in the host of heaven and among the inhabitants of the earth; and none can stay his hand or say to him, 'What doest thou?' " (Dan. 4:34-35). "The LORD brings the counsel of the nations to nought; he frustrates the plans of the peoples. The counsel of the LORD stands for ever, the thoughts of his heart to all generations" (Ps. 33:10-11). "I form light and create darkness, I make weal and create woe, I am the LORD, who do all these things" (Is. 45:7). "We know that in everything God works for good with those who love him, who are called according to his purpose" (Rom. 8:28). God's rule in history is true whether men and women acknowledge it or not. They cannot break God's rule. They can only break themselves upon it like weak iron on an anvil.

The personal dimension of God's kingdom is seen in God's drawing a person out of a state of rebellion and opposition to his rule to a state of glad acquiescence in it. God does this by the new birth. The kingdom is then seen in God's work within that individual to increasingly conform him or her to the standards of that kingdom and to use his or her witness to bring that kingdom to others. When we pray "Thy kingdom come," we are praying for this present realization of God's rule in willing individuals (and not merely a future coming of Christ).

Finally, there will be a future coming of God's kingdom, when Jesus will return to judge the living and the dead.

So the Bible is a revelation of: (1) God's overall guidance

and rule of history, (2) a present reality in which the Spirit of God is bringing many individuals into willing conformity to the goals of God's kingdom and (3) a promise that the kingdom will one day be consummated in the judgment of sinners and the eternal and glorious reign of Christ. Within that framework those who believe in Christ have a two-fold responsibility: to live for Christ and to be his witnesses throughout the world.

4. The *doctrine of redemption* introduces two ideas that have already been alluded to but not adequately discussed: sin and God's unique act in Christ to save the sinner.

The first theme explains why no naturalistic or nonethical explanation of history can ever be adequate. Those who are committed to the modern, progressive understanding of history are particularly vulnerable at this point, since the progress they have envisioned is not pure progress, and in some cases it is questionable whether what they point to is progress at all. The problem is not that so-called progressive elements are not present. They are. But a tragic human flaw —what Christian theology calls original sin—mars those elements of progress and at times perverts them for destructive rather than constructive ends.

Sometimes, particularly in the self-righteous climate of modern times, it is assumed that this destructive element resides in institutions and can therefore be eliminated by social restructuring or revolution. But the problem is deeper than that. It is in the deep nature of men and women and therefore cannot be dealt with except by God for whom all things, even a restructuring of human nature, are possible.

Today some secular thinkers are willing to recognize what *Time* magazine once called "a dark underside" to human na-ture. In the essay "On Evil: The Inescapable Fact," written just after the My Lai massacre at one of the worst periods of the Vietnam war, *Time* sought to get beyond the immediate trag-edy to the underlying evil in human nature. The writers said,

Today's young radicals, in particular, are almost painfully sensi-
tive to these and other wrongs of their society, and denounce them
violently. But at the same time they are typically American in that
they fail to place evil in its historic perspective. To them, evil is
not an irreducible component of man, an inescapable fact of life
but something committed by the older generation, attributable to a
particular class or the "Establishment," and eradicable through
love and revolution. . . .

My Lai is a token of the violence that trembles beneath the
surface of American life; where else, and in what ways will it
explode? How much injustice and corruption distort the reality of
democracy that the U.S. offers to the world?[10]

A few years later a campus magazine made the same observation in reaction to a book by Harvard Divinity School theologian Harvey Cox, in which he had optimistically called for
faith in the "inner world" of human imagination. The magazine objected: "Three generations of American literary artists, however, have testified that the cruelty, the viciousness,
and indeed the insanity rampant in our society are things
which came exactly out of our own 'interiority'; that our
institutions were not flown in from the moon but are in fact
projections of structures envisioned deep in the pits of our
imagination."[11]

Christians concur with that analysis. It is the problem of
history, from the original Fall in Eden up to and including
modern times. But what is the solution? If God did not act
in history, there would be no solution. There would only be a
continuing struggle with evil in which pessimism (the destruction of the race) or escapism (the Greek view of history)
would have to win out. But God does act. He acts decisively,
not merely to guide history or to provide a moral framework
in which the worst sins are inevitably judged, but to redeem
those who are responsible for the evil. He redeems them
through the work of Jesus Christ. The Bible tells us that "in
Christ God was reconciling the world to himself, not counting

their trespasses against them, and entrusting to us the message of reconciliation" (2 Cor. 5:19). As long as Christ stands in history there can be no pessimism for the person who believes in him and the value of his sacrifice.

5. But all are not to be redeemed. That is a hard saying, yet it is the clear teaching of the Word of God. Therefore, to make the Christian view of history complete there must be added to the doctrines already considered—creation, providence, revelation and redemption—the *doctrine of God's final judgment* at the end of history. Christians express belief in this doctrine in the Apostles' Creed: "From thence [that is, from heaven] he [*Christ*] shall come to judge the quick and the dead."

In saying that Christ is to judge the dead as well as the living (the quick), the creed is saying that in the ultimate analysis the meaning of history is not found only at the end of history —as if everything had been building up to one final peak of accomplishment which shall then be judged fit or not fit for glory. The meaning of history is rather found in any given moment in the choice or choices made by any given individual, no matter who that person is, where he or she has come from, or how important he or she may seem to be.

Here we come back to the idea made toward the end of the last chapter, that the important moment in history is always *now.* I quote Butterfield again, who makes this point by an intriguing analogy:

> *History is not like a train, the sole purpose of which is to get to its destination; nor like the conception that my youngest son has of it when he counts 360 days prior to his next birthday and reckons them all a wearisome and meaningless interim, only to be suffered for the sake of what they are leading up to. If we want an analogy with history we must think of something like a Beethoven symphony—the point of it is not saved up until the end, the whole of it is not a mere preparation for a beauty that is only to be achieved in the last bar. And though in a sense the end may lie in the archi-*

tecture of the whole, still in another sense each moment of it is its own self-justification, each note in its particular context as valuable as any other note, each stage of the development having its immediate significance, apart from the mere fact of any development that does take place. . . . We envisage our history in the proper light, therefore, if we say that each generation–indeed each individual–exists for the glory of God.[12]

God's Glory

There is no better example for us at this point than the example of our Lord. Christ came to earth not to do his own will but the will of the Father who sent him (Jn. 5:30; 6:38).

"I glorified thee on earth, having accomplished the work which thou gavest me to do" (Jn. 17:4). How did Christ's work bring glory to God? It did so by revealing God himself clearly. Glorifying God means "to acknowledge God's attributes" or "to make God's attributes known." God's attributes are best seen at the cross of Christ. There above all other places God's sovereignty, justice, righteousness, wisdom and love are abundantly and unmistakably displayed. We see God's sovereignty in the way in which the death of Christ was planned, promised and then took place, without the slightest deviation from the prophecies of the Old Testament concerning it or adjustment to meet some unforeseen circumstance. We see God's justice in sin's actually being punished. Without the cross God could have forgiven our sin gratuitously (to speak from a human perspective), but it would not have been just. Only in Christ is that justice satisfied. We see God's righteousness in recognition of the fact that only Jesus, the righteous One, could pay sin's penalty. We see God's wisdom in the planning and ordering of such a great salvation. We see his love. Only at the cross do we know beyond doubt that God loves us even as he loves Jesus. "For God so loved the world that he gave his only Son, that whoever believes in him should not perish but have eternal life" (Jn. 3:16).

Jesus fully revealed these attributes of the Father by his death. Hence, his obedience to the Father's will in dying fully glorified him. We cannot glorify the Father as Jesus did, perfectly or by a substitutionary atonement, but we can honor God by the way we attempt to accomplish his purposes for us—through obedience.

3 CHRIST, THE FOCAL POINT OF HISTORY

At the beginning of his influential book *Christ and Time,* University of Basel professor of New Testament and early Christianity Oscar Cullmann calls attention to the fact that we in the Western world do not reckon time in a continuous forward-moving series that begins at a fixed initial point, but from a center from which time is reckoned both forward and backward. The Jewish calendar begins from what it regards as the date of the creation of the world and moves on from that point. We, by contrast, begin with the birth of Jesus of Nazareth—fixed within the space of a few years—and then number in two directions: forward, in an increasing succession of years which we identify as A.D. *(anno Domini,* "in the year of [our] Lord"), and backward, in a regression of years which we identify as B.C. ("before Christ").

That system did not come into being all at once. The custom of numbering forward from the birth of Christ was introduced in A.D. 525 by a Roman abbot, Dionysius Exiguus, and came into widespread use during the Middle Ages. The custom of numbering backward from the birth of Christ originated only in the eighteenth century. The interesting point is not so much the time at which those customs originated, but rather the testimony they give to the conviction in Christian hearts that Jesus is the focal point of history.

A secular historian might judge that the coming of Jesus was a pivotal event because of his obvious influence on later history. But the Christian conviction, symbolized by the division of time, goes beyond that recognition. As Cullmann says, "The modern historian may when pressed find a historically confirmed meaning in the fact that the appearance of Jesus of Nazareth is regarded as a decisive turning point of history. But the *theological* affirmation which lies at the basis of the Christian chronology goes far beyond the confirmation that Christianity brought with it weighty historical changes. It asserts rather that from this mid-point all history is to be understood and judged."[1] Christianity affirms that apart from Christ there is no way of determining what history as a whole is all about, nor can we legitimately weigh historical events so that one may be pronounced better or more significant than another. With Christ, however, both those essentials for a true historical outlook are provided. We affirm this by our division of time into two great halves of history.

Fullness of Time

Such a division of time is not stated in the Bible explicitly. But it is pointed to by the fact that our Bible has two Testaments: the Old Testament leading up to the time of Christ, and the New Testament telling of his life and the events which flowed from it. The book of Galatians points to the significance of the specific time in history at which Christ came. It uses a phrase ("the fullness of time") that occurs nowhere else in the Bible. "But when the time had fully come, God sent forth his Son, born of woman, born under the law, to redeem those who were under the law, so that we might receive adoption as sons" (Gal. 4:4-5).

That phrase refers primarily to historical events, so its significance in regard to Christ must first be viewed historically. What is it that made the particular time in which he came, the first century of our era, significant? A number of answers are usually given. First, it would be impossible to imagine the rapid expansion of the Christian gospel in the world as it was prior to the time of Alexander the Great and the subsequent Roman empire. Before Christ's birth, the world was divided into nations and religions that were separate from and hostile to one another. These were insuperable barriers to missionary work, but they had been broken down by the time of Christ's coming. Then the world was truly one world, and the missionaries of the gospel found the doors of the nations wide open as they traveled about to proclaim Christ's message.

A second factor was also important: the heritage of the Greek and Roman civilizations. The Greeks had left their language as the common, trade language of the world. It was spoken everywhere and was therefore the language in which the Christian faith was communicated. The New Testament is written in Greek, for example, rather than in Hebrew, Aramaic or Latin. Rome had brought peace to the world (the *pax Romana)* and had linked the world by a magnificent system of roads, some of which still exist in parts of Italy, France, Switzerland, Britain and elsewhere. On these roads (and at sea), under the general protection of the Roman legions, the apostle Paul and his companions brought the good news of the gospel to Asia Minor, Greece and even to Rome.

Third, the expansion of the gospel was prepared for by the dispersion of Jews throughout the Empire. The Jews had special privileges for the conduct of their religion as a result of their timely help of Julius Caesar during a particularly tense moment in the Egyptian campaign, and they were now present everywhere with their synagogues, Scriptures and general God-consciousness. The early church flourished under the wing of Judaism in its early days, and it was within the synagogues that the first converts to Christianity were made.

A fourth factor in this historical preparation for the coming of Christ was the failure of philosophy to provide sure answers to life's great questions along with the uncertainty that had crept into the various religious systems of the times. It was a time of such moral decline and depravity that even the pagans cried out against it. In such an age the teachings of Christ came.

What this means, when we take it all together, is that Christ's time was the focal point of history. The earlier centuries of the human race, both sacred and secular, were a preparation for him. They may have had meaning on other levels too; undoubtedly they did. But the biblical perspective is that all this was leading to Christ. Emil Brunner has written of this preparation:

> *Plato and Alexander, Cicero and Julius Caesar must serve God, in order to prepare the way for Christ. It is significant that the Gospel of Luke begins with the incident of the census taken by order of Augustus, and the Gospel of Matthew begins with the story of the Magi from the East who prepare to leave their homes to follow the Star which leads to Palestine and the Court of Herod. . . . Long ago, from the very earliest beginnings, God had prepared that which he then willed to give as the salvation of the world "in the fullness of the times," as something which on the one hand–according to its human nature–grows out of this history, as well as something which came into history, as something which could not be explained from itself.* [2]

In the same way, the biblical history now unfolds from Christ through a development of his work and an outpouring of his Spirit, as the New Testament shows.

Time Made Full

To speak of the fullness of time as the preparation in history for the coming of Christ is only one part of the meaning of that phrase, however, and it is not even necessarily the most important part. True, the events of history under the guidance of the sovereign God did prepare for Christ, and in that sense the time of his coming was propitious. But the time was also full in the sense that God made it full through what he did in Christ. The time of Christ bears a relationship to history as has no other time before or since.

We should focus here on three key moments in Christ's life: the initial moment of the Incarnation, the central moment of the crucifixion, and the climactic moment of the resurrection. Each is an unparalleled part of that total moment of Christ's life by which history is to be understood and judged.

The essence of the _Incarnation_ is that by it God became man in order to achieve salvation and establish the rule of God in history and over history. The means by which that was accomplished historically was the virgin birth. The conception of Christ without benefit of a human father is, of course, something that has always staggered the unbelieving mind, both within and outside the church. It has been denied, thereby reducing Jesus to the level of a mere man with certain not-too-well-defined spiritual sensibilities. But that is not the meaning of the Incarnation. The Incarnation means the invasion by God of history through One who is uniquely both God and man. It is a supernatural or miraculous event, and it is this character of the event which the doctrine of the virgin birth both defines and preserves.

Whether or not there was a virgin birth is a historical question which has been definitively handled by J. Gresham Machen in _The Virgin Birth of Christ_,[3] a book that no one has ever refuted or even attempted to answer. Machen defends the virgin birth by an exhaustive study of the original documents (in which he demonstrates their consistency and inherent credibility) and by a devastating critique of all rival theories of the doctrine's origin. The person who wishes to investigate this side of the issue can do no better than to begin with Machen's work. What Machen does not discuss, but which is of great significance for a Christian view of history, is the importance of the doctrine for history itself. The biblical narratives themselves do this.

Let us take Mary's hymn after the Annunciation of Christ's birth and her subsequent visit to Elizabeth, who was then awaiting the birth of John the Baptist (Lk. 1:46-55). It is known as the *Magnificat,* from the opening word of the hymn in Latin.

My soul magnifies the Lord,
And my spirit rejoices in God my Savior,
For he has regarded the low estate of his handmaiden.
For behold, henceforth all generations will call me blessed;
For he who is mighty has done great things for me,
And holy is his name.
And his mercy is on those who fear him from generation to
generation.
He has shown strength with his arm,
He has scattered the proud in the imagination of their hearts,
He has put down the mighty from their thrones,
And exalted those of low degree;
He has filled the hungry with good things,
And the rich he has sent empty away.
He has helped his servant Israel,
In remembrance of his mercy,
As he spoke to our fathers,
To Abraham and to his posterity for ever.

The power of that hymn comes from the view of God's definitive invasion of human history which its author held. Mary was describing nothing less than the total overturning of the entire state of history as we know it, a state in which the mighty usually triumph and the poor starve. The mighty are to be brought down and the poor exalted. The rich will be sent away empty and the hungry will be fed. This is to be done in accordance with God's promises to Abraham and the other fathers of the Jewish nation. It is an event from outside history, but it is also now within history. It is decisive.

We find the same thing further on in the same chapter in the *Benedictus* of the aged Zechariah (Lk. 1:68-80).

> *Blessed be the Lord God of Israel,*
> *For he has visited and redeemed his people,*
> *And has raised up a horn of salvation for us*
> *In the house of his servant David,*
> *As he spoke by the mouth of his holy prophets from of old,*
> *That we should be saved from our enemies,*
> *And from the hand of all who hate us;*
> *To perform the mercy promised to our fathers,*
> *And to remember his holy covenant,*
> *The oath which he swore to our father Abraham, to grant us*
> *That we, being delivered from the hand of our enemies,*
> *Might serve him without fear,*
> *In holiness and righteousness before him all the days of our life.*
> *And you, child, will be called the prophet of the Most High;*
> *For you will go before the Lord to prepare his ways,*
> *To give knowledge of salvation to his people*
> *In the forgiveness of their sins,*
> *Through the tender mercy of our God,*
> *When the day shall dawn upon us from on high*
> *To give light to those who sit in darkness and in the shadow of death,*
> *To guide our feet into the way of peace.*

This hymn is referring in the first instance to the birth of John the Baptist, the "prophet of the Most High" who should "go before" him. Yet it looks beyond the work of the forerunner to the fulfillment of God's promises to Israel in the coming of Christ. In this hymn, as in the Magnificat, the focus is upon God's intervention in history with inevitable historical results.

Rousas J. Rushdoony, who has looked at the historical aspects of the Incarnation in an essay on "The Virgin Birth and History," writes,

> *Prior to Jesus Christ, the movement of history was meager, and in the dark. The pilgrims of history were afraid to move; they could not move, having no direction in the dark. . . . Now, with the fullness of the revelation, God's people move with him in the light of Christ. According to the Benedictus, the great forward movement of man in history began in Christ and with Christ. . . . Every aspect of the nativity narrative is not only historical but directed towards the fulfillment of the historical process.*[4]

The second important moment in Christ's life is the *crucifixion* which, as a part of this central time in history, is the most central of all. It is that for which the Incarnation took place, and to which the resurrection attests.

The cross is the central feature of the New Testament. Each of the Gospels devotes an unusually large proportion of its narrative to the events of Christ's final week in Jerusalem, culminating in his crucifixion and resurrection, and it is no exaggeration to say that the cross overshadows the life and ministry of Christ even before this time. The very name *Jesus,* given to the child by Joseph at the direction of the angel, looks forward to his death on Calvary. The angel explained the choice of the name, saying, "You shall call his name Jesus, for he will save his people from their sins" (Mt. 1:21). Jesus, too, spoke of the suffering which was to come. "And he began to teach them that the Son of man must suffer many things, and be rejected by the elders and the chief priests and the scribes, and be killed, and after three days rise again" (Mk. 8:31). "The Son of man will be delivered into the hands of men, and they will kill him; and when he is killed, after three days he will rise" (Mk. 9:31). Jesus linked the success of his mission to his crucifixion. "And I, when I am lifted up from the earth, will draw all men to myself" (Jn. 12:32). He spoke of the crucifixion as that vital "hour" for which he came (Jn. 2:4; 12:23, 27; 17:1; compare 7:30; 8:20; 13:1). In narrating these events, Matthew gives two-fifths of the Gospel to the final week in Jerusalem; Mark, three-fifths; Luke, one-third; and John, nearly one-half.

Again the crucifixion is a theme of the Old Testament: the Old Testament sacrifices, given to Israel by God for pedagogical purposes, prefigured Christ's suffering. The prophets explicitly foretold it. Jesus probably referred to both those lines of witness when he taught the downcast Emmaus disciples that the Old Testament had foretold his death. "And he said to them, 'O foolish men, and slow of heart to believe all that the prophets have spoken! Was it not necessary that the Christ should suffer these things and enter into his glory?' And beginning with Moses and all the prophets, he interpreted to them in all the scriptures the things concerning himself" (Lk. 24:25-27).

It is not surprising in view of this biblical emphasis that the centrality of Christ's cross has been recognized by Christians in all ages, even before Constantine made the cross the universal badge of Christendom. "The cross stands as the focal point of the Christian faith. Without the cross the Bible is an enigma, and the Gospel of salvation is an empty hope."[5]

Anyone who knows anything at all about the Bible should know why the crucifixion of Christ is central to it. The Bible is a story of man's hopeless fall into sin and of God's perfect remedy for that sin through Christ. The cross is God's solution to the sin problem. But there is even more to the centrality of the cross than this. If the cross is the solution to the sin problem and the *only* solution, then the cross confronts each individual as a crisis to which he or she must respond, and in accordance with which decision he or she will either live or die. People in Old Testament times either looked forward to Christ as the Savior whom God had promised, or did not look forward to him. We either look back in simple faith to what he has done for our salvation, or we do not look back. In that difference hangs our destiny.

The third key moment in the life of Christ is the *resurrection*. It is important in two ways. First, it is important historically. Only because of the resurrection did the church of Christ (and with it Christianity) come into existence. Apart from a true resurrection within history, the early disciples would simply have scattered to their homes, their dreams shattered. They would have said, as did the Emmaus disciples, "But we had hoped [past tense] that he was the one to redeem Israel" (Lk. 24:21). Only because Jesus appeared to them again after the resurrection did the disciples regather as a community, convinced of their message and empowered to go out with it into a hostile world and to persevere in their testimony even in the face of persecution and death. In this historical about-face the resurrection was both climactic and pivotal.

Second, the resurrection is important for each individual. It is part of God's solution to the human problem. What is our problem? It is sin. Sin has three chief areas of expression: it causes us to be ignorant of God; it alienates us from God; and it makes us powerless to live for God—even if we could somehow come to know him and be reconciled to him. The Incarnation is God's answer to the first problem: although God has also revealed himself in Scripture, it is in Christ above all that we see and know him. God's answer to the second problem is the crucifixion: in it God has made an atonement for sin by which the guilt of sin is removed and we, who once were far off, are now brought near by the blood of Christ (Eph. 2:13). God's answer to the third problem is the resurrection. It is not only proof of Christ's divinity and of the value of his death for sinners. It is also the promise and proof of new life and power for all who believe in Jesus. It may be said of the resurrection, as well as of the Incarnation, that with it a new thing came into the world and that the world can never be the same because of it.

The importance of the resurrection was detailed in the second volume of this series, where it was argued that it proves:

1. There is a God, and the God of the Bible is the true God.
2. Jesus of Nazareth is the unique Son of God.
3. All who believe in Christ are justified from all sin.
4. The Christian can live a life that is pleasing to God.
5. Death is not the end of this life.
6. There will be a final judgment on all who reject the gospel.[6]

So there at the middle of history, symbolized by the division into B.C. and A.D., stands the central event, the life and work of Christ. History prepared for it and was changed by it. History is understood by it and is judged by it. The greatest of all human decisions, the eternally determining decision, is how we, each one, will respond to Jesus.

Lord of History

One more thing must be said before leaving this subject. Although we speak of Christ as the focal point of history, that statement is not to be understood as if we are saying that Christ appeared only there—and that, apart from that brief interval in time, he and history are separate. On the contrary, we say that the One who appeared in history is also the Lord of history. He is to be seen at its very beginning; he is currently ruling in history to accomplish his own wise ends, and he will also appear at the end of history as its judge. In other words, he is the One through whom the Father exercises his relationship to history (as we saw in the last chapter).

Cullmann summarizes the biblical evidence like this:

Even the time before the Creation is regarded entirely from the position of Christ; it is the time in which, in the counsel of God, Christ is already foreordained as Mediator before the foundation of the world (Jn. 17:24; 1 Pet. 1:20). He is then the Mediator in the Creation itself (Jn. 1:1; Heb. 1:2; and especially vv. 10ff.;

1 Cor. 8:6; Col. 1:16). . . . The election of the people of Israel takes place with reference to Christ and reaches its fulfillment in the work of the Incarnate One. . . . Christ's role as Mediator continues in his Church, which indeed constitutes his earthly body. From it he exercises over heaven and earth the Lordship committed to him by God, though now it is invisible and can be apprehended only by faith (Mt. 28:18; Phil. 2:9ff.). Thus Christ is further the Mediator of the completion of the entire redemptive plan at the end. That is why he returns to the earth; the new creation at the end, like the entire redemptive process, is linked to that redemption of men whose Mediator is Christ. Upon the basis of his work the resurrection power of the Holy Spirit will transform all created things, including our mortal bodies; there will come into being a new heaven and a new earth in which sin and death no longer exist. Only then will Christ's role as Mediator be fulfilled. Only then will Christ "subject himself to him who subjected all things to him, in order that God may be all in all" (1 Cor. 15:28). At that point only has the line which began with the Creation reached its end.[7]

Although Christ is the focal point of history, he is also and at the same time over and in control of history. It is his history and contains his meaning. It is our privilege to enter into that history consciously through faith in him.

PART II
THE CHURCH OF GOD

*To me . . . this grace was given, to preach
to the Gentiles the unsearchable riches
of Christ, and to make all men see what is
the plan of the mystery hidden for ages in
God who created all things; that through the
church the manifold wisdom of God
might now be made known to the principalities
and powers in the heavenly places.*
(Eph. 3:8-10)

*"God is spirit, and those who worship him
must worship in spirit and truth."*
(Jn. 4:24)

"Do this in remembrance of me."
(1 Cor. 11:24)

*His gifts were that some should be apostles,
some prophets, some evangelists,
some pastors and teachers, to equip the saints
for the work of ministry, for building
up the body of Christ, until we all attain to
the unity of the faith and of the
knowledge of the Son of God, to mature
manhood, to the measure of the stature of
the fulness of Christ.*
(Eph. 4:11-13)

4 CHRIST'S CHURCH

If the life, death and resurrection of Jesus Christ is the focal point of history, then the church of Christ, his body, is a focal point too. It cannot be a focal point in the same sense. Christ's work is the church's foundation; he, not the church, is the point at which history is to be understood and judged. Yet Christ's work continues in the church; the fullness of the mystery of God in redemption is disclosed among his people. A text from Paul's writings says, "To me, though I am the very least of all the saints, this grace was given, to preach to the Gentiles the unsearchable riches of Christ, and to make all men see what is the plan of the mystery hidden for ages in God who created all things; that *through the church* the manifold wisdom of God might now be made known to the principalities and powers in the heavenly places" (Eph. 3:8-10).

Any reader of the New Testament will understand that the church is important in this age, just as God's dealings with Israel were important in the Old Testament period. But the text from Ephesians says more. The fullness of God's wisdom is being revealed in the church even now, and the principalities and powers—the phrase refers to spiritual powers such as angels and demons—are scrutinizing the church to learn of the wisdom and plan of God revealed there.

It is as though the church is a stage upon which God has been presenting the great drama of redemption, a true-life pageant in which it is shown how those who have rebelled against God and wrecked his universe are now being brought back into harmony with him, becoming agents of renewal and healing instead. Those who have become members of the body of Christ are given the privilege of becoming what Ralph Keiper calls "the verifying data of God's grace." "God's will for you and me is to be agents of his wisdom, to show that truly we are the capstone of his creation, that men may behold us as the masterpiece of God. . . . We have been redeemed with such a salvation that in the midst of a sinful and crooked world we can become the sons of God without rebuke, demonstrating the marvelous salvation of which we speak, that we might become, as it were, the picture book leading people to the written Book that they by the Holy Spirit might come to know the living Book, even Jesus."[1]

Because of the church's critical importance for disclosing the redemptive plan of God, our attention in this section must therefore be on this reality. We will study the church's nature, marks, life, organization and responsibilities.

Old Testament Background

Strictly speaking, the church is the creation of the historical Christ and therefore dates from the time of Christ. But the church has roots in the Old Testament and cannot be understood well without that background. This is true theologically because the idea of a called-out "people of God" obviously existed in the Old Testament period, just as in the New. It is also true linguistically since the Greek word for *church* (*ekklēsia*) occurs frequently in relation to Israel in the Greek translation of the Old Testament (the Septuagint) and was therefore known to the New Testament writers. The passages in which _ekklēsia_ occurs may therefore be supposed to have exerted an influence on the thinking of the New Testament writers.

In the Septuagint _ekklēsia_ generally translates the Hebrew term _qhl,_ which, like the Greek term, refers to those who are "called out" or "assembled" by God as his special possession. That is the case in regard to the earliest appearances of this term—in the phrase "the day of the assembly" (Deut. 9:10; 10:4; 18:16); it refers to the nation of Israel assembled at Mount Sinai. This is also its meaning in Psalm 22, where the term is translated "congregation" (vv. 22, 25). It is the idea behind Stephen's reference to the assembly in his sermon in Acts: "This is he who was in the congregation in the wilderness with the angel who spoke to him at Mount Sinai, and with our fathers" (Acts 7:38). In these passages and others the key element is the call of God, followed by the response of the ones called and God's solemn covenant with them to bless them—to be their God and they his people.

We see an illustration of these elements in the call of Abraham, with whom the Old Testament "assembly" begins. We are told that God appeared to Abraham saying, "Go from your country and your kindred and your father's house to the land that I will show you. And I will make of you a great nation, and I will bless you, and make your name great, so that you will be a blessing" (Gen. 12:1-2). In this narrative the initiative was entirely with God. He sought and called Abraham; it was not Abraham who sought him.

Again, we see the beginning of the promise or covenant: "I will make of you a great nation . . . I will bless you." That covenant is elaborated in God's subsequent revelations to Abraham. "Know of a surety that your descendants will be sojourners in a land that is not theirs, and will be slaves there, and they will be oppressed for four hundred years; but I will bring judgment on the nation which they serve, and afterward they shall come out with great possessions.... To your descendants I give this land" (Gen. 15:13-14, 18). "Behold, my covenant is with you, and you shall be the father of a multitude of nations.... And I will establish my covenant between me and you and your descendants after you throughout their generations for an everlasting covenant, to be God to you and to your descendants after you. And I will give to you, and to your descendants after you, the land of your sojournings, all the land of Canaan, for an everlasting possession; and I will be their God" (Gen. 17:4, 7-8).

Abraham's response was to believe God (Gen. 15:6) and worship him (Gen. 12:8).

We see the same pattern in God's dealings with Isaac, Abraham's son, and with Jacob, his grandson. Later there was a special call to Abraham's descendants when they had become slaves in Egypt. On that occasion God told Moses, "I have seen the affliction of my people who are in Egypt, and have heard their cry because of their taskmasters; I know their sufferings, and I have come down to deliver them out of the hand of the Egyptians, and to bring them up out of that land to a good and broad land, a land flowing with milk and honey" (Ex. 3:7-8).

Finally, a call and promise to Israel followed the Babylonian captivity: "Therefore, behold, the days are coming, says the LORD, when it shall no longer be said, 'As the LORD lives who brought up the people of Israel out of the land of Egypt,' but 'as the LORD lives who brought up the people of Israel out of the north country and out of all the countries where he had driven them.' For I will bring them back to their own land which I gave to their fathers" (Jer. 16:14-15).

In each of these passages there is the creation of an *ekklēsia*, an assembly of those who are called out of a normal relationship to the world in order to be a special people of God. That call is accompanied by special promises and is met by faith, worship, love and obedience from those to whom the call comes.

A New Community

Each of these Old Testament elements is present in the New Testament understanding of the church, but the church has characteristics that cannot rightly be applied to the Old Testament assembly and which therefore set it off as something new. The church (1) is founded on the Lord Jesus Christ, (2) is called into being by the Holy Spirit, and (3) is to contain people of all races who thereby become one new people in the sight of God.

The first reference to the church in the New Testament makes the first of these points clearly: the sole foundation on which the church can stand is its master, Jesus Christ. Matthew 16:18 is probably the Bible's best-known text dealing with the church. Jesus had left the dangerous area of Galilee for Caesarea Philippi where he had begun to question his disciples about people's opinion of him. "Who do men say that the Son of man is?" he asked them.

They answered, "Some say John the Baptist, others say Elijah, and others Jeremiah or one of the prophets."

"But who do you say that I am?" he continued.

Peter answered for the rest, "You are the Christ, the Son of the living God." At that point Jesus began to speak of the church and of the sufferings that would precede its founding. "Blessed are you, Simon Bar-Jona! For flesh and blood has not revealed this to you, but my Father who is in heaven. And I tell you, you are Peter, and on this rock I will build my church, and the powers of death shall not prevail against it." He then "began to show his disciples that he must go to Jerusalem and suffer many things from the elders and chief priests and scribes, and be killed, and on the third day be raised" (Mt. 16:13-21).

That passage makes several important points. First, the emphasis is on Peter's confession, which focused on *the person of Christ* and not on Peter himself. Jesus called attention to the fact that this insight had been given to him by a special revelation from God.

The Roman Catholic Church has built its doctrine of the supremacy of the pope on this passage, claiming that Christ founded the church on Peter and his successors. Actually, the Greek underlying this passage contains a play on words between the masculine and feminine forms of the word *petros* meaning stone or rock. Peter's name *(petros,* the masculine form) meant *stone.* But it could be a big stone or a little one; it could even mean what we might call a pebble. *Petra,* the feminine form, meant *bedrock* such as the living rock of a mountain. So the passage really means, "You, Peter, are a little quarried stone, solid (in this confession at least) but easily moved. I, by contrast, am the living rock of ages, and on that solid foundation, which your confession points to, I will build my church." Nowhere in his later New Testament writings did Peter ever suggest that he was the foundation of the church. Yet he often spoke of Jesus as the foundation, using Christ's image which had undoubtedly impressed itself upon his imagination.

Not long after the resurrection Peter and John were preaching and were arrested by the Sanhedrin, the same body that had tried and condemned Jesus, and were asked to give an account of themselves. Peter used the occasion to testify clearly to the Lord. He spoke of Christ's power, through which a crippled man had just been healed. Then he continued on in clear reference to Christ. *"This is the stone* which was rejected by you builders, but which has become the head of the corner. And there is salvation in no one else, for there is no other name under heaven given among men by which we must be saved" (Acts 4:11-12).

We have the same thing in Peter's first epistle, in which he compared Christ to a foundation stone upon which we, as quarried stones, may be fastened. His words are, "Come to him, to that living stone, rejected by men but in God's sight chosen and precious; and like living stones be yourselves built into a spiritual house, to be a holy priesthood, to offer spiritual sacrifices acceptable to God through Jesus Christ. For it stands in scripture: 'Behold, I am laying in Zion a stone, a corner-stone chosen and precious, and he who believes in him will not be put to shame' " (1 Pet. 2:4-6).

A second important point of this first mention of the church in the New Testament is its stress on the *work of Christ.* Peter had pointed to Christ's person, confessing that he was "the Christ, the Son of the living God." But after acknowledging that this was correct, Jesus said that his initial work as Messiah (Christ) would not be what the disciples expected of him. Rather it would be a work of suffering and death. "From that time Jesus began to show his disciples that he must go to Jerusalem and suffer many things from the elders and chief priests and scribes, and be killed, and on the third day be raised" (Mt. 16:21). Peter did not understand that. He thought it unnecessary and rebuked Christ for it. "God forbid, Lord!" he said. "This shall never happen to you."

But Jesus considered his suffering so necessary that he regarded Peter's words as a satanic temptation. He answered Peter, "Get behind me, Satan! You are a hindrance to me; for you are not on the side of God, but of men" (vv. 22-23).

So the first thing that must be said about the church is that the person and work of the Lord Jesus Christ is its foundation. It is based on him. It is the assembled body of those for whose sins he, the eternal Son of God, died to make atonement. Any assembly of people founded on any other foundation is not the church, no matter what it calls itself. On the other hand, all who are united to the crucified but risen Christ by faith are part of his church, regardless of their background or denominational labeling.

This concept has an important application, namely, that the church of Christ is one church and must be seen to be one church by the world. Jesus taught this to the Jews of his day by an image drawn from rural life. He compared himself to a shepherd and his church to sheep. He would die for them, he said, and then he would call forth his sheep from many different sheepfolds to follow him. "I have other sheep, that are not of this fold; I must bring them also, and they will heed my voice. So there shall be one flock, one shepherd" (Jn. 10:16).

We must understand what Christ said in that verse, since it has been badly misused. The initial problem can be traced to Jerome and the Latin Vulgate. In that translation of the Bible, Jerome failed to distinguish between a *fold* (mentioned in the first part of the verse) and a *flock* (mentioned later). They are two entirely different words in Greek. Yet Jerome treated them the same, and many of our translations have followed him. The error is corrected in the RSV and other versions. In Jerome's translation Jesus seemed to be saying that there is only one organization, and the obvious deduction was that there could therefore be no salvation outside the formal organization of the then-existing church. That interpretation became official Roman Catholic teaching, but it is based on that wrong translation.

The church about which Christ was speaking is not an organization (though it obviously has organized parts) but rather the entire company of those who have the Lord Jesus Christ as their shepherd. Thus, the unity comes not from forcing all the sheep into one great organization, but in the fact that all have heard Jesus and have left lesser loyalties to follow him. Moreover, to the degree that they do follow him, a visible (though not necessarily structural) unity follows.

The question is, Do we truly have or acknowledge such unity? We often do not. The error of the older Roman Catholic Church is in supposing that the Holy Spirit must work along ecclesiastical lines. It is a real error. But although it expresses itself differently, the same error often exists within Protestantism. The problem is not so much that there are different denominations within Protestantism. People are different, and there is no reason why there ought not to be different organizations with different forms of service and church government to express those differences. To insist that there must be one Protestant denomination (which some in the ecumenical movement insist on) is a similar error.

The real problem is that believers in one denomination refuse to cooperate with believers in another denomination, justifying it on grounds that other Christians are somehow contaminated by their associations or are disobeying the Lord by remaining in their church or are not actually Christians. That attitude is a great hindrance to the advance of the gospel in the world today. Moreover, it is sin, and we will not have great revival until believers repent of that sin and ask God to cleanse them of it.

What are we to conclude about the church of the Lord Jesus Christ on the basis of these and other biblical passages? We can say:

1. There is one church to whom all who confess Jesus as Lord and Savior belong. All who are Christians are one with all other Christians and should acknowledge that to be true, even though the other believer is wrong about or denies what we consider to be important doctrines.

2. Nothing in the Bible tells us that there should be or even that we should desire to have one all-encompassing organization. Instead we may expect God to call people to faith within various organizations and lead believers into Christian service within those or other organizations. We dare not say that another believer is out of God's will because he or she is serving somewhere else.

3. God's people need one another and must learn from one another, whether Baptists, Presbyterians, Episcopalians, Roman Catholics, Pentecostals, Methodists, independents or members of any other denomination. It does not mean that each of us will therefore think those other believers are completely right in church matters or even in doctrine--we do not dare say that we are totally right—but it does mean that we need to learn something about the body of Christ and receive help for the body of Christ from many Christians.

4. Because of the love which is to bind the true church together, we also have an obligation to demonstrate that love-unity tangibly, over and above denominational programs and concerns. To do so is the indispensible basis for our mission. "By this [your love for one another] all men will know that you are my disciples," said Jesus (Jn. 13:35).[2]

Filled with Power

A second unique characteristic of the New Testament church is that it is brought into being and is empowered by the Holy Spirit. Although the Lord Jesus Christ is the church's foundation, the church did not come into being immediately following his death, resurrection and ascension, but at Pentecost when the Holy Spirit came upon the disciples in power and caused many to respond to the first preaching about Jesus. The Lord prepared the disciples for this coming of the Holy Spirit by commanding them to stay in Jerusalem until that moment. Then they were to go forth as his witnesses. "But you shall receive power when the Holy Spirit has come upon you; and you shall be my witnesses in Jerusalem and in all Judea and Samaria and to the end of the earth" (Acts 1:8).

The Holy Spirit does three things for the church in all times and places. First, as the verse just quoted says, he *empowers the church* to do Christ's bidding and to be effective in doing it. That is the thrust of Christ's command. He was telling the disciples that they were to be his witnesses throughout the whole world, beginning in Jerusalem. But they would not be able to do that until the Holy Spirit came upon them to fill their words with power.

When Peter preached on Pentecost three thousand people responded to the gospel. They then entered into the church's fellowship, devoting themselves to "the apostles' teaching and fellowship, to the breaking of bread and the prayers" (Acts 2:42). When Peter next preached five thousand believed (Acts 4:4). It was a phenomenal response for any age or place but particularly so for a city and people who had earlier rejected Jesus. Two months earlier they had hounded Jesus to his death. Now they were responding in massive numbers. What made the difference? Not the preaching of Peter certainly, or we would have to conclude that he was a more effective communicator than the Lord. It was rather that the Holy Spirit spoke through Peter's message and changed the hearts of his hearers. So it is today. We preach Christ and witness to him, but we cannot change people's hearts. Only the Holy Spirit can do that, and he does.

Second, the Holy Spirit has been sent to develop the _character of the Lord Jesus Christ_ in his people. We are not like him naturally, but we are to become like him as the Spirit of Christ increasingly transforms us into his image. "And we all, with unveiled face, beholding the glory of the Lord, are being changed into his likeness from one degree of glory to another; for this comes from the Lord who is the Spirit" (2 Cor. 3:18).

Finally, by means of the Holy Spirit the risen _Christ is with his people_ to comfort and direct them during this age. The Lord spoke of this even before his crucifixion. "I will pray the Father, and he will give you another Counselor, to be with you for ever, even the Spirit of truth, whom the world cannot receive, because it neither sees him nor knows him; you know him, for he dwells with you, and will be in you" (Jn. 14:16-17). It was because of the Holy Spirit's coming that Christ could say, "Lo, I am with you always, to the close of the age" (Mt. 28:20), and "Let not your hearts be troubled, neither let them be afraid" (Jn. 14:27).

The church of Christ is to be a spiritual reality in which the distinct endowments of the Spirit of Christ are seen. That reality should be true of the organized or visible church. The organized church is not identical with the church of God, and it often fails to show these characteristics. Yet these characteristics should be seen wherever true believers gather together in Christ's name; the world should be able to recognize that there is something spiritual about them. Francis Schaeffer writes, "These are the things that the world should see when they look upon the church—something that they cannot possibly explain away.... The church of the Lord Jesus Christ should be functioning moment by moment on a supernatural plane. This is the church living by faith, and not in unfaith. This is the church living practically under Christ's leadership, rather than thinking of Christ being far off and building the invisible Church, while we build that which is at hand with our own wisdom and power."[3]

A Broken Wall

A third special characteristic of the church was suggested in discussing the church's foundation but was not adequately developed there. It is the universal nature of the church, in which people of all cultures are brought together into its fellowship and all national, racial and other barriers are broken down.

Bannerman writes,

The invisible Church of Christ made up of the whole number of true believers throughout the world, is catholic, or, in other words, not confined to any place or people. In this respect, it stands contrasted with the limited and local economy of the church under the Jewish dispensation. In so far as the Jewish church constituted a society of the worshipers of God, it was local, not catholic. It had its center at Jerusalem, and its circumference at the geographical limits of Judea.... There is a striking contrast between all this and the Christian church under the Gospel. There is now no local center for the religious service of Christ's people—no holy place to which they must repair personally for their worship, or towards which, when at a distance, they must turn their face in prayer. Neither at Jerusalem, nor in the temple, are men now to worship the Father. Wherever on the wide earth there is a true worshipper, there is a true temple of Jehovah, and there he may be worshipped in spirit and in truth.... The narrow barriers of a former economy have

*been thrown down; and in the gift of the Spirit to all believers,
and in the fellowship of the Spirit coextensive with all, there is
laid the foundation of a Church, no longer confined to one nation
as before under the law, but worldwide and universal.* [4]

That union of peoples within the church is *given* to the church
by God, but it is something that must be achieved historically.
The church must actually develop brotherhood, a sense of
family oneness, among those to whom the gospel spreads.
Many barriers to such a union existed in the early church.
There were barriers of race—the Greek despising the Roman,
the Roman contemptuous of the Greek. There were barriers
of nationhood—most captive people chafing under the yoke
of Rome. There were barriers of sex, language and culture
—the same barriers that exist among people today. But they
were broken down as those who were called to faith in Christ
increasingly came to see their oneness in him. "For he is our
peace, who has made us both [Jews and Gentiles] one, and
has broken down the dividing wall of hostility" (Eph. 2:14). To
the Corinthians Paul wrote, "God . . . through Christ reconciled us to himself and gave us the ministry of reconciliation"
(2 Cor. 5:18).

In his commentary on the Gospel of John, William Barclay
tells of an incident from the life of Egerton Young, the first
missionary to the Indians of Saskatchewan, Canada. Young
had gone to them with the message of the love of God the
Father, and they had received it like a new revelation. When
he told his message an old chief said, "When you spoke of the
great Spirit just now, did I hear you say, 'Our Father'?"

"Yes, I did," said the missionary. "We know him as Father
because he is revealed to us as Father by Jesus Christ."

"That is very new and sweet to me," said the chief. "We
never thought of the great Spirit as Father. We heard him in
the thunder; we saw him in the lightning, the tempest and the
blizzard, and we were afraid. So when you tell us that the great
Spirit is *our Father,* that is very beautiful to us." The chief

paused, and then asked, "Missionary, did you say that the great Spirit is *your* Father?"

"I did," said Young.

"And," said the chief, "did you say that he is the Father of *the Indians?*"

"Yes," said the missionary.

"Then," said the old chief, *"you and I are brothers."*[5]

Nothing will abolish distinctions between nations. There will always be nations. Nothing (so far as I can see) will ever abolish denominations. But in spite of that—in spite of race, nations and denominations—there can be a real and visible unity among those who acknowledge the Lord Jesus Christ as their shepherd. As Dr. D. Martyn Lloyd-Jones says in his study of the second chapter of Ephesians, "We are all equally sinners. . . . We are all equally helpless. . . . We have all come to one and the same Savior. . . . We have the same salvation. . . . We have the same Holy Spirit. . . . We have the same Father. . . . We even have the same trials. . . . And finally, we are all marching and going together to the same eternal home."[6] Only a knowledge of the love of the Lord Jesus Christ will draw us together.

5 THE MARKS OF THE CHURCH

The church is founded on the Lord Jesus Christ and is called into being by the Spirit of Christ. The church must therefore be like Christ, possessing at least some of his characteristics. That statement is not only the result of a process of reasoning. It is clearly taught in the Bible. We find the apostle John saying, "As he is so are we in this world" (1 Jn. 4:17).

What does that mean? What should characterize the church? The most comprehensive answer is seen in Jesus' prayer for the church recorded in John 17. He prayed that the church might be characterized by six things: joy (v. 13), holiness (vv. 14-16), truth (v. 17), mission (v. 18), unity (vv. 21-23) and love (v. 26). His life was marked by each of those qualities. These marks of the church are so important that we should study each of them carefully before going on to other items that are also part of the church's life and ministry.

A Joyous Assembly

It is interesting that the characteristic mentioned first by

Jesus is joy. Many of us would not naturally mention it, let alone put it first. We would point to love or holiness or true doctrine. But Jesus said, "I am coming to thee [the Father]; and these things I speak in the world, that they may have my joy fulfilled in themselves" (Jn. 17:13). That most of us do not think of joy as a primary characteristic of the church probably indicates how little we regard it and how far we have moved from the spirit of the early church. The early church was a joyous assembly.

We see their joy immediately when we begin to study the subject in the New Testament. In the Greek language, the verb meaning "to rejoice" or "be joyful" is *chairein;* it is found seventy-two times. The noun, meaning "joy," is *chara;* it occurs sixty times. As we study these usages, we find that joy is not a technical concept, found only in highly theological passages. Rather it most often occurs simply as a greeting, meaning "Joy be with you!" To be sure, *chairein* is not always restricted to the speech of Christians. It is used, for example, in the letter to Felix about Paul by the Roman officer Claudius Lysias, where it means "Greetings" (Acts 23:26). But in Christian hands it obviously meant much more than it did with pagans and is used more frequently.

We notice, for example, that the angel who announced the birth of Jesus to the shepherds said, "Behold, I bring you good news of a great joy which will come to all the people; for to you is born this day in the city of David a Savior, who is Christ the Lord" (Lk. 2:10-11). The word here obviously meant more than "Greetings!" Later Jesus said, "These things I have spoken to you, that my joy may be in you, and that your joy may be full" (Jn. 15:11). The things he had spoken were great promises.

Paul's writings contain many uses of the word. In Philippians, the apostle, wishing to give a final admonition to his friends, wrote, "Rejoice in the Lord always; again I will say, Rejoice" (4:4). As Barclay says in his discussion of this term,

"This last greeting, 'Joy be with you!' rings triumphantly through the pages of the New Testament. . . . There is no virtue in the Christian life which is not made radiant with joy; there is no circumstance and no occasion which is not illumined with joy. A joyless life is not a Christian life, for joy is one constant in the recipe for Christian living."[1]

Is the church today joyful? Are Christians? We need not doubt that we are all far more joyful than we would be if we were not Christians, or that there are places where joy is particularly evident. Joy is often very evident in new believers, for example. But in most churches, if one were to observe them impartially week after week, I wonder if joy would be visible. We think of joy as something that should characterize the church ideally and will doubtless characterize it in that day when we are gathered together around the throne of grace to sing God's glory. But here? Here it is often the case that there are sour looks, griping, long faces and other manifestations of an inner misery.

Is there a remedy for our frequent lack of joy? There is. The remedy is contained in Jesus' promises. We will look at this matter further under the third mark of the church, where the subject of "truth" is taken up.

Separated unto God

A second characteristic of the church is holiness, the characteristic of God most mentioned in the pages of the Word of God. Holiness therefore should characterize God's church. We are to be a "holy" people (1 Pet. 2:9). We are to "strive" for holiness "without which no one will see the Lord" (Heb. 12:14). Jesus spoke of this mark of the church when he prayed that God would keep it from the evil one. "I do not pray that thou shouldst take them out of the world, but that thou shouldst keep them from the evil one. They are not of the world, even as I am not of the world. Sanctify them in the truth; thy word is truth" (Jn. 17:15-17).

Some people have identified holiness with a culturally determined behavioral pattern and so have identified as holy those who do not gamble or smoke or drink or play cards or go to movies or do any of a large number of such things. Their approach betrays a basic misconception. It may be that holiness in a particular Christian may result in abstinence from one or more of these things, but the essence of holiness is not found there. Consequently, to insist on such things for the church is not to promote holiness but rather to promote legalism and hypocrisy. In some extreme forms it may even promote a false Christianity according to which men and women feel they are justified before God on the basis of some supposedly ethical behavior.

The apostle Paul found that to be true of the Israel of his day, as Jesus had also found it before him. So Paul distinguished clearly between that kind of holiness (the term he used is *righteousness)* and true holiness, which comes from God and is always God-oriented. He said of Israel, "For, being ignorant of the righteousness that comes from God, and seeking to establish their own, they did not submit to God's righteousness" (Rom. 10:3).

Israel had imagined that holiness was something that could be graded. That is, as we look around we see some whom we consider low on the scale of human goodness: criminals, perverts, habitual liars and other base characters. We might give them a score in the low teens, for although they are not very good by our standards they are nevertheless not entirely without any redeeming qualities. A little higher up are the average people of society. They score between thirty and sixty. Then there are the very good people. They may score in the seventies. Beyond that, if you push the score up to one hundred (or higher if that is possible) you get to God. His holiness is perfect holiness. According to that way of looking at holiness, God's holiness is only a perfection of the holiness which lies to a greater or lesser degree in all of us.

We are to please him (some would say "earn heaven") by trying harder.

That is what Israel had done, and it is what nearly everybody naturally does. But it does not reflect the biblical idea of holiness. According to the Bible, holiness actually deals (on God's level) with transcendence and (on our level) with a fundamental response to him which we would call commitment or complete dedication.

The biblical idea of holiness is made somewhat clearer when we consider words that are related to it, namely, _saint_ and _sanctify_. Christ used the second one in John 17. A saint is not a person who has achieved a certain level of goodness (although that is what most people think) but rather one who has been "set apart" for God. In the Bible the word is not restricted to a special class of Christians, still less a class that is established by the official action of an ecclesiastical body. Rather it is used of all Christians (Rom. 1:7; 1 Cor. 1:2; 2 Cor. 1:1; Eph. 1:1; Phil. 1:1; and so on). The saints are the "called-out ones" who make up God's church.

The same idea is also present when the Bible refers to the sanctification of objects (as in Exodus 40). Moses was instructed to sanctify the altar and laver in the midst of the tabernacle. That is, he was to "make saints" of them. The chapter does not refer to any intrinsic change in the nature of the stones—they are not made righteous. It merely indicates that they were to be set apart for a special use by God.

In John 17 Jesus prayed, "I consecrate [the word is _sanctify_] myself, that they also may be consecrated [sanctified] in truth" (v. 19). The verse does not mean that Jesus made himself more righteous, for he already was righteous. Instead it means that he separated himself for a special task, the task of providing salvation for all people by his death. If holiness is to be understood at all, it must be understood in that framework.

But if holiness has to do with separation or consecration

and if believers are already holy by virtue of their being set apart for himself by God, why did Christ pray for our sanctification? Why pray for what we already have? The answer is that although we have been set apart for God we often fail to live up to that calling. To paraphrase Wordsworth, it is "trailing clouds of old commitments, sins and loyalties that we come."

God's Truth

What is the cure? That question brings us to the third mark of the church: truth. We are led to truth because both Christian joy and holiness depend almost entirely on how well we know God's Word—that is, how well we know and practice the principles of God's written revelation. Jesus said, *"These things* I have spoken to you, that my joy may be in you, and that your joy may be full"* (Jn. 15:11), and *"These things* I speak in the world, that they may have my joy fulfilled in themselves"* (Jn. 17:13). Again, "Sanctify them in the *truth;* thy word is *truth"* (Jn. 17:17).

A striking thing, which we realize more and more as we grow in the Christian life, is that nearly all that God does in the world today he does by the Holy Spirit through the instrumentality of his written revelation. That is true of sanctification. Since sanctification means to be set apart for God's use, our text is saying that the only way this will ever happen to us is by appropriating God's truth recorded in the Bible.

As far as truth goes, the world lives by an illusion. Its views are an inevitable problem for us unless we have a sure way of countering and actually overturning its influence. Ray Stedman writes of this problem when he says,

The world lives by what it thinks is truth, by values and standards which are worthless, but which the world esteems highly. Jesus said, "What is exalted among men is an abomination in the sight of God" (Lk. 16:15). That is how the world lives. And how can we live in that kind of a world—touch it and hear it, having it pouring into our ears and exposed to our eyes day and night, and not be conformed to its image and squeezed into its mold? The answer is, we must know the truth. We must know the world and life the way God sees it, the way it really is. We must know it so clearly and strongly that even while we're listening to these alluring lies we can brand them as lies and know that they are wrong.[2]

Stedman is saying that Christians should be the greatest of realists, because their realism is that of the truth of God. That by its very nature should lead to greater joy and sanctification.

A Missionary Church

Up to this point Christ's prayer (Jn. 17) has been dealing with things that concern the church itself or that concern individual Christians personally. We have looked at joy, holiness and truth. But while those characteristics are important and undoubtedly attainable to some degree in this life, it does not take much thinking to figure out that all three would be more quickly attained if we could only be transported to heaven. We have joy here. But what is it compared to that abundant joy we will have when we eventually see the source of our joy face to face? The Bible acknowledges this when it speaks of the blessedness of the redeemed saints, from whose eyes all tears shall be wiped away (Rev. 7:17; 21:4). In this life we undoubtedly know some sanctification. But someday we shall be made completely like Jesus (1 Jn. 3:2). In this life we are able to assimilate some aspects of God's truth. "Now we see in a mirror dimly, but then face to face. Now I know in part; then I shall understand fully, even as I have been fully understood" (1 Cor. 13:12). If that is true, why should we not go to heaven immediately?

The answer is in a fourth mark of the church. The church is not only to look inward and find joy, Christward and find sanctification, to the Scriptures and find truth. It is also to look outward to the world and find there the object of its mission. Jesus said, "As thou [the Father] didst send me into the world, so *I have sent them* into the world. And for their sake I consecrate myself, that they also may be consecrated in truth" (Jn. 17:18-19).

The first thing these verses tell us is where our mission is to be conducted. The word *mission* comes from the Latin verb meaning "to send" or "dispatch." But when we ask "To whom (or where) are we sent?" the answer is "Into the world." That answer is probably the explanation of why the evangelical church in America is not the missionary church it claims to be. It is not that the evangelical church does not support foreign missions. It does. The problem does not lie there. Rather it lies at the point of the evangelicals' personal withdrawal from the culture. Many seem afraid of the culture. They try to keep as far from the world as possible, lest they be contaminated by it. They have developed their own subculture. It is possible, for example, to be born of Christian parents, grow up in that Christian family, have Christian friends, go to Christian schools and colleges, read Christian books, attend a Christian country club (known as a church), watch Christian movies, get Christian employment, be attended by a Christian doctor, and finally die and be buried by a Christian undertaker in hallowed ground. A Christian subculture? That is certainly not what Jesus meant when he spoke of his followers being "in the world."

What does it mean to be in the world as a Christian? It does not mean to be like the world; the marks of the church are to make the church different. It does not mean that we are to abandon Christian fellowship or our other basic Christian orientations. But it does mean that we are to know non-Christians, befriend them and enter into their lives in such a way that we begin to infect them with the gospel, rather than their infecting us with their outlook.

A young pastor in Guatemala went from seminary to a remote area known as Cabrican. Cabrican was unpopular; it was located at an altitude of about nine thousand feet and was nearly always damp and cold. The church he went to was small, having only twenty-eight members, including two elders and two deacons. These believers met together on most nights of the week, but they were not growing as a congregation. There was no outreach. In one of his first messages to them the young pastor, Bernardo Calderón, said, "I know God cannot be satisfied with what we are doing." Then he challenged them to this program.

First, they abandoned the many dull meetings at the church, retaining only the Bible-school hour on Sunday. In their place home meetings were established. On Monday night they would meet in a home in one area of Cabrican, and everyone would be invited. As they made their way to that home they were to invite everyone they encountered, even passers-by on the streets. Since the Christians came from different areas of the city and took different paths to get there this meant that quite a bit of the city was covered. On Tuesday the church met somewhere else. This time different paths were used as the twenty-eight members converged, and different villagers were invited. So it was on Wednesday and Thursday and the other days of the week, as the church literally left its four small walls to go out into the world with the gospel. The result? Within four years the church had eight hundred members. The next year a branch church was started, and today there are six churches in that area of Guatemala, two of which have nearly one thousand members. There is even an agricultural cooperative in which the church members buy land for their own poor and then buy and sell the produce their own people supply. The entire area has been revitalized.

The second thing these verses talk about is the character of the ones who are to conduct this mission, which means our character as Christian people. We are to be _as Christ_ in the world. Jesus compared the disciples to himself, both in having been sent into the world by the Father and being sanctified or set apart to that work. He said, "As thou didst send me into the world, so I have sent them into the world. And for their sake I consecrate myself, that they also might be consecrated in truth" (Jn. 17:18-19). We are to be in our mission as Jesus was in his mission. We are to be like the One we are presenting.

That They May Be One

A fifth mark of the church is unity. Christ said, "I do not pray for these only, but also for those who are to believe in me through their word, that they may all be one; even as thou, Father, art in me, and I in thee, that they also may be in us, so that the world may believe that thou hast sent me. The glory which thou hast given me I have given to them, that they may be one even as we are one, I in them and thou in me, that they may become perfectly one, so that the world may know that thou hast sent me and hast loved them even as thou hast loved me" (Jn. 17:20-23).

What kind of unity is this to be? If the unity is to be organizational, our efforts to achieve and express it will be in one direction while, if it is to be a more subjective unity, our efforts will be expended differently.

One thing the church is not to be is a great *organizational unity*. Whatever advantages or disadvantages may be found in massive organizational unity, that in itself obviously does not produce the results Christ prayed for. Nor does it solve the church's other problems. It has been tried and found wanting. In the early days of the church there was much growth but little organizational unity. Later, as the church came into governmental favor under Constantine and his successors, the visible church increasingly centralized until during the Middle Ages there was literally one united ecclesiastical body covering all Europe. Wherever one went—north, south, east or west—there was one united, interlacing church with the pope at its head. Was it a great age? Was there deep unity of faith? Was the church strong? Was its morality high? Did men and women find themselves increasingly drawn to that faith and come to confess Jesus Christ as their own Savior and Lord? On the contrary, the world believed the opposite. Spurgeon wrote, "The world was persuaded that God had nothing to do with that great crushing, tyrannous, superstitious, ignorant thing which called itself Christianity; and thinking men became infidels, and it was the hardest possible thing to find a genuine intelligent believer north, south, east or west."[3]

Certainly there is something to be said for some form of outward, visible unity in some situations. But it is equally certain that this type of unity is not what we most need, nor is it that for which the Lord prayed.

Another type of apparent unity that we do not need is _conformity_—that is, an approach to the church which would make everyone alike. Here we probably come closest to the error of the evangelical church. If the liberal church for the most part strives for organizational unity—through the various councils of churches and denominational mergers— the evangelical church seems to strive for an identical pattern of looks and behavior for its members. Jesus was not looking for that either. On the contrary, there should be diversity among Christians, diversity of personality, interests, lifestyle and even methods of Christian work and evangelism. Uniformity is dull, like rows of Wheaties boxes. Variety is exciting. We see it in the variety of nature and the actions of God.

But if the unity for which Jesus prayed is not an organizational unity or a unity achieved by conformity, what kind of unity is it? It is a unity analogous to the unity that exists in the Godhead. Jesus spoke of it like this: "That they may all be one; even as thou, Father, art in me, and I in thee, that they also may be in us . . . I in them and thou in me, that they may become perfectly one" (Jn. 17:21, 23). The church is to have a spiritual unity involving the basic orientation, desires and will of those participating. "Now there are varieties of gifts, but the same Spirit; and there are varieties of service, but the same Lord; and there are varieties of working, but it is the same God who inspires them all in every one" (1 Cor. 12:4-6).

This is not to say that all true believers actually enter into this unity as they should. Otherwise, why would Christ have prayed for it? Like the other marks of the church, unity is something given to the church but also something for which the body of true believers should strive.

The Greatest Mark

At last we come to love, the greatest mark of all. Love is the mark that gives meaning to the others and without which the church cannot be what God intends it to be. Having written about love and having placed it in the context of faith, hope and love, the apostle Paul concluded, "But the greatest of these is love" (1 Cor. 13:13).

With the same thought in mind, the Lord Jesus Christ, having spoken of joy, holiness, truth, mission and unity as essential marks of the church in his high priestly prayer (Jn. 17), nevertheless concluded with an emphasis on love. Here we see the "new commandment" of John 13:34-35 once again: "that you love one another; even as I have loved you, that you also love one another. By this all men will know that you are my disciples, if you have love for one another." Jesus said that he declared the name of God to the disciples in order that "the love with which thou [the Father] hast loved me may be in them, and I in them" (Jn. 17:26).

We understand the pre-eminence of love if we see it in reference to the other marks of the church. What happens when you take love away from them? Suppose you subtract love from joy? What do you have? You have hedonism, an exuberance in life and its pleasures, but without the sanctifying joy found in relationship to the Lord Jesus Christ.

Subtract love from holiness. What do you find then? You find self-righteousness, the kind of self-contentment that characterized the Pharisees of Christ's day. By the standards of the day the Pharisees lived very holy lives, but they did not love others and thus were quite ready to kill Christ when he challenged their standards.

Take love from truth and you have a bitter orthodoxy, the kind of teaching which is right but which does not win anybody.

Take love from mission and you have imperialism, colonialism in ecclesiastical garb.

Take love from unity and you soon have tyranny. Tyranny develops in a hierarchical church where there is no compassion for people or desire to involve them in the decision-making process.

Now express love and what do you find? All the other marks of the church follow. What does love for God the Father lead to? Joy. Because we rejoice in God and in what he has done for us. What does love for the Lord Jesus Christ lead to? Holiness. Because we know that we will see him one day and will be like him: "Every one who thus hopes in him purifies himself as he is pure" (1 Jn. 3:3). What does love for the Word of God lead to? Truth. If we love the Word, we will study it and therefore inevitably grow into a fuller appreciation of God's truth. What does love for the world lead to? Mission. We have a message to take to the world. Where does love for our Christian brothers and sisters lead us? Unity. Because by love we discern that we are bound together in that bundle of life which God himself has created within the Christian community.

Like all divine things love comes to us by revelation only. God has revealed himself to be a God of love in the pages of the Old Testament. We are told there that he set his love on Israel even though nothing in the people merited it. God is revealed to be a God of love in Christ's teaching. He called him Father, indicating that his was a father's love. The best and fullest revelation of love is at the cross of Jesus Christ. "For God so loved the world that he gave his only Son, that whoever believes in him should not perish but have eternal life" (Jn. 3:16).

In the words that close the prayer in John 17, Jesus said, "I will make it known," meaning the name of God. What was he thinking of? We could understand the phrase if it had occurred in the past tense; it would then clearly refer to his previous teaching. But why the future tense? I am convinced that Jesus was talking about the cross. It is as though he were saying, "I am now going to demonstrate what I have been talking about in a dramatic and tangible way through my crucifixion."

There has never been, there never will be, a greater demonstration of the love of God. So, if you will not have the cross, if you will not see God speaking in love in Jesus Christ, you will never find a loving God anywhere. The God of the Bible is going to be a silent God for you. The universe is going to be an empty universe. History is going to be meaningless. Only at the cross do we find God in his true nature and learn that these other things have meaning.[4]

6 HOW TO WORSHIP GOD

"Christians believe that true worship is the highest and noblest activity of which man, by the grace of God, is capable."[1] Those words by John R. W. Stott find an echo in the hearts of all who know God and desire to serve him. Yet much that passes for worship today is not worship at all.

"What is worship?" some ask. "Who can worship? Where can one worship? How does one worship?" ask others. Many who sincerely desire to worship do not know how to go about it.

A. W. Tozer, a Bible student of the last generation, wrote about the problems he saw in his churches:

Thanks to our splendid Bible societies and to other effective agencies for the dissemination of the Word, there are today many millions of people who hold "right opinions," probably more than ever before in the history of the Church. Yet I wonder if there was ever a time when true spiritual worship was at a lower ebb. To great sections of the Church the art of worship has been lost entirely, and in its place has come that strange and foreign thing called the "program." This word has been borrowed from the stage and applied with sad wisdom to the type of public service which now passes for worship among us.[2]

A person might argue that program nevertheless has a place in the church's activity and that right opinions about God are essential. Tozer would agree with the second point (and perhaps even with the first). But having said that, we cannot avoid the problem. Is the "worship" we often see in the churches really what God would have? Is it genuine worship? The only way to answer those questions is to study what the Bible has to say about the subject.

Biblical Principles

Let us begin by setting down some of the Bible's basic teachings about worship and then go on to discuss the essential nature and form of worship.

1. *God desires worship*—in fact, he commands it. We see that in Christ's words to the woman of Samaria. The woman had asked Jesus a question about the proper place to worship, but he had directed her thoughts away from the place of worship to the nature of worship itself, saying that God desires such worship. "The hour is coming, and now is, when the true worshipers will worship the Father in spirit and truth, for such the Father *seeks* to worship him" (Jn. 4:23). Similarly, when our Lord was tempted by Satan with the gift of the kingdoms of this world if only he would fall down and worship Satan, Jesus replied by quoting Deuteronomy 6:13. "Begone, Satan! for it is written, 'You shall worship the Lord your God and him only shall you serve' " (Mt. 4:10). In Revelation 19:10 an angel says simply, "Worship God."

2. *God alone is to be worshiped.* That truth is explicit in Christ's reply to Satan. It is also the essence of the first and second commandments in the Decalogue: "You shall have no other gods before me. You shall not make yourself a graven image, or any likeness of anything that is in heaven above,

or that is in the earth beneath, or that is in the water under the earth; you shall not bow down to them or serve them" (Ex. 20:3-5). The God who makes these commands is the triune God who has revealed himself in Jesus Christ, his Son. Therefore, the only true and acceptable worship is worship directed to him. If it is not directed to him, it is not true worship no matter how decorous or impressive the ceremony.

3. *The worship of God is a mark of saving faith.* Paul wrote about this in Philippians: "For we are the true circumcision [that is, the true people of God], who worship God in spirit, and glory in Christ Jesus, and put no confidence in the flesh" (Phil. 3:3). That verse speaks of three marks of faith. The last, putting "no confidence in the flesh," is obviously important, for it is a matter of adhering to the true gospel. The second, "glory" in Christ or "joy," is also a mark of faith and of the church, as indicated in John 17 (studied in the last chapter) and in Galatians 5. But who would naturally think of worship as being a mark of saving faith? Not many. Yet Paul included it here along with other essentials.

4. *Worship is a corporate activity.* This does not mean that we are not to worship privately. Indeed, the Lord commanded privacy in regard to prayer ("When you pray, go into your room and shut the door and pray to your Father who is in secret"—Mt. 6:6). But worship in its fullest expression is to involve the entire people of God. This is noticeable in Scripture from the earliest chapters of Genesis ("At that time men began to call upon the name of the LORD"—Gen. 4:26) to the book of Revelation ("And I heard every creature in heaven and on earth and under the earth and in the sea, and all therein, saying, 'To him who sits upon the throne and to the Lamb be blessing and honor and glory and might for ever and ever!' And the four living creatures said, 'Amen!' and the elders fell down and worshiped"—Rev. 5:13-14).

5. *God is not pleased with all worship.* Jesus made that point to the Pharisees of his day. "Well did Isaiah prophesy of you

hypocrites, as it is written, 'This people honors me with their lips, but their heart is far from me; in vain do they worship me' " (Mk. 7:6-7). Jesus taught that God desires worship, but not all that passes for worship is acceptable to him. True worship must be of the heart and not a ceremony only.

It is sobering to note that in the pages of the Bible God says more about unacceptable worship than he does about acceptable or pleasing worship. The prophet Amos quoted him as saying, "I hate, I despise your feasts, and I take no delight in your solemn assemblies. Even though you offer me your burnt offerings and cereal offerings, I will not accept them, and the peace offerings of your fatted beasts I will not look upon. Take away from me the noise of your songs; to the melody of your harps I will not listen. But let justice roll down like waters, and righteousness like an ever-flowing stream" (Amos 5:21-24).

The prophet Isaiah wrote, "What to me is the multitude of your sacrifices? says the LORD; I have had enough of burnt offerings of rams and the fat of fed beasts; I do not delight in the blood of bulls, or of lambs, or of he-goats. When you come to appear before me, who requires of you this trampling of my courts? Bring no more vain offerings; incense is an abomination to me. New moon and sabbath and the calling of assemblies—I cannot endure iniquity and solemn assembly. Your new moons and your appointed feasts my soul hates; they have become a burden to me, I am weary of bearing them. When you spread forth your hands, I will hide my eyes from you; even though you make many prayers, I will not listen; your hands are full of blood. Wash yourselves; make yourselves clean; remove the evil of your doings from before my eyes; cease to do evil, learn to do good; seek justice, correct oppression; defend the fatherless, plead for the widow" (Is. 1:11-17).

David said, "Thou hast no delight in sacrifice; were I to give a burnt offering, thou wouldst not be pleased. The sacrifice acceptable to God is a broken spirit; a broken and contrite heart, O God, thou wilt not despise" (Ps. 51:16-17).

God desires and commands worship, and although worship is an important and essential mark of the corporate people of God, not all that goes by the name of worship is pleasing to God.

God's "Worth-ship"

"What is true worship?" "How can we know that what we are doing in our worship of God is pleasing to him?" Part of the answer is in the early linguistic derivation of the word _worship._ If we had been living in England during the days of the formation of modern English, between the period of Geoffrey Chaucer and William Shakespeare, we would not have used the word _worship_ at all. Instead we would have said _worth-ship,_ meaning that in worshiping God we were assigning to him his true worth. Linguistically speaking, worship of God is the same thing as praising God or glorifying his name.

Here let us ask what it means to "glorify" God. In the early years of the Greek language, when Homer and Herodotus were writing, there was a Greek verb _dokeō_ from which the Greek noun _doxa_ (meaning "glory") came. The verb originally meant "to appear" or "to seem." Consequently, the noun that derived from it meant "an opinion," which is the way something appears or seems to the observer. From that meaning we have acquired the English words _orthodox, heterodox_ and _paradox,_ meaning "straight (or correct) opinion," "other (or incorrect) opinion" and "contrary (or conflicting) opinion." The theological dictionary edited by Gerhard Kittel gives several pages to this early history of the words. In time the verb _dokeō_ was used only for having a good opinion about some person, and the noun, which kept pace with the verb in development, came to mean the "praise" or "honor" due to one of whom that good opinion was held. Kings possessed glory because they merited the praise of their subjects. Psalm

24 speaks of the King of glory: "Who is the King of glory? The LORD, strong and mighty, the LORD, mighty in battle! . . . The LORD of hosts, he is the King of glory!" (vv. 8, 10).

At this point we can see the effect of taking the word over into the Bible and applying it to God, for if a person had a right opinion about God, it meant that she or he was able to form a correct opinion of God's attributes. God is sovereign, holy, omniscient, just, faithful, loving, immutable. God is glorified when he is acknowledged to be so.

The good Anglo-Saxon word *worth* might well have been used to express the essence of "glory" in the English language had not the French word *gloire* predominated. Since the French word did, we normally speak of glorifying God rather than of worth-ifying him. Nevertheless the idea remains in our word *worship,* as we have indicated. To glorify God is to acknowledge his worth-ship. We worship God, just as we glorify God, when we acknowledge his perfections.

Spirit and Truth
Such a definition of the word *worship* must not lead us to think only in terms of orthodox persuasions, however. Those are important—we must worship the true God and not another—but they are not the whole of what is involved. An element that must also be present is our personal response to the one we are worshiping, which means that we must worship "in spirit and truth," as Jesus indicated (Jn. 4:24). True worshipers must worship "in truth" because truth has to do with what God's nature is. They must worship in "spirit" because they can respond to this only spiritually.

Some Bible readers have been misled in understanding this verse by their assumption that when Jesus spoke of "spirit" he was thinking of the Holy Spirit, meaning that it is only by means of the Holy Spirit that worship is made possible. That is true, of course. Nothing spiritual is possible except by the Spirit's work. Nevertheless that is not the meaning of the verse. Here Jesus is speaking of "spirit" generally (without the definite article), not *the* Holy Spirit. He is teaching that, in the age which he was then inaugurating, the place of worship would not matter. A man or woman would not worship merely by being in the right place and doing certain things. The believer would worship in his or her spirit, which could take place anywhere.

Many people worship with the body. They consider themselves to have worshiped if they have been in the right place doing the right things at the right time. In Christ's day the woman of Samaria thought this meant being in Jerusalem at the Jewish temple or on Mount Gerezim at the Samaritans' temple. In our day this would refer to people who think they have worshiped God because they have occupied a seat in a church on Sunday morning, sung a hymn, lit a candle, crossed themselves or knelt in the aisle. Jesus says that those customs are not worship. They may be a vehicle for real worship; in some cases they may also hinder it. But they are not worship in themselves. We must not confuse worship with the particular things we do on Sunday morning.

In addition, we must not confuse worship with feeling. It may be the case, and often is, that emotions are stirred in real worship. At times tears fill the eyes or joy floods the heart. But it is possible for these things to happen and still not to have worship. It is possible to be moved by a song or by oratory and yet not come to a genuine awareness of God and praise him.

True worship occurs only when that part of human beings, their spirit, which is akin to the divine nature (God is spirit), actually meets with God and finds itself praising him for his love, wisdom, beauty, truth, holiness, compassion, mercy, grace, power and other attributes. On this point, William Barclay wrote: "The true, the genuine worship is when man, through his spirit, attains to friendship and intimacy with God. True and genuine worship is not to come to a certain place; it is not to go through a certain ritual or liturgy; it is not even to bring certain gifts. True worship is when the spirit, the immortal and invisible part of man, speaks to and meets with God, who is immortal and invisible."[3]

To worship God in spirit also has bearing on the question of the various types of liturgy used in Christian churches. It means that, with the exception of liturgical elements that suggest wrong doctrine, no liturgy in itself is either inherently better or worse than another. For any given congregation one type of service will presumably be more valuable than another. But decisions about the most valuable type of service should be arrived at, not by asking whether one likes emotional or nonemotional hymns, extemporaneous or read prayers, congregational responses or silence—in short, whether one prefers Anglican, Lutheran, Presbyterian, Methodist, Baptist, Congregational or Quaker liturgies—but by asking how effective the service is in turning the worshipers' attention away from the service itself to God.

In thinking through this particular issue I have been greatly helped by C. S. Lewis. Lewis was a member of the Church of England and was accustomed to various forms of what we generally call a "liturgical" service. Nevertheless, Lewis did not plead for liturgy. He asked merely for what he called *uniformity,* on the grounds that "novelty" in the worship service at best turns our attention to the novelty and at worst turns it to the one who is enacting the liturgy.

Lewis wrote, "As long as you notice, and have to count, the steps, you are not yet dancing but only learning to dance. A good shoe is a shoe you don't notice. Good reading becomes possible when you need not consciously think about eyes, or light, or print, or spelling. The perfect church service would be one we were almost unaware of; our attention would have been on God."[4] We should pray that God will use any form of church service in which we happen to be participating to that end.

But that does not mean that "anything goes" in Christian worship or that some elements are not necessary and that others are not detrimental. In defining worship as "in truth" Christ meant at least three things.

First, we must approach God _truthfully,_ that is, honestly or wholeheartedly. Jesus said of the people of his day, "This people honors me with their lips, but their heart is far from me; in vain do they worship me . . . " (Mk. 7:6-7). According to Jesus, nothing is worship unless honesty of heart characterizes the worshiper. We must not pretend to worship. We must worship truthfully, knowing that our hearts are open books before him.

Second, we must worship on the basis of _biblical revelation._ The above verse goes on to condemn those who have substituted "the precepts of men" for the doctrines of Scripture. "Thy word is truth," says the Scripture (Jn. 17:17). If we are to worship in truth, our worship must be in accord with the principles and admonitions of the Bible.

A true sermon is an exposition of Scripture. Its purpose is to direct the worshipers' attention to the truth of God and invite them to order their lives in accordance with it. The Westminster Confession of Faith speaks of "the reading of the Scriptures with godly fear; the sound preaching and conscionable hearing of the Word, in obedience unto God, with understanding, faith, and reverence" as being "ordinary" parts of our worship (chap. XXI, 5).

When the Protestant Reformation first took place under Martin Luther in the early sixteenth century, there was an immediate elevation of the Word of God in Protestant services. Doctrines and principles of the Word of God, long covered over by the traditions and ceremonial encrustations of the medieval Church, again came into prominence. John Calvin particularly carried this out with thoroughness, ordering that the altars (the center of the Latin mass) be removed from the churches and that a pulpit with a Bible on it be placed in the center of the building. Every line of the architecture would carry the worshipers' gaze to the Book which alone contains the way of salvation and outlines the principles upon which the church of the living God is to be governed.

Third, to approach God in truth means that we must approach him *Christocentrically.* Jesus said to his disciples, "I am the way, and the truth, and the life; no one comes to the Father, but by me" (Jn. 14:6). That is a difficult point for many to accept. Because of the difficulty, God has taken pains to teach throughout Scripture that this is the way of approach to him.

In the Old Testament God gave Moses clear instructions for the design of the Jewish temple. What was the temple? It was not a thing of great beauty or permanence. It had no stained-glass windows, no arches. It was made of pieces of wood and animal skins. But each part was significant. It taught the way to God. Take that temple with its altar for sacrifice, its laver for cleansing, its Holy Place and its Holy of Holies. The altar is the cross of Christ. It teaches that without the shedding of blood there is no remission of sins. It directs attention to the Lamb of God who was to come to take away the sins of the world. The laver is a picture of cleansing, which Christ provides when we confess our sins and enter into fellowship with him. The table of shewbread, which was within the Holy Place, speaks of Christ as the bread of life. The seven-branched candlestick reveals him as the light of the world. The altar of incense is a picture of prayer. Behind the altar of incense was the great veil, dividing the Holy Place from the Holy of Holies. The veil was torn in two at the moment of Christ's death in order to demonstrate that his death was the fulfillment of all those figures. His death is the basis of our approach to the Almighty. Finally, within the Holy of Holies was the ark of the covenant with its mercy seat upon which once a year on the Day of Atonement the high priest placed the blood of the lamb. There, symbolized by the space above the mercy seat, was the presence of God to whom we can now come because of Christ's death on our behalf.

There is no other way to come to God. To come through Christ is to come in truth. He is the truth. We must come in God's way and not in any way of human devising.[5]

7 SALVATION'S SIGNS AND SEALS

The last chapter contained a section of the Westminster Confession of Faith which spoke of "the reading of the Scriptures" and "sound preaching" as being ordinary parts of Christian worship. The Confession goes on to speak of other parts of worship, among which are "the due administration and worthy receiving of the sacraments" (chap. XXI, 5).

There has been much debate in the church about the sacraments—their number, for example, or whether a particular form of administration of the sacraments is necessary for the existence of a true church. To a greater or lesser degree, however, nearly all Christians have acknowledged that there are sacraments instituted by Christ and that these are to have a place in the normal or "ordinary" worship of God's people. The word *sacrament* (like the word *Trinity*) is an extrabiblical term. It entered theology by means of the Latin Vulgate, where it is customarily used to render the Greek word *mysterion*. It designates those "ordinances" (practices) to which the Lord himself gave special significance.

In most Protestant churches the sacraments are two: baptism and the Lord's Supper. In the Roman Catholic Church there are seven: the two sacraments already referred to plus the ceremonies of penance, confirmation, marriage, holy orders and final unction.

Peter Lombard (1100-60) called a sacrament "a sign of a sacred thing."[1] John Calvin wrote that a sacrament is "an outward sign by which the Lord seals on our consciences the promises of his good will toward us in order to sustain the weakness of our faith; and we in turn attest our piety toward him in the presence of the Lord and of his angels and before men."[2]

Four Elements

In what way do the Scriptures represent the sacraments of the church as being different from other practices, such as the reading of Scripture or prayers, which are not sacramental? What constitutes a sacrament? There are four elements.

1. The sacraments are *divine ordinances instituted by Christ himself.* In that respect the sacraments are similar to other necessary ordinances which also form part of the church's worship—prayer, for example. Christ told us to pray. But they differ from things which we may do but which are not commanded. We sing when we assemble, and we have biblical warrant for it, including the example of Jesus and his disciples (Mk. 14:26). But the singing of hymns is not specifically commanded by the Lord and consequently falls in the category of those things which are permissible and even good but not mandatory. The sacraments are mandatory. The Lord's Supper was instituted by Jesus on the night in which he was betrayed. Baptism was instituted shortly before his ascension into heaven.

2. The sacraments are ordinances in which *material elements are used as visible signs of God's blessing.* In baptism the sign is

water. In the Lord's Supper two signs are used: bread, which signifies the broken body of the Lord Jesus Christ, and wine, which signifies his shed blood.

This feature is important in understanding the nature of a sacrament. It sets baptism and the Lord's Supper off from other proper but nonsacramental things, which do not use a material element as a sign. The material element distinguishes the sacrament from the reality that it signifies. A sign is a visible object that points to a reality different from and more significant than itself. A sign saying "New York" points to New York. A sign reading "Drink Coca-Cola" directs our attention to Coca-Cola. The sacrament of baptism points to our identification with Christ by faith. The Lord's Supper points to the reality of our communion with him. In the case of the sacraments, the sign is secondary, outward and visible. The reality is primary, inward and invisible.

An important consequence of this is that neither baptism nor the Lord's Supper make or keep one a Christian. That is, we do not become a Christian by being baptized, nor do we remain a Christian by "taking communion" periodically. Those signs merely point to something that has already taken place internally and invisibly.

Again, a sign frequently indicates ownership, and the sacraments do that too, particularly baptism. Baptism indicates to the world and to ourselves that we are not our own but that we have been bought with a price and are now identified with Jesus. That truth was a great comfort to Martin Luther, who had times when he was confused about everything, no doubt because of the strain of being in the forefront of the Reformation for twenty-eight years. In those bleak periods he questioned the Reformation itself; he questioned his faith; he even questioned the value of the work of the Lord Jesus Christ on his behalf. At such times, we are told, he would write on his table in chalk the two words _Baptizatus sum!_ (I have been baptized!). That would reassure him that he really was Christ's and had been identified with him in his death and resurrection.

3. The sacraments are *means of grace* to the one who rightly partakes of them. In saying this we must be careful to point out that we are not therefore assigning some magical property to baptism or the observance of the Lord's Supper, as if grace, like medicine, is automatically dispensed along with the material elements. That error, in regard both to the sacraments and grace, led to the abuse of the sacraments in the early Roman Catholic Church and then later in some of the groups that emerged from the Reformation. In each case the sacrament rather than faith became the means of salvation. The custom arose even of delaying baptism (in particular) until the last possible moment before death, in order that the greatest number of sins might be washed away by it.

To say that the sacraments are not magical or mechanical, however, does not mean that they do not have value. God has chosen to use them to encourage and strengthen faith in believers. Thus, they presuppose the acknowledgment of God's grace by the one who partakes of them, but at the same time they also strengthen faith by reminding the believer of what the sacraments signify and of the faithfulness of the One who has given them.

John Murray writes,

Baptism is a means of grace and conveys blessing, because it is the certification to us of God's grace and in the acceptance of that certification we rely upon God's faithfulness, bear witness to his grace, and thereby strengthen our faith. . . . In the Lord's supper that significance is increased and cultivated, namely, communion with Christ and participation of the virtue accruing from his body and blood. The Lord's supper represents that which is continuously being wrought. We partake of Christ's body and blood through the means of the ordinance. We thus see that the accent falls on the faithfulness of God, and the efficacy resides in the response we yield to that faithfulness.[3]

4. The sacraments are *seals, certifications* or *confirmations* to us of the grace they signify. In our day the use of seals is infrequent, but the examples we have suggest the idea. The seal of the United States of America appears on a passport, for example. It is stamped into the paper so that the document cannot be altered, thus validating the passport and showing that the one possessing it is a United States citizen. Other documents are validated by a notary public. The notary's seal is confirmation of the oath taken. The sacraments are God's seal on the attestation that we are his children and are in fellowship with him.

Baptism

The first of the two Protestant sacraments is baptism. "All authority in heaven and on earth has been given to me. Go therefore and make disciples of all nations, baptizing them in the name of the Father and of the Son and of the Holy Spirit, teaching them to observe all that I have commanded you; and lo, I am with you always, to the close of the age" (Mt. 28:18-20). It is evident from those verses that baptism is an initiatory sacrament belonging to the task of making disciples; the text speaks of the authority or lordship of Christ and of the baptized person as one who recognizes and professes that lordship.

Major difficulties have arisen in dealing with this subject, as the controversy surrounding it would indicate.[4]

A good beginning for our present purposes may be made by recognizing that there are two closely related words for *baptism* in the New Testament, and that they do not necessarily have the same meaning. The first word, *baptō,* means "dip" or "immerse." The second word, *baptizō,* may mean "immerse," but it also occurs with a variety of other meanings which in turn lead to a proper understanding of what the passages using this word signify. In the English Bible *baptizō* has generally been transliterated to give us the word *baptize.* When a word is transliterated into English from an-other language, it is quite often an indication of a multi-plicity of meanings. Thus, if the word *baptizō* had lent itself to easy translation, an obvious English word would have been used to translate it. If *baptizō* had meant only "immerse," then immerse would be the word used. We would speak of "John the Immerser." Or we would recite, "Go therefore and make disciples of all nations, immersing them in the name of the Father and of the Son and of the Holy Spirit." That is not the case. We therefore must look beyond the purely literal mean-ing of the word *baptize* to the more important metaphorical meanings.

Here we gain help from classical Greek literature. The Greeks used the word *baptizō* from about 400 B.C. to the second century after Christ. In their writings *baptizō* always points to a change having taken place or, as we might properly say, to a change of identity by any means. Thus, to give a few examples, it can refer to a change having taken place by immersing an object in a liquid, as in dyeing cloth, by drink-ing too much wine and thus getting drunk, by overexertion, and by other causes.

Of all the texts that might be cited from antiquity the one that gives greatest clarity to this issue is a text from a Greek poet and physician, Nicander, who lived about 200 B.C. In a recipe for making pickles he used both words. Nicander said that the vegetable should first be dipped *(baptō)* in boiling water and then baptized *(baptizō)* in the vinegar solution. Both had to do with immersing the vegetable in the solution. But the first was temporary while the other, the operation of baptizing the vegetable, produced a permanent change. We could say that the baptizing had identified the vegetable with the brine.[5]

This meaning of the word is obvious in many Old Testa-ment and New Testament texts. Thus, in Isaiah 21:4, we read: "My heart misleads me, lawlessness baptizes me" (literal translation of the Septuagint). The writer was changed from a state of quiet trust in God to fearfulness as a result of seeing great wickedness and knowing that terrible judgments would follow. Similarly, Galatians 3:27 says, "For as many of you as were baptized into Christ have put on Christ." That is, the Christians in Galatia had been identified with him.

That the word *baptizō* may be used metaphorically does not mean that it must be used in that way in passages dealing with the sacrament of baptism. But in point of fact, those passages above all require a metaphorical meaning. They require it because only an understanding of baptism as identification with Christ makes any sense of them.

An example of such verses is Mark 16:16. "He who believes and is baptized *(baptizō)* will be saved." People have read that verse and have drawn the false conclusion that unless a person is baptized (or immersed) in water he or she cannot be saved. We should know that such a conclusion is wrong because of the teaching of the rest of Scripture about the way in which a person is to be saved: by grace through faith in the death of Jesus Christ alone. If baptism is required for salvation, then the believing thief who was crucified with Christ is lost. Once we get away from the idea that the verse is talking about water, and instead think of the believer's identification with Christ, then the statement becomes clear. We recognize that Jesus was calling for an intellectual belief in himself plus personal commitment. "He who believes in me and is identified with me shall be saved." In that form the verse is a theological parallel to John 1:12: "But to all who *received* him, who *believed* in his name, he gave power to become children of God," and Revelation 3:20: "Behold, I stand at the door and knock; if any one *hears* my voice and *opens* the door, I will come in to him and eat with him, and he with me." All three verses teach that there must be a personal identification with Jesus by the person believing.

A second verse illuminated by the metaphorical meaning

of the word *baptizō* is 1 Corinthians 10:1-2. "I want you to know, brethren, that our fathers were all under the cloud, and all passed through the sea, and all were baptized into Moses in the cloud and in the sea." That passage is especially significant in understanding baptism, since the people of Israel were obviously not immersed either in the sea or the cloud. The cloud was behind them, separating them from the pursuing Egyptians. The Egyptians were immersed in the sea, and they drowned in it. The meaning here is a change of identity. Before the crossing of the Red Sea the people were in rebellion against Moses. Their original attitude changed into an attitude of obedience and rejoicing after the Red Sea crossing.[6]

Baptized into Christ

Study of the word *baptize* points to the primary meaning of baptism as a sign of our union with Christ through the work of the Holy Spirit. Hence, we find many references to being baptized with or by the Spirit, or being baptized "into" Christ or "in the name of" Christ.

In what ways are we identified with Christ in our baptism? The answer is, in all ways—in his birth, life, death and resurrection—but chiefly in his death and resurrection. Paul spoke of our identification with Christ in his death when he wrote, "Do you not know that all of us who have been baptized into Christ Jesus were baptized into his death? We were buried therefore with him by baptism into death, so that as Christ was raised from the dead by the glory of the Father, we too might walk in newness of life" (Rom. 6:3-4). We are baptized into Christ's death in two ways. First, when Jesus died on the cross God regarded us as having died with him as far as our sin is concerned. God the Father put God the Son to death, and since all who believe were united to him by the Holy Spirit from before the foundation of the world, they too were put to death. Their sin was punished, and they may now stand boldly in God's presence as his justified people.

Second, there is a sense in which our union with Christ in his death refers to our life here and now. Paul says that believers are to count themselves as dead to sin but alive to God through Jesus (Rom. 6:11). Through our identification with Christ in his death the power of sin over us is broken and we are set free to serve God.

We are also identified with Christ in his resurrection. Paul says, "For if we have been united with him in a death like his, we shall certainly be united with him in a resurrection like his" (Rom. 6:5). As in the case of our union with Christ in his death, that identification means two things—first, our future resurrection. "For as in Adam all die, so also in Christ shall all be made alive" (1 Cor. 15:22). It also means newness of life now (the main point of Romans 6). In Philippians Paul wrote about his desire to "know him [Christ] and the power of his resurrection" (Phil. 3:10). He wanted to experience the holy "resurrection power" of Christ as he went about his life of service for him.

Baptism is our sign and seal of that identification with Christ and hence a proof of our true security as God's people (Eph. 4:30). The book of Ezekiel contains a prophecy that has to do with God's dealing with Israel at the end of history. Six men enter Jerusalem to pronounce judgment on the inhabitants; but before they go in, one man clothed in linen and carrying a writer's case enters to "put a mark upon the foreheads of the men who sigh and groan over all the abominations that are committed in" Israel (Ezek. 9:4). Afterward the others are told, "Slay old men outright, young men and maidens, little children and women, but touch no one upon whom is the mark" (v. 6).

All who believe in the Lord Jesus are identified by the Holy Spirit of God as "Christ's ones," Christians, and are made secure in that identification. The Bible says, "God's firm foundation stands, bearing this seal: 'The Lord knows those who are his,' and, 'Let every one who names the name of the Lord depart from iniquity' " (2 Tim. 2:19).

Remembrance

The second of the two Protestant sacraments is the Lord's Supper, which Jesus instituted on the night before his crucifixion. That event is recorded in each of the synoptic Gospels (Mt. 26:17-30; Mk. 14:12-26; Lk. 22:7-23), but the best and fullest account is in 1 Corinthians in a passage in which Paul was attempting to correct certain abuses of the supper prevailing in the Corinthian church. This passage reads: "For I received from the Lord what I also delivered to you, that the Lord Jesus on the night when he was betrayed took bread, and when he had given thanks, he broke it, and said, 'This is my body which is for you. Do this in remembrance of me.' In the same way also the cup, after supper, saying, 'This cup is the new covenant in my blood. Do this, as often as you drink it, in remembrance of me.' For as often as you eat this bread and drink the cup, you proclaim the Lord's death until he comes. Whoever, therefore, eats the bread or drinks the cup of the Lord in an unworthy manner will be guilty of profaning the body and blood of the Lord. Let a man examine himself, and so eat of the bread and drink of the cup" (1 Cor. 11:23-28).

The Lord's Supper is like baptism in possessing all the elements of a sacrament. But it is unlike baptism in that baptism is an initiatory sacrament (it testifies to a primary identification with Christ without which one is not a Christian at all) while the Lord's Supper is a continuing sacrament meant to be observed again and again ("As often as you drink it") throughout the Christian life. This character of the Lord's Supper is seen in its past, present and future significance.

The *past significance* of the Lord's Supper is made clear by the word *remembrance*. In the Lord's Supper we look back to the Lord's death. We remember his substitutionary atonement, first of all; it is this that the broken bread, representing the Lord's broken body, and the wine, representing his shed blood, most clearly signify. Atonement has to do with our being made right with God. Substitutionary means that this was achieved by the death of another in our place.

Why did Jesus die? The Bible teaches that all who have ever lived are sinners, having broken God's law, and that the penalty for sin is death. The Bible says, "None is righteous, no, not one; no one understands, no one seeks for God. All have turned aside, together they have gone wrong; no one does good, not even one" (Rom. 3:10-12). It says, "The soul that sins shall die" (Ezek. 18:4), and "the wages of sin is death" (Rom. 6:23). This death is not merely physical, though it is that. It is spiritual as well. Death is separation. Physical death is the separation of the soul and spirit from the body. Spiritual death is the separation of the soul and spirit from God. We deserve that separation as a consequence of our sin. But Jesus became our substitute by experiencing both physical and spiritual death in our place.

A vivid illustration of this principle is seen in the early chapters of Genesis. Adam and Eve had sinned and were in terror of the consequences. God had warned them. He had said, "You may freely eat of every tree of the garden; but of the tree of the knowledge of good and evil you shall not eat, for in the day that you eat of it you shall die" (Gen. 2:16-17). At that point they probably did not have a very clear idea of what death was, but they knew it was serious. Consequently, when they sinned through disobedience and then later heard God walking toward them in the garden, they tried to hide.

But no one can hide from God. God found them, called them out of hiding and began to deal with their transgression. What should we expect to happen as a result of that confrontation? Here is God who told our first parents that in the day they sinned they would die. Here are Adam and Eve who have sinned. In that situation we should expect the immediate execution of the sentence. If God had put them to death in that moment, both physically and spiritually, banishing them from his presence forever, it would have been just.

But that is not what happened. Instead, we have God first rebuking the sin and then performing a sacrifice. As a result, Adam and Eve were clothed with the skins of the slain animals. It was the first death that anyone had ever witnessed. It was enacted by God. As Adam and Eve looked on they must have been horrified. Yet even as they recoiled from the sacrifice, they must have marveled as well. For what God was showing was that although they deserved to die it was possible for another, in this case two animals, to die in their place. The animals paid the price of their sin, and they were clothed in the skins of the animals as a reminder of that fact.

That is the meaning of substitution. It is the death of one on behalf of another. Yet we must also say, as the Bible teaches, that the death of animals could never take away the penalty of sin (Heb. 10:4). That event was only a symbol of how sin was to be taken away. The real sacrifice was performed by Jesus Christ, and we look back to it in the communion service.

We also look back to something that Jesus suggested when he spoke of the wine as the "blood of the covenant" (Mk. 14:24) and as "the new covenant in my blood" (1 Cor. 11:25). We look back to that victory on the basis of which God has established a new covenant of salvation with his redeemed people. A covenant is a solemn promise confirmed by an oath or sign. So when Christ spoke of the cup as commemorating a new covenant he was pointing to the promises of salvation that God made to us on the basis of Christ's death. It comes to us by grace alone.

The Lord's Supper has a *present significance*. First, the sacrament is something in which we repeatedly take part, thereby remembering the death of the Lord again and again until he comes. Second, it is an occasion for examining our lives in the light of our profession of faith in his death. Paul says, "Let a man examine himself, and so eat of the bread and drink of the cup. For any one who eats and drinks without discerning the body eats and drinks judgment upon himself" (1 Cor. 11:28-29).

At the heart of the present significance of the Lord's Supper is our communion or fellowship with Christ, hence the term "communion service." In coming to this service the believer comes to meet with Christ and have fellowship with him at his invitation. The examination takes place because it would be hypocrisy for us to pretend that we are in communion with the holy One while actually cherishing known sin in our hearts.

The manner in which Jesus is present in the communion service is a matter that has divided the Christian church. There are three theories. The first is that Jesus is not present at all, at least no more than he is present all the time and in everything. To those who hold that view, the Lord's Supper takes on an exclusively memorial character. It is only a remembrance of Christ's death. The second view is that of the Roman Catholic Church. In it the body and blood of Christ are supposed to be literally present under the appearance of the bread and wine. Before the mass the elements are literally bread and wine. But in the mass, through the ministrations of the priest, they are changed so that, although worshipers perceive only the bread and wine, they nevertheless actually eat and drink the body and blood of Jesus. That process is called transubstantiation. The third view, the view of John Calvin particularly but also of other Reformers, is that Christ is present in the communion service, but spiritually rather than physically. Calvin called this "the real presence" to indicate that a spiritual presence is every bit as real as a physical one.

What are we to think of these theories? To begin with, we must say that there can be no quarrel with the memorial theory, since it is certainly true as far as it goes. The only question is whether more than remembrance is involved. The real division is between the view of the majority of the Reformers and the doctrine of the Roman Catholic Church. Those who favor a literal, physical presence (and Luther was one, though he did not accept the theory of transubstantiation) argue from a literal interpretation of Christ's words, "This is my body" (Mk. 14:22). But that hardly decides the matter, because such expressions occur frequently in the Bible with obviously figurative or representational meanings. For example:

"The seven good cows are seven years . . . "
"You are the head of gold"
"The field is the world"
"The Rock was Christ"
"The seven lampstands are the seven churches"
"I am the door of the sheep"
"I am the true vine"[7]

That Jesus was using figurative language and not performing a miracle of transubstantiation should be evident from the fact that his body was right there with the disciples as he spoke. Today his resurrected body is in heaven.

A reason for taking the presence of Christ in the sacrament to be spiritual is that this is the sense in which every other promise of the presence of Christ with us in this age must be taken. Bannerman writes,

> Such promises as these–"Lo, I am with you alway, even unto the end of the world"; "Where two or three are met together in my name, there am I in the midst of you"; "Behold, I stand at the door and knock: if any man hear my voice, and open the door, I will come in to him, and will sup with him, and he with me"; and such like–plainly give us ground to affirm that Christ, through his Spirit, is present in his ordinances to the faith of the believer, imparting spiritual blessing and grace. But there is nothing that would lead us to make a difference or distinction between the presence of Christ in the Supper and the presence of Christ in his

*other ordinances, in so far as the manner of that presence is con-
cerned. The efficacy of the Savior's presence may be different in
the way of imparting more or less of saving grace, according to
the nature of the ordinance, and the degree of the believer's faith.
But the manner of that presence is the same, being realized through
the Spirit of Christ, and to the faith of the believer.*[8]

Some well-known verses in John 6 also speak of faith in Christ
and of a spiritual feeding on him. They do not speak literally
of the Lord's Supper, since the Lord's sacrament had not yet
been instituted. "Truly, truly, I say to you, unless you eat the
flesh of the Son of man and drink his blood, you have no
life in you; he who eats my flesh and drinks my blood has
eternal life, and I will raise him up at the last day. For my
flesh is food indeed, and my blood is drink indeed" (Jn.
6:53-55).

If we want synonyms for "eat" and "drink," we find them
in John 6 in such concepts as believe (vv. 29, 35, 47), come
(v. 35), see (v. 40), hear and learn of (v. 45). All indicate a
response to Jesus. The terms *eat* and *drink* stress that this
feeding by faith is to be as real as literal eating.

The third significance of the Lord's Supper is *future*. Paul
said, "As often as you eat this bread and drink the cup, you
proclaim the Lord's death *until he comes*" (1 Cor. 11:26). The
Lord suggested the same when he told the disciples who were
eating the last meal with him, "Truly, I say to you, I shall not
drink again of the fruit of the vine until that day when I drink
it new in the kingdom of God" (Mk. 14:25).

We speak of the real presence of the Lord Jesus Christ in
the service as we know it now, and we seek to respond to
him and serve him. We readily admit that there are times
when this is difficult and the Lord does not seem to be present.
Whether because of sin, fatigue or simply lack of faith, Jesus
often seems to be far away. Though we continue on in Christian life and in service, we long for that day when we will
see him face to face and be like him (1 Jn. 3:2). The com-

munion service is a reminder of that day. It is a foreshadowing of the great marriage supper of the Lamb. It is an encouragement to faith and an impulse to a higher level of holiness.

8 SPIRITUAL GIFTS

One of the marks of the church is unity. This mark is inherent in the very definition of the church. The church is (1) founded on the Lord Jesus Christ, (2) called into being by the Holy Spirit and (3) to contain people of all races who thereby become one new people in the sight of God. If the church is founded on Jesus Christ, it has one foundation, meaning one Lord and one theology centered in him. If it is called into being by the Holy Spirit, the fundamental experience of the people of God is identical. They come from various backgrounds, but they are called into a relationship to God by a work of regeneration, justification and adoption. If they have become one new people, they are obviously set off from the world as a separate and holy entity.

A person who becomes a Christian notices this unity. Before, the person was to a greater or lesser extent on his or her own. Now that has changed. As Paul said in writing to the Ephesians, "So then you are no longer strangers and sojourners, but you are fellow citizens with the saints and members of the household of God" (Eph. 2:19).

One is not a member of the church for long, however, before the many diversities within it are also evident. Some are the results of sin and are entirely unjustified. Others are actually the gift of God to the church and are of great importance for the church's proper functioning in the world.

This twofold emphasis, on unity and diversity, appears at important points in the New Testament writings. For example, in Ephesians 4 a number of phrases speak eloquently of our unity. "There is one body and one Spirit, just as you were called to the one hope that belongs to your call, one Lord, one faith, one baptism, one God and Father of us all, who is above all and through all and in all" (vv. 4-6). But no sooner had Paul articulated that truth than he went on to speak of diversity in the area of gifts. "But grace was given to each of us according to the measure of Christ's gift. . . . And his gifts were that some should be apostles, some prophets, some evangelists, some pastors and teachers, to equip the saints for the work of ministry, for building up the body of Christ" (vv. 7, 11-12). In the next verses he illustrated his point by speaking of a body which, although it is one body, nevertheless has many differently functioning parts.

In 1 Corinthians the examples of unity and diversity are mixed. "Now there are varieties of gifts, but the same Spirit; and there are varieties of service, but the same Lord; and there are varieties of working, but it is the same God who inspires them all in every one" (1 Cor. 12:4-6). After listing nine of these gifts the apostle concluded, "All these are inspired by one and the same Spirit, who apportions to each one individually as he wills" (v. 11).

The book of Romans has a similar emphasis. "For as in one body we have many members, and all the members do not have the same function, so we, though many, are one body in Christ, and individually members one of another" (Rom. 12:4-5).

These verses teach that a certain kind of unity and a certain kind of diversity are necessary for the health of the church. Without the unity, a unity of relationship to Christ through the work of God's Spirit, there is no church at all. We are still in our sins. On the other hand, without diversity the church cannot be healthy and will certainly not function properly, any more than a body without arms or legs.

Up to now everything said about the church may be looked at as being in the area of unity: the definition of the church, its marks, the nature of its worship, the sacraments. These things are the experience of all who are God's people. Now we must look at the areas of diversity. First, we want to look at spiritual gifts, including the role of leaders in helping others to discover and develop those gifts. Second, we will look at church offices and how they fit into the larger picture.

To Each a Gift

Spiritual gifts have been widely discussed in the church in recent years. Others in earlier years were poorer for the absence of such discussion. One person who has written about spiritual gifts is Ray C. Stedman of the Peninsula Bible Church of Palo Alto, California. He defines a spiritual gift as "a capacity for service which is given to every true Christian without exception and which was something each did not possess before he became a Christian."[1]

That definition is worth looking at in detail. First, it defines a spiritual gift as being given to the believer by God, as the words "spiritual gift" imply. In the New Testament the word for that kind of gift (the word which is almost always used in speaking of them) is _charisma_ or _charismata_ (plural). We get our word _charismatic_ from it, though the word is far more restricted in its English meaning. The most important thing about the word _charisma_ is that it is based on the Greek noun _charis,_ meaning "grace." Since grace is God's unmerited favor, the emphasis is that spiritual gifts are dispensed by

God according to his good pleasure. One Christian will receive one gift, another Christian another. Some will receive more than one gift. Paul emphasized this in the verse already quoted. "All these are inspired by one and the same Spirit, who apportions to each one individually *as he wills*" (1 Cor. 12:11).

In saying that a spiritual gift is something the Christian did not possess before becoming a Christian, Stedman distinguishes a spiritual gift from what we would call a natural talent. Natural talents are also gifts of God. We are told that "every good endowment and every perfect gift is from above," which is true of talents and for Christians and non-Christians alike (Jas. 1:17). It is also true that a Christian may exercise a spiritual gift through a natural talent. Examples would be one who fulfills the gift of "helping" through a talent for carpentry, baking, financial management or similar things, or one who fulfills the gift of "exhortation" through a natural ability to get close to people. Still, spiritual gifts are not talents for the simple reason that they are given for spiritual ends only, and only to Christians. They are "to equip the saints for the work of ministry, for building up the body of Christ" (Eph. 4:12).

An example of the relationship between a spiritual gift and talent is found in the Old Testament in the case of Bezalel, one of the craftsmen who worked on the art objects of the Jewish tabernacle. The Lord said of this man, "I have filled him with the Spirit of God, with ability and intelligence, with knowledge and all craftsmanship, to devise artistic designs, to work in gold, silver, and bronze, in cutting stones for setting, and in carving wood, for work in every craft" (Ex. 31:3-5). Bezalel had been given the natural talent of craftsmanship, but he had also been given the spiritual gift of knowledge or intelligence which directed him in the way his natural talents were to be used. Because of the spiritual gift he was able to produce objects for Israel's worship.

A third point of Stedman's definition of spiritual gifts is that every Christian has been given at least one. Paul said, "To *each* is given the manifestation of the Spirit for the common good" (1 Cor. 12:7). Peter wrote, "*Each* has received a gift" (1 Pet. 4:10).

Failure to see that truth has led in church history to what John R. W. Stott has termed "the clerical domination of the laity." There has developed within the church (for a variety of reasons) a kind of division between clergy and laity in which the clergy are supposed to lead and do the work of Christian ministry while the people (which is what the word *laity* means) are to follow docilely—and, of course, give money to support the clergy and their work. As an example of that outlook Stott quotes from a 1906 papal encyclical entitled *Vehmenter Nos:* "As for the masses, they have no other right than of letting themselves be led, and of following their pastors as a docile flock."[2]

That is not what the church as the people of God is to be. Where such a view prevails, the church and its ministry suffer by the loss of the exercise of gifts given to the laity. Gifts are for use in serving others. The laity serve the church and the world. The clergy serve the laity, particularly in helping them to develop and use their gifts. As Stott says, "Clergy are not hyphenated to the laity as if they were a separate class; they are 'ministers of the people' because they themselves belong to the people they are called to serve."[3]

Those three points about the nature of spiritual gifts show how important they are. They are important theologically, because they lead us to a fuller understanding of the grace of God. They are important personally and experientially, because they have direct bearing on the individual believer's service to Christ and others within the church. They are important organizationally, because they show how clergy and laity should relate to one another.

What Are the Gifts?

The gifts of the Spirit are listed in four separate chapters of

Spiritual Gifts Listed in the New Testament

	Eph. 4:11	1 Cor. 12:8-10	1 Cor. 12:28-30	Rom. 12:6-8	1 Pet. 4:11
1.	Apostles		Apostles		
2.	Prophets		Prophets	Prophecy	
3.				Service	Service
4.	Evangelists				
5.		Wisdom			
6.		Knowledge			
7.	Pastors				
8.	Teachers		Teachers	Teaching	Speaking
9.				Exhortation	
10.		Faith			
11.		Healing	Working miracles		
12.		Working miracles [Prophecy]	Healing		
13.		Ability to distinguish spirits			
14.				Contributing	
15.			Helpers	Giving aid	
16.				Mercy	
17.			Administrators		
18.		Tongues	Tongues		
19.		Interpretation of tongues	Interpretation of tongues		

the New Testament and in one of those chapters in two places. That makes five lists in all (Eph. 4:11; 1 Cor. 12:8-10; 1 Cor. 12:28-30; Rom. 12:6-8; and 1 Pet. 4:11). These lists vary in regard to the gifts listed. The shortest is 1 Peter 4:11, which contains only two gifts, speaking and service. The lists in 1 Corinthians 12 each contain nine, though those nine are not identical. In all there may be nineteen gifts mentioned, but that is not an absolute figure: different words can conceivably be used to describe the same or nearly identical gifts, and there may be gifts not mentioned.

1. *Apostles and prophets.* First in the lists found in Ephesians 4:11 and 1 Corinthians 12:28-30 is the gift of apostles and prophets. Some who have written about the gifts have tried to show that apostles and prophets are present today. They point out that the word *apostle* does not mean only the original band of authoritative spokesmen commissioned by Christ; it can also refer to anyone who is sent forth as a witness, particularly to establish churches. Similarly, *prophet* does not always mean one who receives a special inspired word from God; it also refers to anyone who speaks boldly in his name (as in 1 Cor. 14). Those points are well taken. But they do not really apply to the use of the words in the two lists mentioned. In these lists both *apostle* and *prophet* must be taken in their most technical sense. Therefore, *apostles* refers to those witnesses who were specifically commissioned by Christ to establish the church on a proper base, and *prophets* refers to those who received God's message (like prophets of old) and recorded it in the pages of what we call the New Testament.

Neither one of these gifts exists today. We no longer have apostles or prophets in that sense. But we are not deprived of the benefits of those first gifts of God to the Christian community. The apostles did establish the first churches and taught them authoritatively, and those who spoke from God have left us the New Testament.

2. *Evangelists.* The second category of gifts contains just

one item. Obviously the gift of evangelism has not ceased. An evangelist is one who possesses a special ability in communicating the gospel of salvation from sin through Jesus Christ. The existence of such a spiritual gift does not mean that others who are not evangelists are excused from the obligation to tell others about Jesus. On the contrary, that is a task we all share. The Great Commission declares it. But it does mean that some are especially gifted in this area.

The evangelist does not necessarily have to be a well-educated or highly intelligent person. True, evangelists must know their message. They must be able to answer questions about it. But their primary gift is in being able to communicate the basic gospel clearly and well. The gift of evangelism is not limited to those who are "professionals," like Billy Graham. It is more often the gift of laypersons. In his study of spiritual gifts in *The Holy Spirit*, Graham points out that the only person in the entire Bible who was actually called an evangelist is Philip, and he was a deacon. Speaking personally, I can say that I have known quite a few men and women who have had this gift, and none of them was ordained. Rather, they were people who enjoyed and were particularly effective in speaking about Christ to others.

3. *Pastors, teachers and the gift of exhortation.* I put the three gifts of pastoring, teaching and exhorting in one category because they often go together and may in fact actually be one gift. In Ephesians 4:11 the words *pastors* and *teachers* may be joined together due to the nature of the Greek phrasing in that sentence, so that we could speak of the gift of pastor-teacher.

Pastor refers to one who has a pastoral oversight of others. It is based on the idea of shepherding and looks back to the pattern of Jesus, who described himself as "the good shepherd" (Jn. 10:11) and who is referred to as "the great shepherd" (Heb. 13:20) and "chief Shepherd" of the sheep (1 Pet. 5:4). As in the case of evangelists, many have this gift who are not ordained. For example, pastoring should be the gift of elders, and also of deacons if they have duties involving spiritual oversight. It should also be a gift of Sunday-school teachers.

The word _teacher_ is self-explanatory. It is always an important gift and may be one of the gifts most needed at the present time. We see the importance of the gift of teaching when we recognize that this is a key idea in Matthew's version of the Great Commission. There Jesus says, "Go . . . and make disciples of all nations, baptizing them in the name of the Father and of the Son and of the Holy Spirit [and then, in order to explain how that specifically is to be done], _teaching_ them to observe all that I have commanded you" (Mt. 28:19-20). Those who are brought to faith in Christ are to be discipled primarily through teaching.

In Romans 12:8 "exhortation" follows immediately after teaching. Having been taught in the Word, the disciple next needs to be encouraged to press on in the things he or she has learned. Again, this is a pastoral responsibility. In fact, when Paul used this word in Romans he may have had pastors in mind particularly, since the word _pastor_ does not occur elsewhere in the passage.

Another listing of the gifts should be considered at this point, since it throws light on the gifts in this category. In 1 Corinthians 12:8-9, Paul did not mention any of the gifts already considered which, however, occur first in each of the other Pauline passages: apostles, prophets, evangelists, pastors and teachers in Ephesians 4:11; apostles, prophets and teachers in 1 Corinthians 12:28-30; prophecy, service, teaching and exhortation in Romans 12:6-8. Instead he mentions "wisdom" and "knowledge." Perhaps in this passage the apostle is substituting those two items for his customarily longer list. Wisdom and knowledge are gifts particularly associated with the evangelistic, pastoral and teaching ministries. This fact is helpful in trying to determine whether

God has given an individual the gift of being an evangelist, pastor or teacher, a matter we will come to more fully later. We may ask, Does that one have spiritual wisdom? Does he or she have the gift of knowledge? The point is also a helpful indication of areas in which one can profitably pray for his or her pastor. We can pray that God will give him true spiritual knowledge, based on careful study of the Bible and wisdom to apply it properly.

4. *Faith.* The word *faith* is one of the most important terms in the Christian vocabulary. It has several uses. It can refer to "saving faith" (Eph. 2:8). It can refer to the content of the gospel (Rom. 10:8; Acts 6:7; 13:8; 14:22). It can mean faithfulness (Gal. 5:22). It can refer to trust in God in adversity (Eph. 6:16). In the list of gifts in 1 Corinthians 12:8-10, faith probably refers to the ability to look ahead to something God has promised and act as if it were already present. Stedman says that faith in this sense is what we today would probably call vision. "It is the ability to see something that needs to be done and to believe that God will do it even though it looks impossible."[4]

The heroes of faith listed in Hebrews 11 had this gift. In each case their lives demonstrated the "assurance of things hoped for, the conviction of things not seen" (v. 1). Abel, who had been promised salvation through the seed of the woman who would crush Satan's head, testified to his faith in that future reality through obedience in the matter of the blood sacrifice. Enoch believed God and lived a righteous life. Noah accepted God's word about a future destruction of the ungodly and acted upon that conviction by building an ark in which he and his family were saved. Abraham exhibited faith throughout his lifetime. He left his homeland for a land not yet seen, endured hardship in the land of promise, changed his name as a symbol of his faith in God's ability to provide him with a son when both he and Sarah were past the age of childbearing, was willing to offer Isaac as a sacrifice on an altar on Mount Moriah—all because he believed God was able to do what he had promised (compare Rom. 4:21).

After noting these persons and in anticipation of other examples of outstanding faith to follow—Isaac, Jacob, Joseph, Moses, Rahab, Gideon, Barak, Samson, Jephtha, David, Samuel—the author of Hebrews declared, "These all died in faith, not having received what was promised, but having seen it and greeted it from afar" (v. 13). Isaac Watts referred to such persons in a stanza of his hymn "Am I a Soldier of the Cross?"

Thy saints, in all this glorious war,
Shall conquer, though they die;
They view the triumph from afar,
And seize it with their eye.

5. _Healings and miracles._ The gifts of healings and miracles occur at two separate places in 1 Corinthians 12 and are therefore obviously related. This conjunction of gifts is important in interpreting the nature of the gift of healing. Although it is true that the word _healing_ (actually, _healings_—plural) can refer to various types of cures—emotional as well as bodily ailments, and healing by natural as well as miraculous means —the use of the word in these verses must refer to the miraculous.

The question arises as to whether such gifts exist today, a matter on which Christians are divided. We may note, on the one hand, that some gifts (such as the gifts of apostleship and prophecy) no longer occur in their biblical sense. The gifts of healings and miracles could be like them.

Yet gifts like evangelism, teaching and faith continue to exist and clearly must continue to the end of church history. Healings and miracles could be like them.

A third possibility exists. Healings and miracles could exist but could occur infrequently. There are several reasons for preferring this interpretation. Miracles and healings are bracketed by other gifts which continue: in the case of 1 Corinthians 12:8-10, by wisdom, knowledge and faith before, and by the discerning of spirits afterward; in the case of 1 Corinthians 12:28-30, by teaching before and the gift of helping after. The working of miracles is similar to the case of speaking in tongues, which is treated at great length two chapters later and in regard to which we receive an explicit warning: "Do not forbid speaking in tongues" (1 Cor. 14:39). Paul is not encouraging tongues-speaking, but he recognizes that God may continue to give this gift and it should therefore not be discouraged. Nowhere does Paul indicate that either healings, miracles or tongues will cease. Further, accounts of healings and other miracles exist from every period of church history. (Although it may be true that many of them are myths, mistakes or even deliberate deceptions, it would be brash indeed to declare that they all are.)

We dare not put God in a box on this matter, saying that he cannot give the gifts of healings or miracles today. He can. On the other hand, to say that is not the same thing as saying we have a right to expect healings or that what passes for the miraculous today is authentic.

A man whose opinion in this area should be highly valued is Dr. C. Everett Koop, surgeon-in-chief of Children's Hospital in Philadelphia, Pennsylvania, and professor of pediatric surgery at the University of Pennsylvania School of Medicine. Koop is a strong Bible-believing Christian whose testimony in and outside the hospital has been used to lead many persons to faith in Christ. He has solid technical understanding of the development of disease and the process of healing. He is an expert in the area of surgery for birth defects and childhood cancers, a field of medicine where the question of supernatural healing quite often arises. Koop believes in miracles. But—and this is the point—in spite of believing in miracles and in spite of a lifetime of work with many families who have undoubtedly prayed in faith that God would heal their deformed or suffering children, in nearly forty years of active practice he has never seen one. He writes, "I believe in miracles. I understand that all healing comes from God. I would love to see a miracle of healing where God supervenes his natural law and heals by miracle. If I were to see such a miracle, I would be overjoyed. I would give God the praise. But now, in spite of believing that all healing comes from God and in spite of believing in miracles, I have never seen one."[5] His experience has led him to conclude that truly supernatural healings are not occurring in our time. Whether one would fully agree with him in that conclusion or not, his experience and opinion should be a warning to those who talk loosely about this matter and even claim miracles in questionable cases.

6. _Ability to distinguish spirits._ The gift of discernment is mentioned at only one place in the various lists of gifts, but it is nevertheless important. The gift of discernment relates to a prophet's or a teacher's teaching. In 1 Corinthians 12:10 discernment occurs immediately after the reference to prophecy, which makes one think that Paul was referring to the ability to discern whether a person who is speaking in the name of God is actually inspired by the Holy Spirit or is speaking in his or her own strength or by means of a demonic spirit. On the other hand, discernment can refer merely to discerning the truth or error of a religious teacher's instruction (compare 1 Jn. 4:1-6). Peter exercised this gift when he saw through the deception being perpetrated by Ananias and Sapphira. "Ananias, why has Satan filled your heart to lie to the Holy Spirit... ?... How is it that you have agreed together to tempt the Spirit of the Lord?" (Acts 5:3, 9).

Some people today are easily taken in by any new "Christian" fad. Others are not. The latter may have the gift of discernment. The church should recognize such persons and seek their judgment in areas where true discernment is needed.

7. *Helpers.* The reference to helpers in 1 Corinthians 12:28 is amplified in Romans 12:7-8 by the gifts of contributing [financially], giving aid, showing mercy and perhaps also rendering service (which occurs earlier). We could add many more things. Some individuals exhibit this gift in doing the work necessary to keep a home, business or church running smoothly. They see what needs to be done and do it. Some care for older people, buying groceries for them when they are unable to go out, cleaning, shoveling snow, taking them back and forth to medical appointments or to visit friends or to church. Some help the poor. Some assist the sick by sending in food or doing the necessary errands until the sick person recovers. What distinguishes their service from the similar service that non-Christians may give is that it is done in the name of Jesus Christ and for his glory. Peter encourages those who render service to do it "by the strength which God supplies; in order that in everything God may be glorified through Jesus Christ" (1 Pet. 4:11).

8. *Administrators.* Some versions of the Bible call this gift "governments," but it really refers to administrative rule or leadership. Most of us know situations when there was obviously work to be done and many people available to do it. But the job did not get done because there was no one around to take charge, make assignments and then see that the various responsibilities were carried out. On the other hand, there have been times when the necessary gifts and people did not seem to be present. Then someone came along who saw how the work could be done and did it through those who were available.

Here we must avoid two errors. One is the error of being superspiritual, distrusting strong administration on the ground that it is of the flesh and that God must therefore work in other ways. People who feel that way, or are intimidated by others who do, frequently fail to exert the leadership God has given them. The other error is in thinking that what is done in the area of strong leadership is always of God or that God is working only when such leadership is present. That is not true either. People need to recognize the difference between the gift of administration and mere force of personality, willfulness or an aggressive success-oriented mentality.

The Lord obviously had all the spiritual gifts. But he did not boss people about, trample on feelings or press on obstinately like a steamroller in order to accomplish some goal.

9. _Tongues and the interpretation of tongues._ None of the gifts mentioned anywhere in the New Testament has been so controversial as the gift of tongues and the accompanying gift, interpretation. Some people have insisted that the gift of tongues means being able to speak so that other people hear in their own but different languages. That kind of miracle took place at Pentecost (Acts 2:1-11); but it does not seem to be identical with the gift of tongues as it was practiced at Corinth. At Corinth interpreters were necessary because the listeners were not hearing in their own language.

Other people speak of the exercise of tongues as being the ability to speak in "heavenly tongues," that is, in no known human language. Others deny that either possibility exists today; they say that what passes for tongues is either a self-induced psychological phenomenon or the work of demons.[6] The only way to proceed is to limit oneself to what is said in the one portion of Scripture that deals with the phenomenon.

That section of Scripture is 1 Corinthians 12 and 14, in which Paul made the following points. First, _the gift of tongues can be counterfeited._ That is, there is a genuine gift; but there is also a duplication of that gift by other spirits, whether the spirit of Satan or merely the spirit of the individual. Paul was talking about this when he reminded the Corinthians that before their conversions they were "led astray to dumb idols" and warned them that it was necessary to test the spirits on the basis of their confession or lack of confession of Christ. "No one speaking by the Spirit of God ever says 'Jesus be cursed!' and no one can say 'Jesus is Lord' except by the Holy Spirit" (1 Cor. 12:3). Apparently before their conversion to Christ the Christians at Corinth had been fooled by the ecstatic utterances of pagan priests. Now they were being fooled by some who professed to speak in the power of the Holy Spirit but were not actually empowered by him.

It is worth noting that in many parts of the world glossolalia (the technical term for speaking in tongues) is well known in non-Christian circles even today. Unitarian groups sometimes speak in tongues. Buddhist and Shintoist priests often speak in tongues when in a trance. The phenomenon exists in much of South America, India, and Australia in a variety of environments. So speaking in tongues is itself no proof of the Holy Spirit's presence.

A second principle that Paul laid down is that *there are many different and valuable gifts of the Holy Spirit, and the gift of tongues is just one.* He said this in verses 4-11 of 1 Corinthians 12, stressing that there were different needs in the church and that it was the Holy Spirit's prerogative to meet those needs by giving the necessary gifts to those people he had called to work in those areas. Paul's emphasis was on the fact that it was by one and the same Spirit that the gifts were given (vv. 8-11). If the Holy Spirit gives a gift to each Christian and for his own purposes, then obviously we are unable to take pride in our particular gift. The fact that Paul later minimized the gift of tongues indicates that pride was a particular danger for those at Corinth who possessed that gift.

The third of Paul's points is that *the gifts of the Spirit are for* a purpose: *the edification and unity of the church* (12:12-27). In one sense these are two separate purposes. But Paul treated both through the image of the body to which each part contributes. He stressed that: (1) there are "many members" of the body (v. 12); (2) all "are indispensable" (v. 22); and (3) there should be "no discord" (v. 25). If a particular exercise of the gift of tongues does not promote growth or, worse yet, leads to schism, then either the gift is not of God or it is being exercised in a way contrary to God's purposes for it.

Fourth, Paul indicated (perhaps in this case to humble those who were boasting of their gift of tongues) that _if the gifts were to be listed in the order of importance, tongues would always come relatively low on the list_ (12:28—14:12). We see this in several ways. Whenever he listed the gifts, tongues and the interpretation of tongues always came last. This is most marked in 1 Corinthians 12:28, where Paul actually numbered the gifts: "And God has appointed in the church first apostles, second prophets, third teachers, then workers of miracles, then healers, helpers, administrators, speakers in various kinds of tongues." Another way Paul made that point was by emphasis on the importance of love. His concern for love was so great that he interrupted his discussion of the problems of gifts to talk about it (chap. 13). Finally, he concluded that if any gift was to be sought after, it was the gift of prophecy, by which in this passage he meant the ability to preach and teach the Word clearly (14:1). Although he too spoke in tongues, he would rather speak five words in an intelligible language than ten thousand in an unknown tongue (14:19).

Paul's fifth principle is that _the gift of tongues is fraught with particular dangers and must therefore be exercised with safeguards_ (14:13-38).

The first danger is disorder. Paul regarded disorder as a disgrace; God's work should not be done in a disruptive way. Here he laid down guidelines. First, do not allow anyone to speak in church at the same time another person is speaking; people should speak one at a time. Second, do not allow everyone to speak, but at the most two or three. Third, do not permit even those two or three to speak in tongues unless someone can interpret. In these verses Paul was exercising concern lest he quench the voice of the Spirit (which he had no desire to do) while, at the same time and for the same reasons, guaranteeing that the voice of the Spirit would be heard in the assembly. The Holy Spirit obviously could not be heard if everyone was shouting and crying out at the same time under his supposed influence.

A second danger is the danger of a contentless Christianity, which Paul countered by insisting on interpretation. Then, as now, Christianity was threatened by an outlook that made experience central. Content was secondary. The emotional "high" was everything. But Paul would not allow it. True, he did not want to suppress any valid emotional response to the truth of Christianity (and neither must we). There is and should be emotion within Christianity. But it cannot be allowed to become the basis of faith. The objective revelation of God in history and in the Scriptures is the basis of Christianity. If experience is trusted above revelation, it will lead to a distortion of true Christianity and to excesses.

We see this today and not just in the tongues movement. We see a kind of emotional, almost contentless Christianity in which experience is everything. Following Paul's example, we must stress content. Francis Schaeffer writes, "We must stress that the basis for our faith is neither experience nor emotion but the truth as God has given it in verbalized, propositional form in the Scripture and which we first of all apprehend with our minds—though, of course, the whole man must act upon it."[7] John Stott makes this same point in arguing against what he terms "mindless Christianity."[8]

One last point should be noted in Paul's presentation of the tongues question. It is simply that, notwithstanding the dangers of this gift, *no Christian should forbid its exercise.* Specifically he said, "So, my brethren, earnestly desire to prophesy, and do not forbid speaking in tongues" (1 Cor. 14:39). If tongues is not your gift, you are not to desire it—at least not more than any other gift. (You are to desire the gift of prophecy.) But, on the other hand, if another has been given the gift, you are not to forbid its exercise. Who are you to tell that person that he or she cannot use what God has given? To forbid it would be to the church's impoverishment.[9]

Finding Your Gift

At this point someone may be saying, "I recognize the importance of the spiritual gifts and am aware now of what they are. But I am still puzzled because I don't know where I fit into the picture. How can I discover what my own gifts are?" A good question.

First, _we can begin by studying what the Bible has to say about spiritual gifts._ The Bible is God's primary provision for spiritual growth and sanctification. God speaks to us in the Bible. Without a knowledge of what God's Word explicitly teaches in this area we can easily be led to desire experiences that are not his will for us. We can even begin to think of spiritual gifts in secular terms. As we study the Bible's teaching we must be careful to discern what God's purpose in giving spiritual gifts is. It is for the growth of the body and not merely for personal growth or satisfaction.

Second, _we must pray._ This is not a matter to be taken lightly or one in which we may feel free to trust our own judgment. We do not know our hearts. We may find ourselves wanting a gift that exalts our sense of self-importance but that God does not have in mind for us. We may find ourselves resisting the gift he actually has in mind. The only way we will get past this hurdle is to lay the entire matter before the Lord in serious, soul-searching prayer and ask him, as he speaks through his Word, to show us the gift he actually has given us.

Third, _we will be helped by making a sober assessment of our own spiritual strengths and abilities._ If we do not do this on the basis of a careful study of the Word of God and through prayer, we will be misled. But if we have first sought the wisdom and mind of God, we can then go back and look at ourselves through spiritual eyes. We can ask, What do I like to do? That is not a sure guide to what our gift or gifts are, but it is one indication. God's leading is always toward that for which he has prepared us and which we therefore naturally find enjoyable and satisfying. Stedman writes,

Somewhere the idea has found deep entrenchment in Christian circles that doing what God wants you to do is always unpleasant; that Christians must always make choices between doing what they want to do and being happy, and doing what God wants them to do and being completely miserable. Nothing could be more removed from truth. The exercise of a spiritual gift is always a satisfying, enjoyable experience though sometimes the occasion on which it is exercised may be an unhappy one. Jesus said it was his constant delight to do the will of the one who sent him. The Father's gift awakened his own desire and he went about doing what he intensely enjoyed doing.[10]

Another question we can ask is, What am I good at? If you are seeking to fulfill a certain ministry in the church but are constantly failing and feel frustrated, it is quite likely that you are working in the wrong area and have assessed your gifts improperly. If God is blessing your work, if you see spiritual fruit from your efforts, you are probably on the right track and should pursue it even more vigorously. As skill in exercising this gift develops, you will find that the results are even better.

You can ask, What are my talents? Spiritual gifts are not talents, but they are often related. We are seldom wrong if we try to exercise our talents spiritually and for spiritual ends.

A fourth thing you can do is *seek the wisdom of other Christians.* The church does not always function as it should, but where it functions properly one of the things that should happen is that others with the gift of insight or wisdom should be able to sense what your gifts are and point them out in terms of the needs of your particular Christian congregation. Others are almost always more objective about ourselves than we are. We must cultivate the ability to listen to these other members of the family of God and follow their guidance.

9   EQUIPPING THE SAINTS

At the beginning of the last chapter I pointed out that within the overall unity of the church there are nevertheless two areas of difference or distinction: spiritual gifts and church office. We come to the second of these now. I want to approach it indirectly, first seeing not what those offices are and who qualifies for them—that will come in the next chapter—but rather what the purpose of the various offices, particularly the office of elder, teacher or pastor, is.

The reason for an indirect approach is that we must get over a common misunderstanding of how the church is to function: the idea that the work of the church is to be done by ministers or clergy. In that view, the role of laymen and laywomen is, at best, merely to follow where the ordained persons lead. Nothing could be farther from the biblical pattern. The New Testament makes clear that the work of ministry is to be done by all Christians. The job of the clergy or other church officers is to equip other Christians for that task. That is the meaning of those verses quoted earlier: "And his [the Spirit's] gifts were that some should be apostles, some prophets, some evangelists, some pastors and teachers, to equip the saints for the work of ministry, for building up the body of Christ, until we all attain to the unity of the faith and of the knowledge of the Son of God, to mature manhood, to the measure of the stature of the fulness of Christ" (Eph. 4:11-13).

Those verses are so basic to understanding the nature of the ministry of all Christians that the simplest questions must be asked of them: Whom are they about? What are the persons involved to do? Why are they to do it? How are they to do it? When or how long must the work in question be done?

The first two questions go together. The verses mention both those whom we would call clergy (apostles, prophets, evangelists, pastors, teachers—elders are also included, though we will come to that later) and all other Christians (the saints). The former are to equip the latter to do the church's work. All Christians are to be active in the church's work in some way—either equipping others, doing the work of ministry or building up the body of Christ. Each has a gift and is to use it. None is to be inactive. The difference between professional clergy and lay Christians is to be one of function only, not a difference of status, holiness, domination or prestige.

Recent years have seen a new readiness in many evangelical circles to see and welcome this truth, just as many have also recognized the importance of spiritual gifts. That was not always the case. Earlier ages of the church were often characterized by false patterns of ministry rather than biblical ones, though, of course, there have always been properly functioning churches and ministries.

John R. W. Stott points out that three false answers have been given to the question of the relationship of clergy to other Christians.[1] The first he calls *clericalism,* the view that the work of the church is to be done by those paid to do it;

the role of laypeople is at best to support those endeavors financially. How did that false picture arise? Historically it resulted from the development of the idea of the priesthood in the early Roman Catholic Church. In those days the professional ministry of the church was patterned after the Old Testament priestly system, with the mass taking the place of the Old Testament blood sacrifices. Only "priests" were authorized to perform the mass, and that meant drawing a false and debilitating distinction between clergy and laity. Those who favor this view of the church say that it goes back to the days of the apostles, but that claim is demonstrably false. As reflected in the New Testament, the early church often used the word _minister_ or _ministry_ to refer to what _all_ Christians are and must do. It never used the word _hiereus_ (priest) of the clergy. As Robert Barclay pointed out in the seventeenth century and Elton Trueblood has emphasized in modern times, "the conventional modern distinction between the clergy and laity simply does not occur in the New Testament at all."[2] There are pastors, as distinct from other Christians, but the difference is one of spiritual gifts and service, rather than of ministry versus nonministry. Above all, it is not a matter of priests versus those who can serve only a lesser function.

There are historical reasons for the development of clericalism then, but those reasons in themselves are not the whole or even the most significant. We see this when we ask why such developments took place. Was it a matter of biblical interpretation, or did other factors enter in and perhaps even distort the interpretation?

Some causes of clericalism lie deep in the human constitution. Some people always want to run the show, to dominate others. That tendency can lead to outright abuse or tyranny. An example in the New Testament was Diotrephes, who liked "to put himself first" (3 Jn. 9-10). A warning against such a pattern is found in a New Testament passage conveying instruction to church elders: "Tend the flock of God that is your charge, not by constraint but willingly, not for shameful gain but eagerly, not as domineering over those in your charge but being examples to the flock" (1 Pet. 5:2-3). The chief biblical example of the right way is the Lord Jesus Christ who, though Lord of all creation, nevertheless put on a servant's garment and performed a servant's job in washing his disciples' feet.

A third reason for the rise of clericalism is the tendency of laypeople to sit back and "let the pastor do it." Stott quotes a remark of Sir John Lawrence: "What does the layman really want? He wants a building which looks like a church; clergy dressed in the way he approves; services of the kind he's been used to, *and to be left alone.*"[3] Thus laypersons abandon their God-given tasks and responsibilities and the professional clergy pick them up—to the church's impoverishment.

A second false answer to the relationship of clergy to laymen and laywomen is, understandably enough, *anticlericalism.* If the clergy despise the laity or think them dispensable, it is no surprise that the laity sometimes return the compliment by wanting to get rid of the clergy.

That is not always bad. We can imagine situations in which the church has become so dominated by a corrupt or priestly clergy that a general housecleaning is called for. That has happened historically. We can think of areas of the church's work which are best done by laypeople; the clergy are not at all necessary. But that does not give grounds for anticlericalism as the normal stance of Christian people. On the contrary, where the church wishes to be biblical it must recognize not only that gifts of teaching and leadership are given to some within the church for the church's well-being but also that there is ample biblical teaching about the need for such leadership. The apostle Paul appointed elders in every church he founded and entrusted to them the responsibility for training the people for ministry (Acts 14:23). In the pastoral epistles the appointment of such leaders is specifically commanded (Tit. 1:5) and the qualifications for such leadership are given (1 Tim. 3:1-13; Tit. 1:5-9).

Some who have understood the idea of ministry as belonging to the whole church have begun to wonder whether there is room for clergy. But that insight about ministry, good as it is, does not lead to such a conclusion. As Trueblood says, "The earliest Christians were far too realistic to fall into this trap, because they saw that, if the ideal of universal ministry is to be approximated at all, there must be some people who are working at the job of bringing this highly desirable result to pass."[4]

A third false model of the relationship between the professional clergy and laity is what Stott calls _dualism_. The idea is that clergy and laypeople are each to be given their sphere, and neither is to trespass on the territory of the other. For example, in the traditional Roman Catholic system a "lay status" and a "clerical status" are very carefully delineated. That dualism also characterizes certain forms of Protestantism. In such a system the sense of all being part of one body and serving together in one work easily evaporates. The church is partitioned and rivalry is apt to enter in instead.

What then is a proper pattern? The proper relationship of clergy to laypersons is _service_. According to Ephesians, the clergy are to direct their energy to equipping the saints. They are to assist them and train them to be what they should be and to do the work entrusted to them—which is the main or essential work of the church as it relates both to the world and to the body of the church itself. Jesus exemplified that pattern of service. He "came not to be served but to serve, and to give his life as a ransom for many" (Mk. 10:45).

Work in Two Areas

We are now ready for the third of the five questions we asked at the start of this chapter. Why are pastors or teachers to serve the body of the Christian community in this way? The answer is that the saints might be equipped to do the work of the church in two areas: the work of ministry, and building up the body of Christ.

The contrast between the work of ministry and building up the body of Christ is the contrast between service in the world and service within the Christian community. It is important to stress the first of these because the church is often in danger of forgetting it. As is the case with families, the church sometimes becomes entirely wrapped up in itself and forgets that it is in the world to be of service to the world. It is to minister to the world as Christ did.

In *Body Life,* Ray Stedman turns to Christ's description of his ministry in the world on the occasion of his reading the Scripture in the synagogue of Nazareth, early in his ministry. He read from the book of Isaiah where it is written, "The Spirit of the Lord is upon me, because he has anointed me to preach good news to the poor. He has sent me to proclaim release to the captives and recovering of sight to the blind, to set at liberty those who are oppressed, to proclaim the acceptable year of the Lord" (Lk. 4:18-19; compare Is. 61:1-2). Some of those prophesied actions involve natural activities, some supernatural ones in the case of Christ—healing the blind, for example—but, as Stedman points out, there is a sense in which those who are Christ's are nevertheless to do each one. First, there is a work of *evangelism,* described as preaching good news to the poor. Second, there is a *service* ministry in which captives are freed and the blind healed. That service may be literal; our equivalent would be work among prisoners and various forms of medical service, such as Dr. Victor Rambo's work in India among the curably blind. It may also be spiritual service in the sense that those who are captive to sin are set free by the truth of God (Jn. 8:32) and those who are spiritually blind are made to see (compare

Jn. 9). Third, there is a ministry of _mercy_ to those who are oppressed, a ministry of liberation. Fourth, there is the proclamation of _hope_ to a world that has almost lost sight of hope. It is a ministry of assurance that this is the age of God's grace, and he is accepting those who turn from sin to faith in his Son, the Lord Jesus Christ.

Each of those forms of gospel ministry may be viewed spiritually, but we must not lose sight of the fact that they also involve true physical service in the world. Stedman writes, "We must never forget our Lord's story of the sheep and the goats, and the basis of their judgment. The whole point of the story is that Christians must not evade activities that involve them in the hurt of the world. The hungry must be fed, the naked clothed, the sick visited, and those in prison encouraged. We must put our gifts to work. We dare not hide them in the ground as that unfaithful steward did in one of the Lord's parables, for we must someday meet him for an accounting."[5]

The Christian can perform these forms of ministry in many spheres: in the home, on the job, through voluntary welfare agencies, even through church-directed public service projects. The important point is that Christians perform them as one part of their high calling.

The second end for which Christians are to be equipped is building up the body of Christ. This is the churchward side of ministry. It includes such things as the training of children, the discovery and development of spiritual gifts in all the church's members, the bearing of one another's burdens, praying for one another, encouraging one another and helping one another to grow in the knowledge and love of Christ. The goal is Christian maturity, not merely for the individual (though that is part of it and is a necessary step to the greater end), but for the whole church. Paul put it like this: " . . . until we all attain to the unity of the faith and of the knowledge of the Son of God, to mature manhood, to the measure of the stature of the fulness of Christ" (Eph. 4:13).

The health of the church is related to the first area of service in that an unhealthy church cannot minister to the world properly. What keeps the church from being the good and godly influence that Christ intended it to be? Disunity is one factor. A church expending all its energies fighting within itself can hardly be of much use elsewhere. Ignorance is another cause of failure. If the church does not understand the issues of the day or the solutions provided by the gospel it cannot help the world even though it is not divided internally and is anxious to help. The church can also be hindered by immaturity. It can be weakened by sin. Each of those faults can ruin the church's effectiveness.

How are we to reach the maturity that Paul described? Each Christian is to help others. It is not the job of the minister alone.

Feed My Sheep

The fourth and fifth questions asked at the beginning of this chapter were: How are evangelists, pastors and teachers to equip the saints for this work? and When or how long must the work of equipping be done? The answer to the final question is "until we all attain to the unity of the faith and of the knowledge of the Son of God, to mature manhood"—that is, throughout the entire church age until Christ returns for us. The answer to the other question is by teaching and preaching the Word of God—in biblical language often described as "feeding the sheep."

The work of pastor-teacher is similar to the work of a shepherd in caring for sheep. The idea is present in the Old Testament (Ps. 77:20), but it is more predominant in New Testament usage. It is based on Christ's special words of instruction to Peter, "Feed my sheep" (Jn. 21:15-17).

The sheep are called Christ's sheep. They are his first by creation (he made them) and second by redemption. Earlier, the Lord had said, "I am the good shepherd. The good shepherd lays down his life for the sheep" (Jn. 10:11). If the flock were ours, whether as ministers or elders or even as parents (thinking of our children of whom we are overseers), we could do with it as we wished or as we thought best. But if it is Christ's, we must do as he wishes, recognizing our responsibility to him.

Those with the gift of being a pastor-teacher (clergy, elders, Sunday-school teachers, youth leaders) are to "feed" those entrusted to their spiritual care. They are to do that by teaching, sharing and in any other way communicating the Word of God. The job of the equipper is to teach the Bible both by word and example.

Very few of us do not have some degree of responsibility for someone. We are all usually undershepherds in some way. But we need to say a special word to preachers, for the task of teaching the Word of God is particularly theirs. Normal preachers have many functions. They must administer, counsel, visit and do scores of other things. But just as the primary responsibility of a carpenter is to build and a painter to paint, so the primary responsibility of pastors is to teach the Word of God.

This area is in decline today, first in regard to teaching and then in preaching generally, for several reasons. First, attention has been shifted from preaching to other needed aspects of the pastoral ministry, things like counseling, liturgics, small group dynamics and similar concerns. Those things are important. They are part of a minister's work. But they must not shift attention away from the primary responsibility, which is to teach the Word of God. Further, the two are not in opposition. When the Word of God is best preached, those other concerns are best cared for. An example is the age of the Puritans. Preachers in that period were noted for their mature expository sermons. Their material was so weighty in some instances that few today are even up to reading it. Yet other aspects of the ministry were not neglected. Worship services were characterized by a powerful sense of God's presence, and those who preached and led such services were intensely concerned with the problems, temptations and growth of those God had placed under their care.

A second reason for the decline in preaching is the contemporary distrust of oratory. People are sensitive to being manipulated and dislike it. Since preaching is clearly directed to moving people (and not merely instructing them), it may seem to be manipulative and some therefore turn from it.

The trouble with those explanations is that, although they have an element of truth about them, they are based on external matters or external situations and so miss the internal or fundamental cause of preaching's decline. The current decline in preaching and teaching the Word of God comes from a prior decline in belief in the Bible as the authoritative and inerrant Word of God on the part of many of the church's theologians, seminary professors and ministers who are trained by them. It is a loss of confidence in the existence of a sure word from God.

Here the matter of inerrancy and authority go together. It is not that those who abandon inerrancy as a premise on which to approach the Scriptures necessarily abandon a belief in scriptural authority. On the contrary, they often speak of the authority of the Bible most loudly precisely when they are abandoning the inerrancy position. Yet, lacking the conviction that the Bible is without error in the whole and in its parts, those scholars and preachers inevitably approach the Bible differently from those who believe in inerrancy, whatever may be said verbally. In their work the Bible is searched for whatever light it may shed on the world and life as the minister sees them and not as that binding and overpowering revelation that tells us what to think about the world and life and even formulates the questions we should be asking of them.[6]

Yet the work of equipping is to be done not only by speaking the Word of God but also by living it, by example. In describing his work, Jesus said, "When he [that is, himself] has brought out all his own, he goes before them, and the sheep follow him" (Jn. 10:4). Jesus has set the pattern that others are to follow. So should those whose task it is to equip other Christians.

10 CHURCH GOVERNMENT

Our first approach to the subject of church offices has shown that the primary reason for these offices is service to the people of God. Everything else relates to that. When that end is not perceived, troubles follow. In *One People* John Stott reports a saying current in the Roman Catholic Church but (with the exception of its reference to bishops) true of many Protestant churches too: "The bishops are the servants of the clergy, the clergy are the servants of the laity, the laity are kings with a servant problem."[1] Many churches have that problem either through failure to understand and act on biblical principles of church leadership and government or through a determined effort on the part of some, principally the clergy, to circumvent them. It is strange that it should be so. Basic to Christian life, whether of leaders or other Christians, is service. To be a Christian is to minister, and that means "to serve."

An article on the ministry of deacons by George C. Fuller, although it is about the forms of service peculiar to deacons, begins with an emphasis on the diaconal or service ministry of each believer in Christ. Fuller points out that the world measures greatness by the service a person receives. In business the "important" people are those at the top of the organizational pyramid. The bigger the organization the more important the top person is. In personal affairs the "great" are those who have servants, and the greater the number of servants the greater the great one is. Jesus reversed all that. He "turned the whole thing upside down, making, as it were, the first last and the last first." In God's eyes, greatness consists not in the number of people who serve us but in the number of people we serve. The greater that number, the better the Christian. Fuller writes, "If Jesus had not taken upon Himself the 'form of a servant'; if the Lord of glory had not 'humbled himself and become obedient unto death, even death on a cross,' the world's standard would have remained unchallenged." Having done those things, Jesus changed that standard. Now "he is *the* 'deacon,' our ultimate example, and in fulfilling that charge from God he assured power for his people, his body on earth, to do his ministry."[2]

In the church of God all are deacons, ministers or servants for the benefit of the world and the building up of Christ's body.

A Service Ministry

Although all Christians are to be engaged in service to the world and to each other, special responsibilities for service are given to some specifically equipped for that task. To be specific in terms of the offices outlined in the New Testament, elders (or bishops) are to serve by teaching and encouraging others to serve, and deacons are to lead the way in actual service.

It is important to start with the office of deacon. The word itself means "servant" and the role of the servant is clearly seen in this office. As far as we can judge from the New Testament, it was the first office instituted by the apostles in the church. The "apostles" had been chosen by Jesus himself and were present from the beginning, but the diaconate was the first office instituted. The record of the institution of this office is found in Acts 6:1-6. "Now in these days when the disciples were increasing in number, the Hellenists murmured against the Hebrews because their widows were neglected in the daily distribution. And the twelve summoned the body of the disciples and said, 'It is not right that we should give up preaching the word of God to serve tables. Therefore, brethren, pick out from among you seven men of good repute, full of the Spirit and of wisdom, whom we may appoint to this duty. But we will devote ourselves to prayer and to the ministry of the word.' And what they said pleased the whole multitude, and they chose Stephen, a man full of faith and of the Holy Spirit, and Philip, and Prochorus, and Nicanor, and Timon, and Parmenas, and Nicolaus, a proselyte of Antioch. These they set before the apostles, and they prayed and laid their hands upon them."

Although brief, that account of the choice of the first deacons teaches essential principles of sound church leadership and contains particular insight into the nature of the deacons' ministry. There are four clear principles.

First, there is to be a *division of responsibility*. It is true that all Christians are to serve one another and the world, but any one person cannot fulfill that responsibility in all ways. In this case, the apostles simply were not able to deal with the heavy responsibility of prayer and teaching *and* the care of needy persons within the church. So, certain men were appointed to that third task in order to give the apostles ample time to pray and teach.

Second, there is to be a *plurality of leadership*. The church did not install merely one person to do this job but several. In fact, there is no reference anywhere in the New Testament to the appointment of only one elder or one deacon to a work.

We would tend to appoint one leader, but God's wisdom is greater than our own at this point. In appointing several persons to work together, the church at God's direction provided for mutual encouragement among those who shared in the work as well as lessened the chance for pride or tyranny in office.

Third, there is a concern for *spiritual qualifications*. The apostles did not ask the believers to consider whether those elected to this office had private wealth so that they could minister out of their own pockets should the church's funds run out. They did not ask whether they were in positions of secular power or influence. Such concerns did not enter in at all. They were simply asked to pick out men who were of good repute, and full of the Spirit and of wisdom.

We find that emphasis in every passage dealing with qualifications to church office. Qualifications for elders are listed in 1 Timothy 3:1-7, Titus 1:5-9 and 1 Peter 5:1-4. In regard to deacons the key passage is 1 Timothy 3:8-13. "Deacons likewise must be serious, not double-tongued, not addicted to much wine, not greedy for gain; they must hold the mystery of the faith with a clear conscience. And let them also be tested first; then if they prove themselves blameless let them serve as deacons. The women likewise must be serious, no slanderers, but temperate, faithful in all things. Let deacons be the husband of one wife, and let them manage their children and their households well; for those who serve well as deacons gain a good standing for themselves and also great confidence in the faith which is in Christ Jesus." Some of those qualifications are the same as those for elder, but others are different. An elder, for example, must be an "apt teacher" (1 Tim. 3:2; Tit. 1:9), which is not said of deacons. On the other hand, a deacon must not be "double-tongued," which is not said of elders specifically. Since deacons are to be closely involved in the lives of many people they must have their tongue under control even more than others.

Otherwise there will be no end of gossip, misunderstandings, hurt feelings and jealousies.

Fourth, leaders are to be _elected by the people they serve._ In Acts 6 we are not told how the believers chose the first deacons, but we _are_ told that _they_ chose them. They were not appointed by the apostles. Moreover, the people did a good job in choosing. Note that the complaint about the administration of church funds was brought by Greek Christians, Hellenists, and those who were chosen were apparently Greek, to judge by their names—a shrewd move, which undoubtedly hushed complaints and furthered unity.

Ministry of Mercy

The Acts passage is important not only for what it teaches about sound principles of church leadership, particularly as those principles apply to deacons. It also contains insight into the nature of the deacons' ministry. We must be careful at this point, however. Since the passage is a historical one, dealing with a specific problem in the early church and, therefore, while it illustrates what is undoubtedly a true diaconal function, it is obviously not intended to limit the deacons' work to that sole responsibility.

What are deacons to do? Starting with this passage but also taking into account the nature of leadership itself and the particular significance of the word _deacon,_ we may say that there are at least three key areas of responsibility.

The first is what Fuller calls the ministry of mercy[3]— service to those in need, obviously to those within the church (widows) but also to others (if only because this is a universal Christian responsibility). There is a division among deacon boards at this point, whether the deacons' financial responsibility is to members of their own congregation alone or to other people as well. What are we to say to those who insist that their responsibility is to the household of God alone? Obviously, we must recognize that the concern this view expresses is a valid one: Christians are to care for Christians. Not to do so would be a disgrace. Again, we can agree that if funds are limited, the work of mercy should begin with those who are part of our spiritual family. Paul says as much when he instructs the Galatians, "So then, as we have opportunity, let us do good to all men, and especially to those who are of the household of faith" (Gal. 6:10).

But is this all that deacons are to do? How can it be if they are to lead the church in its ministry to the world as well as to those within the Christian community? No doubt, priorities must be set. No body of Christians can meet all the needs that present themselves. But if deacons are to lead the way in the church's service, they must show that our compassion is aroused by need wherever we find it and not merely among ourselves.

Here we have the example of the Lord Jesus Christ who, although he showed a special concern for Israel, nevertheless also performed acts of mercy among the half-gentile masses of Galilee (Mt. 14:13-21; 15:32-39) and to individuals in such gentile areas as Tyre and Sidon (Mk. 7:24-30) or the Decapolis (Lk. 8:26-39).

If deacons minister only to the needy in the local congregation, that is a good thing and will undoubtedly encourage other members of the church to serve widely. But if a board can conceive of its ministry more broadly, it can be even more helpful. Fuller writes,

A board of deacons, functioning properly, will give creative attention to the neighborhood in which it is called by God to function. It will also work to devise a plan to give every member of the congregation a clear opportunity for ministry to others. As the apostles, even after the appointment of the 'seven,' continued to minister to people in need, we should not withhold that privilege from many Christians who simply wait for direction. The problems of our cities need study, reflection, prayer.... The disfavor that many of us have toward the pronouncements and postures of many

> *Church bodies on varied political matters ought not to prohibit us from seeking wisdom for positive contributions in world affairs when survival is at stake. At the very least the board of deacons might ask for authority to sponsor an annual drive for funds for hunger, in an effort to bring that offering above the level of a collective pittance.*[4]

Apart from finances, the deacons might organize a ministry of prison visitation, services to the elderly, or visitation in hospitals and nursing homes. In most large cities the majority of those in nursing homes never receive a visit from anyone.

Another key area of responsibility is *evangelism.* This naturally follows the ministry of mercy, in that numerous opportunities to share the gospel arise in such situations. Various biblical examples encourage us to think along these lines. Philip, one of the original deacons, is called "the evangelist" (Acts 21:8). God used him to take the gospel to the Samaritans (Acts 8:5) and later to an Ethiopian nobleman (Acts 8:26-40). He had a gift for cross-cultural evangelism. Another of the original deacons, Stephen, preached with great power before the Jewish Sanhedrin, the same body that had condemned Jesus. His preaching brought such conviction that they killed him too. He was the first martyr. It is no small honor to be in a succession going back to such examples.

Third, deacons have an *obligation to train others.* The responsibility of an elder is primarily to teach, as we shall see in the next section; that is not the calling of all Christians. But all are called to acts of mercy and evangelism, and therefore in those areas the deacons have an obligation not only to train but also to lead the *whole* family of God. One way is by example, particularly as a deacon takes along one who is not a deacon as works of mercy and evangelism are done. Another is by more formal training, in adult classes or seminars. Deacons who also have the gift of administration may organize the congregation in more comprehensive efforts:

to penetrate a neighborhood, to have a voice in the political affairs of the city, to render service in prisons or nursing homes or hospitals.

Fuller suggests that where this is done: (1) Christians will become bound together as never before, (2) they will be responding properly to Christ's service to us, (3) hypocrisy will be removed from Christians' intercessory prayer, and (4) people will be helped. Even more, we will be demonstrating the reality of the presence of God in our lives.

We must not forget that in our Lord's parable of the sheep and goats, told just before his arrest and crucifixion, it was the presence or absence of genuine service to others that marked the corresponding presence or absence of a saving relationship to him. What was done to and for others was regarded as service to himself. "Then the King will say to those at his right hand, 'Come, O blessed of my Father, inherit the kingdom prepared for you from the foundation of the world; for I was hungry and you gave me food, I was thirsty and you gave me drink, I was a stranger and you welcomed me, I was naked and you clothed me, I was sick and you visited me, I was in prison and you came to me.' Then the righteous will answer him, 'Lord, when did we see thee hungry and feed thee, or thirsty and give thee drink? And when did we see thee a stranger and welcome thee, or naked and clothe thee? And when did we see thee sick or in prison and visit thee?' And the King will answer them, 'Truly, I say to you, as you did it to one of the least of these my brethren, you did it to me' " (Mt. 25:34-40).

Oversight and Teaching

Deacons are not the only ones who are to serve the people of God in the local church, however. They are to lead the way in practical, outward service. Others, elders or bishops, are to serve by their oversight of the congregation and by a ministry of teaching. Since these persons have the chief responsibility in the church, it is no surprise that greatest attention is given to their qualifications for ministry.

Acts 20:28 is a key verse. It occurs in the middle of the account of the apostle Paul's last meeting with the elders of the church of Ephesus, with whom he had spent several years earlier in his ministry. At that point Paul was on his return to Jerusalem for what proved to be the last time, and he had called the elders to the nearby city of Miletus for a final meeting. He used the time to instruct these men and warn them of their responsibilities as well as of the dangers to come. He said, "Take heed to yourselves and to all the flock, in which the Holy Spirit has made you overseers, to care for the church of God which he obtained with the blood of his own Son." That verse is important chiefly because of its delineation of the two main areas of responsibility of the eldership: spiritual oversight (or rule) and teaching.

Spiritual *oversight* is the thrust of the word *episcopos* (translated "overseer"), which in other places is sometimes translated "bishop." It occurs in 1 Timothy 3:1, where Paul began to list the qualifications for those to be elected to this office. "If any one aspires to the office of bishop, he desires a noble task." It occurs in Titus 1:7, "For a bishop, as God's steward, must be blameless." In each of these passages and others, the word *episcopos* is used as a descriptive term for elder and is therefore to be considered synonomous with that term. That is, *bishop* does not denote another higher office in the church of Jesus Christ which would have authority over local clergy, but rather speaks of a particular function of the elder's office,[5] namely, spiritual oversight.

The function of oversight is seen in the meaning of the word *episcopos* itself. *Bishop* is merely an Anglicized pronunciation of the Greek word, but the word itself means "guardian." *Epi*, the prefix, means "over." *Scopos* means "guardian." So *episcopos* refers to one who is a guard over other persons. An elder has a responsibility for oversight. Elders are to be concerned for others' welfare.

The word often occurs in the context of pastoral imagery, as it does here. The function of an elder is comparable to that of a shepherd. In Acts 20:28 Paul referred to the church as a "flock" and reminded the elders of Ephesus that they had a responsibility to feed it. Similarly, Peter instructed the elders of a church to which he was writing, "So I exhort the elders among you, as a fellow elder and a witness of the sufferings of Christ as well as a partaker in the glory that is to be revealed. Tend the flock of God that is your charge, not by constraint but willingly, not for shameful gain but eagerly, not as domineering over those in your charge but being examples to the flock. And when the chief Shepherd is manifested you will obtain the unfading crown of glory" (1 Pet. 5:1-4).

Elders must take Peter's charge seriously, and when they do, it will inevitably involve them deeply in the lives of those in their keeping. They must be concerned for the spiritual health and growth of these people. At times they must be concerned with discipline.

In Presbyterian churches, in which the role of elder is taken seriously, the body of elders is generally called the "session." The word is taken from a word meaning "sit" and means "a sitting together." It has been chosen to highlight the highest duty of this body which is to sit together as a church court. But the difficulty with so many Presbyterian churches (and perhaps with others also) is that the persons who sit on sessions seem to think that sitting is all elders have to do. As Lawrence R. Eyres points out in a valuable study of the responsibilities of elders, "They forget that elders, as Christ's undershepherds, must also *stand* to minister to the saints; they must *walk* (and sometimes *run*) to seek Christ's wandering sheep; they must *kneel* daily to lift up the flock before the throne of grace in prayer!"[6]

The second responsibility of elders is *teaching*. The struc-

uarrelsome, no lover of money (1 Tim. 3:3), *not ar-*
uick-tempered (Tit. 1:7). These six items are related,
do with how a person gets on with other people.
the church must not possess flaws of character
arm their witness or make trouble for the church
might be said that these are the negative char-
corresponding to those positive traits considered
tion 3.

ar statement of what is required in this area is Paul's
fruit of the Spirit in Galatians 5:22-23. "But the
he Spirit is love, joy, peace, patience, kindness, good-
hfulness, gentleness, self-control."

elder must *not be a novice* (1 Tim. 3:6). This refers
ual maturity, not physical age. Anyone who is to lead
rch must not be a neophyte or new convert. That is
, of course. But strangely enough, hardly a qualifica-
these lists is more regularly or clearly flouted by the
porary church. We seem to do the opposite. Instead
ing for new converts to mature, we tend to push them
d into positions of responsibility or visibility on the
that it will cause them to grow. Paul said that to do
ay cause the novice to be "puffed up with conceit and
to the condemnation of the devil."
ristians need to grow in the faith and prove themselves.
writes, "Paul's concern is that a new convert has not had
to develop the qualities of a mature man of God. He
have lots of experience in business, he may be highly
d in some profession. Or he may be very talented as a
ician, actor or sportsman. But he has not had opportunity
time to develop a good reputation, to prove himself
rally and ethically."⁹ It is no favor either to the new Chris-
or to the church to push a novice into a place of visib'
ponsibility.

. An elder must be *well thought of by outsiders* (1 Tim.
metimes Christians look down on non-Christians to s'

ture of Acts 20:28 makes clear that the ministry of oversight is to be exercised chiefly through teaching. In other words, the rule which has been given to them is not some form of autocratic, absolute authority according to which the elders sit back and decide what should be done, who should do it, who is not doing it and who should be disciplined. Rather it is an oversight in which authority is established on the basis of the teaching of the Word of God.

This does not mean that every elder must necessarily be able to teach large groups publicly. But all elders must know the Scriptures and have the ability to bring them to bear upon any particular problem encountered in the lives of those (perhaps an individual or small group of individuals) in their charge.

During the days of his earthly ministry, Jesus exercised his authority in this way. One author writes,

> He was not limited to a classroom, but rather taught anywhere he saw people in need—on a hillside, in an upper room, in the synagogue, by a well, on a rooftop, in a boat in the middle of a lake, on a mountain top, and even as he hung between two thieves on the cross. Sometimes they came to him; other times he went to them. At times he delivered a discourse and at other times he asked questions. Sometimes he told stories. Frequently he visualized his words by referring to the fowls in the air, the water in the well, the sower on the hillside, or even to people themselves. He was never stereotyped; never rigid; never without the right words. He was always meeting their needs, getting them intellectually and emotionally involved, and always penetrating to the deepest recesses of their personality. He was indeed the master *Teacher!*[7]

The teaching patterns of Jesus can be an example to the elders as they seek to fulfill this important area of their responsibility.

Spiritual Qualifications

Who is to have this responsibility? What are the spiritual

qualifications? Qualifications for elder are given in two sections of Paul's pastoral letters. The first, 1 Timothy 3:1-7, contains fourteen of these requirements. The second passage, Titus 1:5-9, contains most of these plus six more. There are twenty items in all. They may be considered in the following categories.

1. An elder must be *blameless* or *above reproach* (1 Tim. 3:2; Tit. 1:6-7). This item comes first in both of Paul's lists and clearly deserves to stand by itself, inasmuch as it aptly summarizes everything that comes afterward. It has to do with a person's reputation. Because elders have the chief position of responsibility in the church and most clearly represent the church before the world, they must be without blame in order that the cause of Christ might not be slandered.

2. An elder must be the *husband of one wife* (1 Tim. 3:2; Tit. 1:6) and have his *children in subjection* (1 Tim. 3:4; Tit. 1:6). It was necessary to stress the first of those qualifications in a culture in which a man frequently had more than one wife or several mistresses. But it is also linked to a proper rule of one's children. Paul was saying that elders must be proper leaders and managers of their own households if they are to be considered as possible leaders and managers of the household of God. Paul said, "If a man does not know how to manage his own household, how can he care for God's church?" (1 Tim. 3:5).

In my opinion, it follows from this latter reason especially that elders in the church should be men and not women. That is not necessarily true of deacons though the qualification "husband of one wife" is also applied to them. The phrase shows that Paul was thinking of deacons being men when he wrote that requirement, but that is not the same thing as saying that a woman cannot be a deacon. (Phoebe, described in Romans 16:1 as *diakonov,* may be an example of a woman deacon.) On the other hand, though Paul does not say that a woman cannot be a deacon, he does seem to say that a woman cannot be [an elder. In 1 Tim]othy 2:12, the two key resp[onsibilities are men]tioned specifically: "I permi[t no woman to teach or to have] authority over men."

3. An elder must be *temper[ate]* (1 Tim. 3:2; Tit. 1:8) and [? The two] words may be taken as expre[ssing a pleasant demeanor or] stance before the world.

4. An elder must be *hospitabl[e]* (1 Tim. 3:2; Tit. 1:8). Hos-pitality is not often discussed as [a qualification for] leadership in the church, but fo[r this reason more atten]tion should be paid to it. The [importance of it is em]phasized throughout the New [Testament:] "Practice hos-pitality" (Rom. 12:13); "Do not [forget to show hospitality] to strangers" (Heb. 13:2); "Practice [hospitality] to one another" (1 Pet. 4:9). We mu[st notice the seriousness] with which a lack of hospitality is ju[dged. Diotrephes, about] whom the apostle John wrote, is one [such case. John said of] him that he "refuses . . . to welcome [the brothers. He also] stops those who want to welcome them [and puts them out of] the church" (3 Jn. 10). John called [it an evil, for he also] said that he would rebuke Diotrephes pu[blicly.]

Hospitality is not merely opening one[s home to those who] have need of it. A far more basic mat[ter is the opening of] one's heart. As Eyres says, "The hospitab[le elder is one whose] heart is first open to the lonely, the reject[ed . . . to] men of all kinds and in all conditions. . . . [Hospitality is] a matter of faith, the faith without which [it is impossible to please] God."[8]

5. An elder must be *able to teach* (1 Ti[m. 3:2). This re-]quirement is made of elders but not of de[acons and is essen-]tial to the elder's role. It has been discusse[d in an earlier] section of this chapter.

6. An elder must also be marked by the [absence of the] following negative characteristics: *no drunkard[ness,* ...]

gentle, not q[uarrelsome,] rogant, not q[uick-tempered] in having t[...] Leaders o[...] that will h[...] of God. I[...] acteristics [...] under sec[...]

A simil[ar...] list of th[e...] fruit of t[he...] ness, fai[th...]

7. An [elder must be given] to spirit[ual leadership in] the chu[rch...] obvious[...] tion in [...] contem[...] of wai[t...] forwar[...] theory [...] this m[...] fall in [...]

Ch[...] Getz [...] time [...] may [...] skill[...] mus[...] nor[...] mo[...] tia[...] res[...]

So[...]

degree that they consider their opinion unimportant. But non-Christians are certainly able to see when a Christian's profession is contradicted by his or her conduct. Since elders represent the church before the world in a special way they must be beyond reproach at this point. Many New Testament passages speak of this goal in regard to Christians generally (1 Cor. 10:31-33; Col. 4:5-6; 1 Thess. 4:11-12; 1 Pet. 2:12).

9. An elder must be a *lover of goodness, master of himself, upright, holy* and *self-controlled* (Tit. 1:8). Each of these terms is self-explanatory, and some seem to be speaking of nearly the same thing that 1 Timothy 3:1-7 speaks of. Two terms, master of himself and self-controlled, have to do with self-discipline. Being upright refers to justice. Holiness refers to personal piety; it may also be translated "devout." These qualities are developed by walking closely with God.

10. Finally, an elder must *hold firm to the sure word*, "so that he may be able to give instruction in sound doctrine and also to confute those who contradict it" (Tit. 1:9). Ability to hold fast to the truth of God when that truth is under attack is essential. An elder should not be shaken by conflicting secular theories or by deviations from the truth within the church. Such developments characterize every age and will occur increasingly as the return of Christ draws near. Paul wrote, "But understand this, that in the last days there will come times of stress. For men will be lovers of self, lovers of money, proud, arrogant, abusive, disobedient to their parents, ungrateful, unholy, inhuman, implacable, slanderers, profligates, fierce, haters of good, treacherous, reckless, swollen with conceit, lovers of pleasure rather than lovers of God, holding the form of religion but denying the power of it" (2 Tim. 3:1-5). Paul warned Timothy to avoid such people and to continue instead in his calling in Christ Jesus.

When the elders of Tenth Presbyterian Church in Philadelphia, the church I serve, meet to discuss these qualifications we find the list quite sobering. Yet we find it encouraging as well. We realize that Paul did not provide these qualifications to discourage anyone—rather he encouraged Christians to seek this office (1 Tim. 3:1). What makes a good leader after all? Paradoxical as it may sound, a good leader is one who is a good follower, a follower of Christ. When Christ came to earth he said, "I have come down from heaven, not to do my own will, but the will of him who sent me" (Jn. 6:38). He said of the Father, "I always do what is pleasing to him" (Jn. 8:29). To be a leader is to be a close follower of the Lord Jesus Christ, who follows the Father.

11 BODY LIFE

At the beginning of part II, I listed three characteristics that set the church off from any other institution either in the Old or New Testament periods. Those are (1) its being founded on the Lord Jesus Christ, (2) its being called into being by the Holy Spirit, and (3) its containing people of all races who thereby become one new people in the sight of God. The first four chapters of this section dealt with the first characteristic. The next three chapters dealt with the second. The last characteristic is to be considered now.

The church from its earliest days consisted of people of many races. That undoubtedly commended it to those who were observing it from outside. The ancient world was divided in hundreds of ways by nation, race, religion. But in Christianity from the beginning Parthians, Medes, Elamites and residents of Mesopotamia, Judea, Cappadocia, Pontus, Asia, Phrygia, Pamphylia, Egypt, Libya, Crete and Arabia entered into the church as equals and experienced a common life together (Acts 2:9-11).

It was not merely an organizational togetherness. It was more. Members of the church were aware of being something new in Christ. Barriers that had previously divided them were broken down. They were a family, or, as Paul put it, they were "one body" in Christ. "For he [Christ] is our peace, who has made us both one, and has broken down the dividing wall of hostility, by abolishing in his flesh the law of commandments and ordinances, that he might create in himself *one new man* in place of the two, so making peace" (Eph. 2:14-15). "So then you are no longer strangers and sojourners, but you are *fellow citizens* with the saints and *members of the household* of God" (Eph. 2:19). Later on in the book he put this in terms of a goal. "Speaking the truth in love, we are to grow up in every way into him who is the head, into Christ, from whom the whole body, joined and knit together by every joint with which it is supplied, when each part is working properly, makes bodily growth and upbuilds itself in love" (Eph. 4:15-16).

Fellowship
Life in common is no less a goal of the church of Christ today, though it is perhaps less often achieved than at the beginning. The Greek word for fellowship is *koinonia,* which in turn is based on the Greek noun *koinos,* meaning "common." It has reference to the things one shares. A partner is a *koinonos.* The Greek language of the time of Christ and the apostles is called Koine because it was so widely spoken. So the fellowship or *koinonia* of the church is based on what we hold in common.

In many churches it would be hard to recognize that Christians have anything in common except that they tend to worship together at a certain fixed time on Sunday morning. Apart from that their lives go in different and almost totally unrelated directions. They do not pray for one another or help one another. Sometimes they do not even know one another. As Ray C. Stedman says, "What is terribly missing is the experience of 'body life'; that warm fellowship of Christian with Christian which the New Testament calls *koinonia,* and which was an essential part of early Christianity."[1]

What is wrong? Possibly a number of things. First, it may be the case—it often is in our day—that those coming together for church services are not in fact Christians. They may have a Christian background. Their parents may have been Christians. But they are not Christians themselves, and since they are not it is no wonder that true Christian fellowship is lacking. Christian fellowship includes many things but at its heart is a common experience of God's grace in Jesus Christ. If a person is not a Christian, he or she does not share in that.

A second problem may be sin in the lives of the Christians involved. I mean not merely that we are all sinners. I mean specific, unconfessed sin which first of all destroys the Christian's fellowship with God and then necessarily also destroys fellowship with other believers. The apostle John spoke of a twofold fellowship, with God and with one another. "That which we have seen and heard we proclaim also to you, so that you may have fellowship with us; and our fellowship is with the Father and with his Son Jesus Christ" (1 Jn. 1:3). The two go together. Then John went on to show how fellowship may be disrupted. "If we say we have fellowship with him [that is, God] while we walk in darkness, we lie and do not live according to the truth; but if we walk in the light, as he is in the light, we have fellowship with one another, and the blood of Jesus his Son cleanses us from all sin" (vv. 6-7). Sin erects a barrier between ourselves and God. If that has happened, the solution is confession of the sin, cleansing and restoration of fellowship, first with God and then also with others.

Lack of fellowship may result from the way the church is organized. It may be stiffly formal. It may be so large that people get lost in the bigness. John Stott recognized this latter difficulty with his own relatively large church in London. He wrote, "There is always something unnatural and subhuman about large crowds. They tend to be aggregations rather than congregations—aggregations of unrelated persons. The larger they become, the less the individuals who compose them know and care about each other. Indeed, crowds can actually perpetuate aloneness, instead of curing it."[2]

The problem of bigness may be countered in several ways. One is to divide the church into two or more churches. That is sometimes done and should probably be done more often. But division is difficult to bring about and is not always desirable. It would certainly be regrettable if all large churches were to divide up into smaller units, since large churches can accomplish things that smaller churches cannot. They can launch pioneer works, for example. Under the umbrella of a large church other smaller works can function.

Another way to establish *koinonia* in a large assembly is to subdivide the church into smaller fellowship groups. That is the solution we have found to be most effective at Tenth Presbyterian Church in Philadelphia. We have tried to do three things at once. First, we have tried to divide the congregation according to age levels. Thus we have a fully graded Sunday school, and on the upper levels we have tried to establish groups for college students, postcollege students, young couples, other adult classes, and meetings for senior citizens. Part of this is an adult elective program. Second, we have tried to divide the congregation geographically. Tenth Church comes from a large and scattered metropolitan area. Some of the members drive twenty, thirty or more miles to get there. Midweek meetings at the church are impractical for most. Therefore, we have established over thirty area Bible studies, where people can meet weekly with those in their area. They meet to study the Bible, share concerns and pray together. These area groups are probably the least structured but also are the most exciting and profitable of all the church's activities. Finally, we have begun to divide the church according to professional interests. There are meetings of groups of artists, musicians (we have a choir and chamber orchestra), medical students and nurses, and at times ministerial candidates and young pastors.

The experience of our church is similar to that of All Souls in London. Stott wrote, "The value of the small group is that it can become a community of related persons; and in it the benefit of personal relatedness cannot be missed, nor its challenge evaded. . . . I do not think it is an exaggeration to say, therefore, that small groups, Christian family or fellowship groups, are indispensable for our growth into spiritual maturity."[3]

What We Owe One Another

To speak of small churches or small fellowship groups does not in itself solve the problem of lack of Christian fellowship. What should happen in such gatherings? Here we must turn to the specific biblical teaching about Christian fellowship. The many verses that use the words "one another" tell us what our relationship to others should be.

1. We are to *love one another*. That demand is emphasized most and in a sense includes everything else that can be mentioned. We find it in John 13, where Jesus gave his new commandment: "A new commandment I give to you, that you love one another; even as I have loved you, that you also love one another. By this all men will know that you are my disciples, if you have love for one another" (Jn. 13:34-35). It is repeated twice in that Gospel. "This is my commandment, that you love one another as I have loved you" (15:12). "This I command you, to love one another" (15:17). In Romans Paul said, "Owe no one anything, except to love one another; for he who loves his neighbor has fulfilled the law" (Rom. 13:8). Paul described how he prayed for the Thessalonians: "May the Lord make you increase and abound in

love to one another and to all men, as we do to you" (1 Thess.
3:12). He wrote, "You yourselves have been taught by God
to love one another" (1 Thess. 4:9). In 1 John the command
to "love one another" occurs five times (3:11, 23; 4:7, 11-12)
and appears again in the second letter (v. 5).

This love is not to be mere sentiment, still less a profession
in words only. It is to be "in deed and in truth," as John says
in his description of it (1 Jn. 3:18). It is to be seen in such practical matters as giving money and other material goods to
those of our fellowship who lack those necessities (1 Jn. 3:17).

Our love is to cross racial and cultural lines. Francis Schaeffer writes,

*In the church at Antioch the Christians included Jews and Gentiles
and reached all the way from Herod's foster brother to the slaves;
and the naturally proud Greek Christian Gentiles of Macedonia
showed a practical concern for the material needs of the Christian Jews in Jerusalem. The observable and practical love among
true Christians that the world has a right to be able to observe
in our day certainly should cut without reservation across such
lines as language, nationalities, national frontiers, younger and
older, colors of skin, levels of education and economics, accent,
line of birth, the class system in any particular society, dress, short
or long hair among whites and African and non-African hairdos
among blacks, the wearing of shoes and the non-wearing of shoes,
cultural differentiations and the more traditional and less traditional forms of worship.*[4]

The expression of fellowship along such lines is so important
that Jesus held it out as a sign by which the world will know
that we actually are his disciples.

2. We are to *serve one another*. Paul said that service is an
outgrowth of love. "You were called to freedom, brethren;
only do not use your freedom as an opportunity for the flesh,
but through love be servants of one another" (Gal. 5:13). Our
example is Jesus, who demonstrated the servant character of
love by removing his robes, dressing himself in the garb of a

servant and stooping before each of his disciples to wash their dusty feet. "I have given you an example, that you also should do as I have done to you" (Jn. 13:15).

Is our fellowship to be expressed in foot washing? It could, but the obvious meaning of the Lord's act was that we are to be servants generally, that is, in all ways. The deacons are to lead in such service. As small groups we may serve together in supporting a Christian work in the area of the city in which we meet, helping in special projects needed by the church, visiting the sick, taking turns caring for the elderly, helping members of the church to move from one dwelling to another, and scores of other such things. After speaking of some of those projects as they have been conducted in his own church Stott writes, "Certainly without some such common concern and service, the fellowship of any Christian group is maimed."[5]

3. We are to _bear one another's burdens._ "Bear one another's burdens, and so fulfil the law of Christ" (Gal. 6:2). We love by helping shoulder the cares that are wearing down our fellow Christians.

Small groups are important in doing this effectively. How are we to bear another's burdens unless we know what they are? How are we to learn about them unless we have a context in which Christians can share with one another honestly? Many problems can arise at this point, of course, one of which is our natural reluctance to let our hair down and confess what is really bothering us. If we have problems with our schoolwork or at home with our children, we hesitate to say so because admitting to what may be a failure leaves us vulnerable. We worry about what others will think. If we are having marital difficulties, we are afraid to admit it. We keep it in, and the problems build to a point where they sometimes prove unsolvable. How are Christians to learn to share their burdens? The easiest way is through a natural building of acceptance and confidence in the small-group setting.

4. We are to *forgive one another*. Quite a few texts talk about this necessary element in true *koinonia*. The obvious reason is that we frequently wrong one another or are wronged and so we need to forgive and be forgiven. "Let all bitterness and wrath and anger and clamor and slander be put away from you, with all malice, and be kind to one another, tender-hearted, forgiving one another, as God in Christ forgave you" (Eph. 4:31-32). "Put on then, as God's chosen ones, holy and beloved, compassion, kindness, lowliness, meekness, and patience, forbearing one another and, if one has a complaint against another, forgiving each other; as the Lord has forgiven you, so you also must forgive" (Col. 3:12-13). "I therefore, a prisoner for the Lord, beg you to lead a life worthy of the calling to which you have been called, with all lowliness and meekness, with patience, forbearing one another in love, eager to maintain the unity of the Spirit in the bond of peace" (Eph. 4:1-3).

We learn from these verses that although the early church had a high degree of true fellowship, it also had troubling moments in which bitterness and wrath erupted and the peace of the church was threatened. Christians had to learn to be patient with one another and forgive the slights, whether real or imagined.

5. We are to *confess our sins to one another*. "Therefore confess your sins to one another, and pray for one another, that you may be healed" (Jas. 5:16).

In opposition to the traditional Roman Catholic doctrine of confession, in which confession is made to a priest and absolution or remission of sins is received from him, Protestants have stressed that the proper biblical pattern is mutual confession. One Christian may confess to another and be assured by that person that God has pardoned the sin and has forgiven him or her through Christ. This reformation doctrine of the priesthood of all believers is an important concept. Confession of that type, however, is more theory than practice among us. Perhaps most Protestants go through life without ever confessing anything to anybody. To judge from our speech one would think that we do not sin and never have problems.

How destructive this is of true fellowship! Ray Stedman writes,

It goes against the grain to give an image of oneself that is anything less than perfect, and many Christians imagine that they will be rejected by others if they admit to any faults. But nothing could be more destructive to Christian koinonia *than the common practice today of pretending not to have any problems. It is often true that Christian homes may be filled with bickering, squabbling, angry tantrums, even bodily attacks of one member of the family against another, and yet not one word of this is breathed to anyone else and the impression is carefully cultivated before other Christians that this is an ideal Christian family with no problems of any serious consequence to be worked out.*

To make matters even worse, this kind of conspiracy of silence is regarded as the Christian thing to do, and the hypocrisy it presents to others (not to mention how it appears to individual members of the family) is considered to be part of the family's "witness" to the world. How helpful, how wonderfully helpful, it would be if one of the members of this family (preferably the father) would honestly admit in a gathering of fellow Christians that his family was going through difficulties in working out relationships with one another, and needed very much their prayers and counsel through this time of struggle. The family members would immediately discover at least two things: (1) that every other Christian in the meeting identified with his problem and held him in higher esteem than ever because of his honesty and forthrightness; and (2) a wealth of helpful counsel would be opened to him from those who had gone through similar struggles and had learned very valuable lessons thereby. Further, the prayers of other Christians willing to help him bear his burden would release great spiritual power into the situation so that members of the family would be able to see much more clearly the issues to be resolved and be empowered to bear with patience and love the weaknesses of each other.[6]

James obviously intended this last result. In encouraging us to confess our sins to each other he linked such confession to prayer and promised that it would be helpful: "The prayer of a righteous man has great power in its effects" (Jas. 5:16).

6. We are to *instruct one another*. If we do not know the Word of God and do not walk closely with him, we cannot do this. We have no right to teach another. On the contrary, if we do know the Scriptures and are close to God, it should be true of us as Paul said it was of the Christians at Rome: "I myself am satisfied about you, my brethren, that you yourselves are full of goodness, filled with all knowledge, and able to instruct one another" (Rom. 15:14). In a small group fellowship we learn to learn from other Christians.

7. Finally, we are to *comfort one another*. Paul spoke of this to the Thessalonians, where there had recently been some deaths among the Christians. Confusion had then arisen about the doctrine of Christ's Second Coming, and Paul wrote to them to explain what Christ's coming again would mean in regard both to them and to all who had died. Christ would return, and those who had died in Christ would be the first to be raised in their new, Christlike bodies. Clothed in their resurrection bodies, they would be united again with believers then still living. "Therefore comfort one another with these words" (1 Thess. 4:18).

God's Fire

One last point. Whenever we talk of fellowship, however hard we try to be practical, our words are always filtered through the rather bland idea of fellowship that most of us have. Fellowship is something like sitting together around a warm fire on a cold day. That concept leaves out something important: the radical nature of true biblical fellowship. Far from being bland and passive, it is actually an active, burning thing.

A wonderful portrayal of this appears in the last chapter of Elton Trueblood's study of the church, _The Incendiary Fellowship._ He shows that in the Old Testament the word _fire_ characteristically carried overtones of judgment, but in the New Testament it became a symbol of the contagious, spreading nature of the gospel of Christ and the church's fellowship. John the Baptist said that when Christ came he would baptize "with fire" (Lk. 3:16). Jesus spoke of people being "salted with fire" (Mk. 9:49). At Pentecost the disciples experienced "tongues as of fire, distributed and resting on each one of them" (Acts 2:3). Trueblood says that, whatever else may be said about the fellowship of the early church, "it was certainly intense." Those who had been set on fire by Christ and who maintained the blaze by their close contact with one another literally set the world on fire.[7] We will see this even in our day where "body life" becomes a reality.

12 THE GREAT COMMISSION

It is impossible to discuss the responsibility of believers within the church fellowship without also emphasizing that part of their activity must be directed outward to the world. Gene Getz notes this in reference to the church's health and vitality: "Believers need . . . three vital experiences to grow into mature Christians. They need good Bible teaching that will give them theological and spiritual stability; they need deep and satisfying relationships both with each other and with Jesus Christ; and they need to experience seeing people come to Jesus Christ as a result of corporate and individual witness to the non-Christian world."[1]

The church does not exist for its members' self-interest. We are in the world to bear witness to the grace of God in Christ. We are "a chosen race, a royal priesthood, a holy nation, God's own people, that you may declare the wonderful deeds of him who called you out of darkness into his marvelous light" (1 Pet. 2:9).

The most common error that Christians make at this point

is to admit the importance of the Great Commission but then relate it solely to the work of those who are specially appointed to it: missionaries. Some are called to missionary work as a special vocational assignment, but witnessing is not their work alone. It is every Christian's job.

Acceptance of that responsibility was an important factor in the astounding outreach and expansion of the early church. It was not simply that Paul and other leaders carried the gospel to the farthest corners of the Roman world. On the contrary, many of the church's leaders were apparently not particularly zealous about missionary effort. Rather, Christians, whoever they were, wherever they were, told others about the Lord. Historian Edward Gibbon, who was by no means sympathetic to Christianity, showed that the gospel had reached the shores of India by A.D. 49 and even the borders of China by A.D. 61.

Tertullian, writing around the year 200, declared to his contemporaries, "We are but of yesterday, and we have filled every place among you—cities, islands, fortresses, towns, market-places, the very camp, tribes, companies, palace, senate, forum,—we have left nothing to you but the temples of your gods."[2]

How did that phenomenon occur? Gibbon wrote that in the early church "it became the most sacred duty of a new convert to diffuse among his friends and relations the inestimable blessing which he had received."[3] Adolf Harnack, a great church historian, declared, "The most numerous and successful missionaries of the Christian religion were not the regular teachers but Christians themselves, in virtue of their loyalty and courage. . . . It was characteristic of this religion that everyone who seriously confessed the faith proved of service to its propaganda. . . . We cannot hesitate to believe that the great mission of Christianity was in reality accomplished by means of informal missionaries."[4]

Informal missionaries. That is what all Christians every-where should be.

Motivations for Missions

Why should Christians risk their comfort, even their lives, in order to bring the gospel of Christ to people who some-times hate and often ridicule them and their message? There are several reasons, but chief among them is the fact that followers of Christ are not at liberty to set their own pri-orities. We have been told to evangelize.

That command, referred to as the Great Commission, is found five times in the New Testament: once in Matthew, Mark, Luke and John, and once in the opening chapter of Acts. We can hardly miss its importance when it is repeated so often.

In each case of repetition the emphasis of the Great Com-mission is slightly different, which suggests that we are to study it and reflect on it from different angles. In Mark, emphasis is on final judgment. "And he said to them, 'Go into all the world and preach the gospel to the whole creation. He who believes and is baptized will be saved; but he who does not believe will be condemned' " (Mk. 16:15-16). In Luke, emphasis is on fulfillment of prophecy. "Then he opened their minds to understand the scriptures, and said to them, 'Thus it is written, that the Christ should suffer and on the third day rise from the dead, and that repentance and forgiveness of sins should be preached in his name to all nations, beginning from Jerusalem' " (Lk. 24:45-47). In John's account, Christ placed the Great Commission in the context of his own commissioning by the Father: "As the Father has sent me, even so I send you" (Jn. 20:21). In Acts, the command is linked to a program for world evangelization: "But you shall receive power when the Holy Spirit has come upon you; and you shall be my witnesses in Jerusalem and in all Judea and Samaria and to the end of the earth" (Acts 1:8).

The best-known statement of the Great Commission is in Matthew, where the emphasis falls on Christ's authority: "All authority in heaven and on earth has been given to me. Go therefore and make disciples of all nations, baptizing them in the name of the Father and of the Son and of the Holy Spirit, teaching them to observe all that I have commanded you; and lo, I am with you always, to the close of the age" (Mt. 28:18-20).

Dr. R. C. Sproul, founder and staff theologian of the Ligonier Valley Study Center in western Pennsylvania, was once a student at Pittsburgh Theological Seminary where he took a course from Dr. John H. Gerstner, professor of church history. The professor had given a lecture on predestination and then, as was his custom, began to ask questions of the students. Sproul was seated on one end of a large semicircle. Gerstner began at the other end. He asked, "Now if predestination is true, why should we be involved in evangelism?"

The first student looked back at the professor and said, "I don't know."

Gerstner moved on to the next student, who replied, "It beats me."

The next seminarian answered, "I am glad you raised that question; I have always wondered about it myself, Dr. Gerstner."

The professor kept going around the semicircle, inquiring of students one by one. Sproul was sitting in the corner feeling like a character in one of Plato's dialogs. Socrates had raised a difficult question. He had heard from the lesser stars. But he still awaited the lofty answer to the impenetrable mystery of the question. Sproul was scared to death. Finally Gerstner came to him and asked, "Well, Mr. Sproul, suppose you tell us. If predestination is true, why should we be involved in evangelism?"

Sproul says that he slid down in his seat and began to apologize. "Well, Dr. Gerstner, I know this isn't what you're looking for, and I know that you must be seeking some profound, intellectual response which I am not prepared to give. But just in passing, one small point that I think we ought to notice here is that God commands us to evangelize."

Gerstner laughed and said, "Yes, Mr. Sproul, God does command us to be involved in evangelism. And, of course, what could be more insignificant than the fact that the Lord of glory, the Saviour of your soul, the Lord God omnipotent, has commanded you to be involved in evangelism?"[5]

Jesus not only commands us to evangelize, he also tells us how to do it. First, we are to _make disciples_ of all nations. We are to preach the gospel to them so that through the power of the Scriptures and the Holy Spirit they are converted from sin to Christ and thereafter follow him as their Lord. Evangelism is the primary and obvious task in this commission. On the other hand, without what follows, evangelism is at best one-sided and perhaps even unreal.

Jesus went on to say, second, that those who are his must lead their converts to the point of being publicly _baptized_ "in the name of the Father and of the Son and of the Holy Spirit." This does not mean that suddenly empty rites or ceremonies are to take place. Far from it. Rather, it means two things. First, at some point a total heart commitment to Jesus as Savior and Lord must go public. Baptism is a public act. It is a declaration before other believers and the world that the person being baptized intends to follow Jesus. Second, he or she is now uniting with the church, Christ's visible body. If we are truly converted, we will want to be identified with other converted people.

Finally, Jesus instructed those carrying out his commission to _teach_ others all that he has commanded them. A lifetime of learning follows conversion and church membership. Proper missionary work is to go out with the gospel, win men and women to Christ, bring them into the fellowship of the church and then see that they are taught the truths recorded in the Scriptures.

As we obey the Lord in this matter we are encouraged by two things: an announcement that all authority has been committed to Christ (which comes before the specific command to evangelize) and a promise of his continuing presence with us to the end of the age (which comes afterward). The promise reads: "Lo, I am with you always, to the close of the age."

We think back to the passage at the beginning of Matthew's Gospel where the newborn Christ was named. " 'Behold, a virgin shall conceive and bear a son, and his name shall be called Emmanuel' (which means, God with us)" (Mt. 1:23). We are told that the great God of the universe has become "God with us" through the Incarnation. It is a great thought. But in the closing chapter of the book we are told, not only that God was with us during the thirty-three or so years of Christ's earthly life, but that as a result of his death and resurrection he is now to be with us forever. He is with us always in all places equally. The all-powerful Christ will be with us to bless us as we go forth with his gospel.

God's Wrath

A second motivation for the missionary enterprise is the need of men and women. They are lost without Christ. Their greatest need is to escape the fearsome judgment of the wrath of God which hangs over them. Are men and women really lost? The weight of opinion in our day is against that conclusion. But the Bible clearly teaches it, and Christians must be impelled by God's Word.

Paul wrote to the Ephesians that before their conversion they were "separated from Christ, alienated from the commonwealth of Israel, and strangers to the covenants of promise, having no hope and without God in the world" (Eph. 2:12). Jeremiah described people as "lost sheep" (Jer. 50:6).

Jesus told pointed stories about lostness: a sheep, a coin and a son (Lk. 15). John wrote, "He who believes in [Jesus] is not condemned; he who does not believe is condemned already, because he has not believed in the name of the only Son of God" (Jn. 3:18). Paul's teaching in the book of Romans begins, "For the wrath of God is revealed from heaven against all ungodliness and wickedness of men who by their wickedness suppress the truth" (Rom. 1:18). In Revelation 20:11-15 we are told about the judgment of the great white throne. At that judgment all will be called to account, and those whose names are not found written in the book of life will be lost.

Nothing is so important to any individual as to escape the wrath of God, whether the person is aware of that need or not. Although persons outside of Christ may be unaware of their danger, there is no excuse for Christians to be unaware of it. Awareness of that terrible need should impel all of us who have found the grace of God in Christ to speak the gospel as wisely, widely and relevantly as we can.

Christ's Love

Finally, the love of the Lord Jesus Christ should be a strong missionary motivation. Paul wrote, "For the love of Christ controls us, because we are convinced that one has died for all; therefore all have died. And he died for all, that those who live might live no longer for themselves but for him who for their sake died and was raised" (2 Cor. 5:14-15). Those verses are not referring to our love for Christ, though that may perhaps also be a motivation for mission, but rather to Christ's love working through those who are his people. He loves through us, and his love should cause us to reach out and identify with those who need the gospel.

Do we? Here are two stories by which we can evaluate the presence or absence of the love of Christ for others in our lives.

During the years I spent in Basel, Switzerland, doing graduate study I met a woman named Sheila. She had come from a bad background in England and had gone to Switzerland when still young in order to make a better life for herself. She was lonely. Having no one to turn to, she fell in with a young man who did not marry her but left her with a child. By the time I met her, the child was about four years old, and Sheila herself was on guard against most people and was very hostile to the church and Christianity.

In time, through the witness of the English-speaking community, she became a Christian, and about the time I left Switzerland to return to America she immigrated to Canada. My wife and I corresponded with her for about six months after she arrived in Canada and had the impression that she was not fitting in with any Christian group in her area. We went to visit her and found that we were right. We began to talk about her with various Christian people we knew in her city. There was interest to a degree, but no real love. They told us, "Oh, there is a very good church in our city." They gave us the name. Sometimes it was a Presbyterian church, sometimes Baptist, sometimes independent. But in all our conversations no one said, "Give me her name and address. I'll stop by and invite her to go with me on Sunday morning."

Finally, being very unhappy, she left that city for another and (I am afraid) once again fell in with bad company. Eventually, in spite of much effort, we lost touch with her.

The second story is more promising. It was told at the Berlin Congress on Evangelism (1966) by the Rev. Fernando Vangioni, now an assistant evangelist with the Billy Graham Evangelistic Association. He said that he was in South America for a series of meetings, and after one of them a woman came to him and said, "I wonder if you would take time to speak to a girl I am bringing to the meeting tomorrow night. She went to New York some years ago, full of hope, thinking that America was the land of opportunity. Instead of doing well she went through terrible times in the city. She was used by one man after another. All treated her badly. Now she has returned to this country very bitter and hostile to all forms of Christianity." The evangelist said he would speak to her.

On the next night the girl was there. Vangioni said he had never looked into such hard eyes or listened to a voice so hostile. At last, seeing he was making no progress in talking with her, he asked, "Do you mind if I pray for you?"

"Pray if you like," the girl said, "but don't preach to me. And don't expect me to listen."

He began to pray, and as he prayed he was greatly moved. Something in the tragedy of her life caused tears to run down his face. At last he stopped. There was nothing to add. He said, "All right, you can go now."

But the girl did not go. Touched by that manifestation of love for her, she replied, "No, I won't go. You can preach to me now. No man has ever cried for me before."

We need to ask if we have ever been touched at all for one who is lost and ignorant of Christ's love. Do we say, "We have a wonderful church; she (or he) should go there"? Or do we go out of our way to know and communicate? We should be able to say as Paul did, "For if we are beside ourselves, it is for God; if we are in our right mind, it is for you. . . . We are ambassadors for Christ, God making his appeal through us. We beseech you on behalf of Christ, be reconciled to God" (2 Cor. 5:13, 20).

PART III
A TALE OF TWO CITIES

The king said, "Is not this great Babylon,
which I have built by my mighty power as a
royal residence and for the glory of
my majesty?"
(Dan. 4:30)

But understand this, that in the last days
there will come times of stress. For men will
be lovers of self, lovers of money, proud,
arrogant, abusive, disobedient to their
parents, ungrateful, unholy, inhuman,
implacable, slanderers, profligates, fierce,
haters of good, treacherous, reckless, swollen
with conceit, lovers of pleasure rather than
lovers of God, holding the form of religion
but denying the power of it. Avoid such
people.
(2 Tim. 3:1-5)

Then I saw a new heaven and a new earth;
for the first heaven and the first earth had
passed away, and the sea was no more. And
I saw the holy city, new Jerusalem, coming
down out of heaven from God, prepared
as a bride adorned for her husband.
(Rev. 21:1-2)

Jesus answered him, "You would have no
power over me unless it had been given
you from above; therefore he who delivered
me to you has the greater sin."
(Jn. 19:11)

13 THE SECULAR CITY

In A.D. 410 a Visigoth king, Alaric, laid siege to Rome and sacked it. The capital of the Roman empire had been besieged by barbarians before. Parts of the empire had already been overrun by foreign armies. But the sack of Rome was politically and psychologically devastating in a way those other events had not been. Rome had been master of the world. The empire had stood for more than one thousand years. When Rome fell, the citizens of the empire (who no doubt could hardly assimilate the depths of the tragedy) searched about for someone or something to blame.

It was not long before blame fell on the Christians, as it had nearly four hundred years before for less serious troubles. The pagans charged that the fall of Rome had resulted from neglect of worship of the old gods under whose tutelage Rome had grown great. The cause of that neglect, so they said, was Christianity.

In God's providence there was a man particularly suited for that era of history: Augustine of Hippo (in North Africa).

In A.D. 412 he began a wise and spirited defense of Christianity called *The City of God,* perhaps the best known of all his writings except *The Confessions.* Augustine was a long time in writing that work, finishing it in A.D. 426. The result was what scholars have since called the first true philosophy of history. It contains twenty-two books or chapters. The first ten answer the pagans' charge, showing that the worship of the old gods had not protected Rome in earlier times—there had been many military and other disasters—nor had they protected other cities or cultures. Rather, the worship of pagan deities had plunged Rome into increasing vice, for which the gods were notorious. Rome fell as a result of its own corruption. Then, in the next twelve books, Augustine developed his philosophy of history proper, showing that from the first rebellion of the fallen angels against God "two cities have been formed by two loves: the earthly by the love of self, even to the contempt of God; the heavenly by the love of God, even to the contempt of self."[1]

In his work Augustine used *city* to refer to two societies. One is the church, composed of God's elect. It is destined to rule the world. The other is the earthly society, having as its highest representatives the city cultures of Babylon in ancient times and Rome in what was for Augustine immediate past history. The earthly city is destined to pass away. In the second part of his work, Augustine traces the origins, history and final destiny of the two humanities.

Not all have agreed with Augustine's interpretation of history, of course. Certainly secular thinkers have not, and even Christians have often dissented from one or more parts of it. Still, the central thesis of *The City of God* is one that needs rehearing. *The City of God* was influential at the time of the Reformation, forming the basis of Martin Luther's and John Calvin's doctrine of the two kingdoms. It needs to be influential again, particularly in our own age in which the line between sacred and secular has been so systematically

smudged. Christians need to recapture what it means to be
"children of God without blemish in the midst of a crooked
and perverse generation" among whom they are to "shine
as lights in the world" (Phil. 2:15).

Two Cities

There has been so much emphasis on the secular in the
twentieth century (even the secularization of Christianity)
that one might wonder if the doctrine of the two cities is
valid. Is not the church to be in the world in order to minister
to the world? Are not the concerns of the world to be the concerns of Christians also? The answer to each of those questions is Yes. The church is to minister to the world. It is to
share the world's concerns. But that is not the whole story.
Although the church is in the world, it is not to be of the world.
Although it shares many of the concerns of non-Christian
men and women, it has concerns they do not know of.

The most important thing to be said about the two cities
(by whatever name they are known) is that the distinction
is found throughout the Word of God.

The first appearance is in Genesis 3:15 in the words of
God to the serpent following the temptation and fall of Adam
and Eve. The serpent, who was himself in rebellion against
God, had led the man and woman to rebellion, and God had
now appeared to judge each of them. He cursed the serpent.
Then he gave this word of decree and prophecy: "I will put
enmity between you and the woman, and between your seed
and her seed; he shall bruise your head, and you shall bruise
his heel." We see three sets of antagonists: the serpent and
the woman, the descendants of the serpent and the descendants of the woman, and Satan himself and the ultimate descendant of the woman, Jesus Christ. Here are divisions in
conflict with one another. But the victory of the godly seed
of the woman is to be assured by the ultimate victory of her
specific descendant, Jesus.

If Genesis 3:15 was the only text to go on, we might think its second contrast is between demons (the seed of the serpent) and humanity. But that is not the case, as the next two chapters of Genesis make plain. It is true that there is antagonism between the fallen angels and *believing* men and women. But there is also conflict between the holy angels and the fallen angels and between believing men and women and those who do not believe. Genesis 4 and 5 show that the antagonism in view in 3:15 is between godly and ungodly men and women.

The first illustration is the conflict between Abel and Cain. Cain was the first child of Adam and Eve (born after the Fall), and the essential meaning of his Hebrew name is "Possession," or colloquially "Here he is!" Adam and Eve had heard God's promise of a deliverer who would crush the head of Satan. So when Cain was born they may have assumed that he was this deliverer. As things turned out, instead of a savior, Cain became a murderer. In later years, Cain grew jealous over God's acceptance of his brother Abel's offering rather than his own and killed him.

The cause of Cain's jealousy is very important, because it concerns the means of approaching God. Cain had brought an offering from the field, the result of his own labor. Abel had brought a lamb which was then killed and offered as the innocent substitute bearing the guilt which Abel recognized as his own. We do not know how much Abel understood about the proper means of approaching God through sacrifice (which anticipated the ultimate and only truly effective sacrifice of Christ). But he is praised in the book of Hebrews as having done what he did through faith. "By faith Abel offered to God a more acceptable sacrifice than Cain, through which he received approval as righteous, God bearing witness by accepting his gifts" (Heb. 11:4). The essential point is that Abel came to God in the right way and Cain did not. When God accepted Abel's offering and not his own, Cain grew angry and murdered his brother. In these brothers we see the first examples of the two humanities.

The remainder of Genesis 4 and the next chapter show how the stance of these two individuals gave birth to two different societies or cultures. Cain is driven away to be a wanderer in the earth, and his descendants are listed: Enoch, who built a city; Irad, the son of Enoch; Mehujael; and finally Methushael, the father of Lamech. Lamech received special mention as an illustration of what was happening in the line of these who walked in "the way of Cain" (Jude 11). He had three sons: Jabal, who, we are told, "was the father of those who dwell in tents and have cattle"; Jubal, "the father of all those who play the lyre and pipe"; and Tubal-cain, "forger of all instruments of bronze and iron" (Gen. 4:20-22).

Although brief, those descriptions speak of a fairly well-developed culture. But it was a godless and cruel culture: "Lamech said to his wives: 'Adah and Zillah, hear my voice; you wives of Lamech, hearken to what I say: I have slain a man for wounding me, a young man for striking me. If Cain is avenged sevenfold, truly Lamech seventy-sevenfold'" (vv. 23-24). It is the story of a man boasting about murder and, since the boast seems to be in poetic form, actually writing a song about it. He is saying, "Look what a neat guy I am. A fellow hurt me, and I killed him. I just killed him. That will teach people not to mess around with Lamech." As Francis Schaeffer says in his discussion of this incident, "Here is humanistic culture without God. It is egotism and pride centered in man; this culture has lost the concept not only of God but of man as one who loves his brother."[2]

At that point in Genesis 5 the godly line of Seth is introduced. Seth took the place of the murdered Abel, and his line continued through Noah and his family, the sole survivors of the flood. The names in this line are Seth, Enosh, Kenan, Mahalalel, Jared, Enoch, Methuselah, Lamech and Noah. Two are mentioned in Hebrews 11: Enoch, who is said to have "pleased God" (v. 5) and Noah, of whom it is written, "By faith Noah, being warned by God concerning events as yet unseen, took heed and constructed an ark for the saving of his household; by this he condemned the world and became an heir of the righteousness which comes by faith" (v. 7).

These lines may be traced through history, as Augustine did in *The City of God*. The godless line is traceable in the world's cultures. The godly line is in Abraham and his descendants, the faithful within Israel, and the church.

"Great Babylon, Which I Have Built"
The two societies are traceable not only by a succession of godly and godless individuals. The Bible also makes the contrast by a comparison of two literal cities: Babylon, which epitomizes the earthly society and its goals, and Jerusalem, which symbolizes the goals and society of God's people. Babylon was founded in ancient times, grew, eventually besieged and overthrew the earthly Jerusalem and was in turn overthrown and abandoned. Today it is a desert. Jerusalem was founded, besieged, overthrown by Babylon—but was then refounded. In the book of Revelation these literal cities are raised into significance as symbols of the two cultures. There, as in actual history, Babylon is overthrown ("Fallen, fallen is Babylon the great!"—Rev. 18:2). Jerusalem is reconstituted as a new "holy city . . . coming down out of heaven from God" (Rev. 21:2), which is to endure forever.

The chief characteristic of the secular city, illustrated by earthly Babylon, is its radical secular humanism, which may be described as its being *of* man, *by* man and *for* man exclusively. When we say that it is *of* man we mean that it is bounded by man and his horizons; it has no place for God. *By* man means that man is the creator of this city; it has his values. *For* man indicates that its goal is man's glory.

The Babylon of Nebuchadnezzar in the days of Daniel the prophet is the clearest biblical illustration of these elements.

It is the story of the struggle between Nebuchadnezzar, who embodied the secular city, and God, who operated through Daniel and his friends. The key to the book is in the opening verses, which say that after Nebuchadnezzar had besieged and conquered Jerusalem (though it was "the Lord [who] gave Jehoiakim king of Judah into his hand"), he took some of the sacred vessels of the temple treasury to Babylon and there "placed the vessels in the treasury of his god" (Dan. 1:2). That was Nebuchadnezzar's way of saying that his gods were stronger than Jehovah. And so it seemed. God had permitted Nebuchadnezzar to triumph over the people of Judah in punishment for their sins. Still, Nebuchadnezzar's rebellion was more than that. It was the rebellion of a humanism that would seek to eliminate God entirely. We might think, because of the disposition of the temple vessels, that this is the story of a struggle between the Lord and Nebuchadnezzar's _gods_. But it is actually a struggle between the Lord and Nebuchadnezzar himself, as the unfolding story shows.

One evening Nebuchadnezzar had a dream that involved a large image of gold, silver, brass and iron. The head was gold. It represented the kingdom of Nebuchadnezzar and was God's way of acknowledging that Babylon was indeed magnificent. But, as God went on to point out, Babylon would be succeeded by another kingdom, represented by the silver arms and chest of the figure; that second kingdom would be succeeded by another, represented by the figure's brass middle portions; and then that by a kingdom represented by iron legs. Only at the end of this period would the eternal kingdom of God in Christ come and overthrow all others, grow up and fill the earth. In this vision God was telling Nebuchadnezzar that he was not so important as he thought he was and that God himself rules history.

In the next chapter we are told that Nebuchadnezzar set up a huge golden statue on the plain of Dura. On the surface this seemed to be only the foolish gesture of a vain monarch who insisted that the statue be worshiped as a symbol of the unity of the empire. When the story is read with the vision of the statue of chapter two in view, however, one realizes that the later episode actually shows Nebuchadnezzar's rebellion against God's decree. It is not a question of God struggling against Nebuchadnezzar's gods, but of Nebuchadnezzar defying God's pronouncements. God had said, "Your kingdom will be succeeded by other kingdoms, kingdoms of silver, brass and iron." Nebuchadnezzar replied, "No, my kingdom will endure forever; it will always be glorious. I will create a statue of which not only the head will be of gold, but the shoulders, thighs and legs also. It will all be of gold, and it will represent me and my descendants forever." The king's personal involvement with the statue explains his violent reaction when the three Jewish men refused to bow down to it.

It also explains the violent reaction of the secular mind to Christian claims today. It is not just a question of the Christian God versus other gods, each individual adherent presumably thinking that his or her god is the true one. It is the rebellion of human beings against God. God is the One to whom we are responsible, but fallen men and women do not want to be responsible to anyone. They want to rule themselves. They want to exclude God even from his own universe and limit their horizons to the secular.

In twentieth-century America secularism is strikingly noticeable in our current doctrine of the separation of church and state. The doctrine of the separation of church and state used to mean that each functioned separately, kings or presidents not being allowed to appoint clerical authorities or run the church, and clerical authorities not being allowed to appoint kings or presidents. Nevertheless, it was always understood that both church and state were responsible to God in whose wisdom each had been established. They were two independent servants of one master. Although neither was permitted to rule the other, each was to remind the other of its God-appointed duties and recall it to upright, godly conduct if it should stray. Today, however, the doctrine of the separation of church and state is taken, primarily by church people, to mean that the church is irrelevant to the state— though the state increasingly brings its secular philosophy to bear on the church. Thus Christians withdraw from politics, neglect even to inform themselves of national and international issues. And as a result, the articulation of spiritual or moral principles is eliminated from debates on national and international policy. The state becomes its own god with its chief operating principle being pragmatism.

A second example of current society being humanistic to the point of excluding God is the philosophy of evolution, which is dominant in most contemporary thinking and extends to everything. There are different reasons for evolution's popularity, of course. First, according to evolutionary thought, everything is knowable. Everything is the result of something prior, and the sequence of cause and effect can be traced backward indefinitely. Such an outlook has obvious appeal. Second, reality has _one_ explanation: the fittest survive, whether a biological form, a government or an ideal. Third, and this is undoubtedly the chief reason for evolution's popularity, evolution eliminates God. If all things can be explained as the natural outworking or development of previous causes, then the need for God is eliminated. God may be safely banished to an otherworldly kingdom or even be eliminated altogether, as many, even so-called theologians, have done.[3]

That the secular city is also _by_ man and _for_ man comes out in the remainder of Nebuchadnezzar's story. One day, a year or more after the earlier incident, Nebuchadnezzar was walking on the roof of his royal palace in Babylon and looked out over the city. He was impressed with its magnificence. Judging himself to be responsible for that magnificence, he then took to himself the glory that should have been given to God. He said, "Is not this great Babylon, which I have built by my mighty power as a royal residence and for the glory of my majesty?" (Dan. 4:30). His statement was a claim that the earthly city had been constructed *by* man and *for* man's glory.

In a sense it was true. Nebuchadnezzar had constructed the city, and his conquests had brought it to its present level of architectural splendor. He had constructed it for his glory, as his self-satisfied boasting shows. His mistake was that he had forgotten that ultimately it is God who rules in human affairs and that the achievements of any ruler are made possible only through God's gifts to humanity.

Is the spirit of Nebuchadnezzar present today? Undoubtedly. It has always been present either overtly or just beneath the surface of the secular city's culture. Algernon Charles Swinburne's "Hymn of Man" is an example.

> *But God, if a God there be, is the*
> *Substance of men which is Man.*
> *Thou art smitten, thou God, thou art smitten;*
> *Thy death is upon thee, O Lord.*
> *And the love-song of earth as thou diest*
> *Resounds through the wind of her wings—*
> *Glory to Man in the highest!*
> *For Man is the master of things.*[4]

The Most High God

Man is not the master. The presumption of that claim is a sin God will not tolerate. God promises to bring the secular city down.

He did it in the case of Nebuchadnezzar. Nebuchadnezzar had judged himself superior to those around him because of his political achievements, so superior that he had no need of God. Then God spoke to show how mistaken Nebuchadnezzar was. He said, "O King Nebuchadnezzar, to you it is spoken: The kingdom has departed from you, and you shall be driven from among men, and your dwelling shall be with the beasts of the field; and you shall be made to eat grass like an ox; and seven times shall pass over you [that is, seven years shall go by], until you have learned that the Most High rules the kingdom of men and gives it to whom he will" (Dan. 4:31-32). That judgment was immediately put into effect. Nebuchadnezzar's mind went from him, and he was driven out of the city. The text says, "He was driven from among men, and ate grass like an ox, and his body was wet with the dew of heaven till his hair grew as long as eagles' feathers, and his nails were like birds' claws" (v. 33). When God caused Nebuchadnezzar to be lowered from the pinnacle of pride to the baseness of insanity and to behave like a beast, God was indicating that this is the result when humans take his glory to themselves and attempt to eliminate him from their lives. Indeed, they become worse than beasts—because beasts, when they are beastlike, are at least behaving the way beasts should behave, while we, by contrast, commit crimes of which they cannot even conceive.

The City of God

Over against the secular city stands the city of God. It is not a visible city, as the kingdoms of this world are visible. The world may call the city of God an illusion. But though invisible it is not illusory. In fact, it alone is substantial, in contrast to the cities of this world which are in the process of passing away.

God is its life. This is so even now, but it will be so in full measure when the new Jerusalem rises on the ruins of the old. In his description of the holy city, John said that there is no temple in that city because "its temple is the Lord God the Almighty and the Lamb" (Rev. 21:22). He wrote, "Behold, the dwelling of God is with men. He will dwell with them, and they shall be his people, and God himself will be with them" (Rev. 21:3). This city is brought into being by God and not by man. It exists for his glory.

All men and women are born into the secular city. No one is

born into the heavenly city naturally. But the city of God can be entered by new birth through faith in the Lord Jesus Christ as Savior. Jesus said, "Unless one is born anew, he cannot see the kingdom of God" (Jn. 3:3). The doors of that city stand open for any who will come. The New Testament says of Abraham: "By faith he sojourned in the land of promise, as in a foreign land, living in tents with Isaac and Jacob, heirs with him of the same promise. For he looked forward to the city which has foundations, whose builder and maker is God" (Heb. 11:9-10).

As you seek to come you can be encouraged by the fact that evidently even Nebuchadnezzar got the message. After the seven years of his punishment had passed and he returned to his senses, he confessed that the God whom he had earlier called Daniel's God (Dan. 2:47) was now his God as well. "At the end of the days I, Nebuchadnezzar, lifted my eyes to heaven, and my reason returned to me, and I blessed the Most High, and praised and honored him who lives for ever; for his dominion is an everlasting dominion, and his kingdom endures from generation to generation; all the inhabitants of the earth are accounted as nothing; and he does according to his will in the host of heaven and among the inhabitants of the earth; and none can stay his hand or say to him, 'What doest thou?' " (Dan. 4:34-35). His last words were "Now I, Nebuchadnezzar, praise and extol and honor the King of heaven; for all his works are right and his ways are just; and those who walk in pride he is able to abase" (v. 37).

As we humble ourselves, we find ourselves exalted in the role God has called us to fill and rejoice as citizens of that heavenly city that shall never pass away.

14   THE SECULAR CHURCH

Discussion of the secular city leads naturally to the city of God, the direction in which the last chapter was moving. But before we come to further consideration of God's city we need to deal with a view that emerged into prominence in the 1960s and may be said to characterize much if not most modern theology.

This view denies the distinction between the sacred and secular, saying either that life has no sacred dimension or that the sacred and secular are one. It says that Christians are called, not to be other-worldly, but to be this-worldly. They are to forget God and get on with the business of being human in a world from which God has vanished. What makes this a unique position, and not just another expression of the secular mind, is that it is maintained by a number of so-called Christian theologians as well as the hierarchy of many Christian denominations.

The "death of God" theologians, who received so much publicity in the mid-'60s, were a clear example: Thomas J. J.

Altizer, William Hamilton, Gabriel Vahanian and Paul van Buren. The views of Harvard Divinity School professor Harvey Cox and John A. T. Robinson, England's bishop of Woolwich, were widely quoted. Since then, hosts of church functionaries and lesser-known but more original theologians have arisen, all of whom were trying to be radically secular. They wrote of "man come of age," a phrase drawn from the writings of Dietrich Bonhoeffer. Some referred to their outlook as "worldly Christianity."

Life without God

The best example of "Christian secularization was Harvey Cox, whose book *The Secular City* hit the religious world as a bombshell in 1965. Although Cox later repudiated some of his ideas, *The Secular City* is still the best example of this view for two reasons: (1) Cox regarded the secular city as a good thing, something to be affirmed and applauded rather than denied; and (2) Cox maintained that the Judeo-Christian tradition itself leads us to regard secularization positively.

Cox finds a biblical base for the second assertion in three areas. First, he believes that the Genesis account of creation teaches the "disenchantment" of nature. Presecular man lived in a world where trees, rocks, glens, groves, droughts and storms were alive with friendly or hostile spirits. Everywhere people looked they were confronted with mysterious forces to be managed, appeased or warded off. In Genesis that view was radically subverted. There both God and human beings were distinguished from nature, with the result that humans could then regard nature in a matter-of-fact way. Now nature is merely nature, natural. It is there to be used. Cox calls this disenchantment of the natural world "an absolute precondition" for the development of natural science and hence for the emergence of the modern technopolis. He says that in this sense the Genesis account of creation is really a form of "atheistic propaganda."[1]

A second area in which the Judeo-Christian tradition has led to secularization is politics, which Cox traces to the Jewish exodus from Egypt. In presecular society anyone who ruled, ruled by divine right. Therefore, rebellion against any duly installed ruler was a rebellion against God or a god. The exodus changed all that. Here was an act of civil disobedience or rebellion sanctioned by the Hebrew God. Cox writes, "As such, it symbolized the deliverance of man out of a sacral-political order and into history and social change, out of religiously legitimated monarchs and into a world where political leadership would be based on power gained by the capacity to accomplish specific social objectives."[2] The old, sacred view of politics did not disappear at once, of course. Jewish people were often tempted to return to sacral politics, especially in the time of the monarchy.

The struggle of pope against emperor re-enacted the same temptation in the Middle Ages. In contemporary history the British state church, presided over by the archbishop of Canterbury, and the use of the Bible for the taking of the oath of office by the president of the United States are remnants of the earlier view. But these have little substance, and politics can now be seen to be thoroughly secular except in some Third World countries such as Nepal.

A third area of biblical desacralization is the Sinai covenant, which Cox calls the "deconsecration of values." He means that values or moral norms are made relative. If we ask how anyone can say such a thing—in that Sinai was the place, above all others, in which God gave what has always been regarded as an absolute and binding moral law—the answer, according to Cox, is in the opposition to idolatry seen there (Ex. 20:3). It was because the Jews believed in Yahweh rather than the gods of the heathen that their values were relativized.

On this so-called biblical basis Cox believes that modern man in his technology, urbanity and pragmatism is the product of biblical faith and divinely directed historical forces.

This man lives in the secular city from which for all practical purposes God is banished. He enjoys a freedom made possible by technology and undergirded by almost total privacy. Values are private, as each is left free to live as he or she desires. Cox calls on Christians to support this outlook. He writes, "Clearly, those whose present orientation to reality is shaped by the biblical faith can hardly in good faith enter the lists as adversaries of secularization. Our task should be to nourish the secularization process, to prevent it from hardening into a rigid world view, and to clarify as often as necessary its roots in the Bible. Furthermore, we should be constantly on the lookout for movements which attempt to thwart and reverse the liberating irritant of secularization."[3]

The World's Wisdom

How can we explain the tremendous attention and acclaim that Cox's book received on its appearance? The reason for that acclaim was that the secularization of the church which Cox described was already well under way, in fact, even entrenched in some church bureaucracies. Consequently, when *The Secular City* appeared, those persons naturally hailed it as a theoretical justification of a lifestyle and denominational policy they were already following.

One element in this secularization of the church, which clearly preceded Cox, was its exchange of the ancient wisdom of the church (embodied in Scripture) for the world's wisdom. In earlier ages Christian people stood before the Word of God and confessed their ignorance of spiritual things. They even confessed their inability to understand what was written in the Scriptures except through the grace of God in the ministry of the Holy Spirit. Christian people confessed their natural resistance to God's teaching. In our time this old wisdom, the strength of the church, has been set aside. The authoritative, reforming voice of God through the Scriptures has been forgotten.

Once I was taking part in a series of Moderator's Conferences in the United Presbyterian Church, U.S.A. In one of these a professor from a theological seminary disagreed with everything I said. I had expected this from some source, but the words this man used were so forceful they stuck in my mind. I had spoken of the historical Christ, but this professor violently disagreed with my position. He said, "We must understand that each of the Gospels was written to correct the other Gospels. So it is impossible to speak of the historical Christ." Then, since I had also said something about the return of the Lord, he added, "We must get it into our heads that things are always going to continue as they are now and that Jesus Christ is never coming back."

That is not an isolated incident. A pastor, who has been an active leader for the evangelical cause, told me that after he had spoken to a particular issue at a presbytery meeting, another minister demanded, "Why are you always talking about the Bible when you argue a point? Don't you know that nobody believes the Bible anymore?" Then, because my friend had referred to the apostle Paul on this occasion, his critic added, "After all, the apostle Paul was not infallible."

I see four consequences of this capitulation to the world. First, it has produced a pitiful state of uncertainty and insecurity in church leaders. It is often covered up, of course. But at times it is honestly stated, as in these words from the inaugural address of Robin Scroggs, professor of New Testament at the Chicago Theological Seminary: "We are thus in no secure place. We have found no single authoritative standard from the past of what to say or how to live. Neither have we a secure self-understanding erected on the basis of our immediate experience. We in fact find ourselves in the abyss of a continual uncertainty, but we are kept from falling into chaos by the very tension between past and present. . . . We have no assurance that where we happen to be is the best or final place to stand."[4]

A second result is the church's turning to the world and its values. One analyst of the secularizing movement in today's theology is John Macquarrie (variously classified as a secular or process theologian). In his study of the intellectual history of many secular theologians, *God and Secularity,* he describes many of these men as "disillusioned Barthians."[5] Since Karl Barth denied that the Bible was the Word of God, calling it only man's witness to the word of God, and since Barth stressed the transcendence or hiddenness of God, those who followed him wondered if anything could honestly be termed a revelation. And if not, or if one could not be certain of such a revelation, then the secular world with its vacillating but audible words was the only place to which one could turn for direction.

A third result of abandonment of the Scriptures as the wisdom of God given to the church is a pragmatic dependence upon the fifty-one-percent vote, the validation of values, goals, objectives and programs by consensus. If people throw out a transcendent authority, an earthly authority will inevitably come in. Reject Scripture, and a poorer authority will take Scripture's place.

This is the true meaning of the well-publicized Kenyon decision, in which a qualified young man was barred from ordination in the United Presbyterian Church, U.S.A. solely on the basis of his views on women's ordination. Kenyon believed that the Scriptures forbid the ordination of women as teaching or ruling elders in the church, but he was moderate in his attitude. He recognized that others saw things differently; he was willing to work with ordained women. Yet he was barred from ordination, even over his presbytery's objection. Why? He was not barred constitutionally, because nothing in the constitution required a minister to participate in any ordination. Obviously he could not be barred for saying that he would not do something he was not required to do. He was not barred biblically, because there was not a word of argument showing that the texts to which he referred were misinterpreted by him and should be understood in other ways. He was barred simply because the consensus of the denomination at that time was that such a view was detrimental to the women's liberation cause.

Christians need to understand that such controversies are being fought, not on biblical or theological grounds, but on grounds of consensus. Decisions are determined as much by what secular spokespersons say on the six o'clock TV news as they are by deliberations within church councils.

A final consequence of the church's abandonment of God's wisdom is that the church becomes irrelevant (as indeed even Cox's _Secular City_ must seem to secular men and women). This is being noted widely and not just by evangelicals. Speaking in the early 1970s at a meeting of the Consultation on Church Union in Denver, Peter Berger of Rutgers University criticized the lack of authority in the churches, which leads to their irrelevance. He argued,

> If there is going to be a renaissance of religion, its bearers will not be people who have been falling all over each other to be "relevant to modern man." . . . Strong eruptions of religious faith have always been marked by the appearance of people with firm, unapologetic, often uncompromising convictions—that is, by types that are the very opposite from those presently engaged in the various "relevance" operations. Put simply: Ages of faith are not marked by "dialogue" but by proclamation. . . . I would affirm that the concern for the institutional structures of the Church will be vain unless there is also a new conviction and a new authority in the Christian community.[6]

Theology, Agenda, Methods
It is not only in the area of the world's wisdom that the church has fallen into secularism. It has also capitulated in the areas of the world's theology, agenda and methods. The world's theology is easy to define. It is the view that human beings are

basically good, that no one is really lost, that belief in Jesus
Christ is not necessary for salvation. Such capitulation is common in some church circles. When I was speaking at those
Moderator's Conferences, a section of my paper had to do
with human lostness. I discussed it as a motivation for mission:
we take the gospel of Jesus Christ to others because they are
lost without it. In every consultation that point in my paper
aroused anger on the part of those listening. Some were infu-
riated. Nearly all were dissatisfied. Each time as I moved into
that section of the paper, people began to shift, cough, move.
When I finished, it was the part of the paper they brought up
for objection.

Thus, the theological terms that we have always used and
which the church continues to use (because it is part of its
heritage) are being redefined. People still speak of sin, salvation, faith and many other biblical terms. But having adopted
the world's theology they no longer mean by those terms what
evangelicals mean when they use them biblically. Thus, *sin*
means, not rebellion against God and his righteous law, for
which we are held accountable, but rather ignorance or
merely the kind of oppression found in social structures.
Since sin is located in the system, the way to overcome it is
clearly not by the death of Jesus Christ but rather by changing
the structures either through legislation or revolution.

In that outlook, *Jesus* becomes, not the incarnate God who
came to die for our salvation, but rather the pattern for
creative living. We are therefore to look to Jesus as an example, but not as Savior. In some forms of this theology he is even
considered to be what we might call the evolutionary peak of
the race, a peak we are all supposed to attain.

Salvation is defined, not as the old theology would say, as
"getting right with God" or even "God moving to redeem us in
Christ," but rather as liberation from the oppression of this
world's structures.

Faith is no longer believing God and taking his Word seriously, but rather awareness of the situation as we see it. This approach is closely related to Marxism, because Marxists say that commitment to communism arises from becoming aware of oppression and beginning to do something about it.

Evangelism is also redefined. It no longer means carrying the gospel of Jesus Christ to a perishing world, but rather working to overthrow injustice.

Again, there is the matter of agenda. In mainline church circles the phrase "the world's agenda" is quite popular. It means that in order of priority the church's concerns should be the concerns of the world, even to the exclusion of the gospel. If the world's first concern is hunger, that should be our first concern too. If it is the problems of underdeveloped countries, that should be our primary concern. Racism. Ecology. The energy crises. Aging. Alcoholism. Anything you read about in the evening paper should be uppermost in our thinking. In recognizing this danger we do not want to go to the opposite extreme and suggest that there are areas of life about which God, and therefore also the church, is unconcerned. That would be a dualism that denies the sovereignty of God over all things. It is simply that these concerns must not be allowed to eclipse the gospel. If that happens, the church loses the framework from which alone she can say something truly unique and actually help with these problems.

Finally, the capitulation to the world of large segments of the organized church is seen in the church's methods. God's methods are prayer and the power of the gospel, through which the Holy Spirit moves to turn God's people from their wicked ways and heal their land. That has always been the strength of the church of Christ. Today that power is despised by the great denominations. It is laughed at, because the methods that those laughing want to use (and do use) are politics and money.

Some time ago I came across a cartoon in *The New Yorker*

magazine. Two Pilgrims were coming over on the *Mayflower* and one was saying "Religious freedom is my immediate goal, but my long-range plan is to go into real estate." In a sense that is what we are seeing today. Prayer and the power of the gospel are being crowded out by commitment to real estate, money, politics and all those things with which we are so familiar from secular sources.

The nineteenth-century English playwright George Bernard Shaw saw it clearly years before these developments actually took place, saying that in his view the religion of the future would be politics. The idea is in several of his plays. It is in *Caesar and Cleopatra,* where Caesar becomes a religious figure in these terms. It is most explicit in *Major Barbara.* Barbara is a major in the Salvation Army, and she is converted in the play from Salvation Army religion to political activism. Politics is the new religion. Politics and money.

Let me illustrate how money is equated with God's work. A little brochure was published by the program agency of one denomination entitled "God's Work in God's World." Looking at that title one might think that it would be a report on what was being done in evangelism, social services, the mission field, church building or such things. Opening it, one found in bold type the words "The Good News." At that point we might imagine the report to have something to do with the gospel. What was this "good news"? It was that the results of a special emergency appeal had "provided the first increase" in general mission receipts since 1967. In other words, the "gospel" was that the church had received more money recently. The brochure then went on to show what could be done with the money. "In 1975, these additional dollars for mission have: 1) provided the capacity to increase the overseas missionary force by twenty-four persons." Wonderful. But if one read carefully, it did not say that the missionary force *was* increased by twenty-four persons. All it said was that there was enough money to do that if those in charge would like to. Did they? They did not. In fact, the total missionary force went down that year just as it had declined both before and since. It is now less than three hundred fifty in a church which once had a missionary force in excess of two thousand.

A Challenge

The story does not stop at this point (though the chapter must), because we will go on to show that evangelicals are not exempt from this criticism and must therefore not be self-righteous. What we can say here is that the situation calls for a major effort on the part of God's people. We should not be surprised by ecclesiastical secularism. This is the point of those verses that say that "in the last days there will come times of stress. For men will be lovers of self, lovers of money, proud, arrogant, abusive, disobedient to their parents, ungrateful, unholy, inhuman, implacable, slanderers, profligates, fierce, haters of good, treacherous, reckless, swollen with conceit, lovers of pleasure rather than lovers of God, holding the form of religion but denying the power of it" (2 Tim. 3:1-5).

That is the secular church: "holding the form of religion [and sometimes not even that] but denying the power of it." The challenge for God's people is to be the opposite. If the secular church employs the world's wisdom, the world's theology, the world's agenda and the world's methods, the church of the Lord Jesus Christ must do the opposite. It must employ the wisdom of God, the theology of the Scriptures, the agenda of God's written revelation and the methods that have been given to us for our exercise in the church until the Lord comes again. Only as the church does that can it affirm what is actually good in secular culture and be bold enough to challenge what is not.

15

GOD'S CITY

The vision of the city of God in Revelation 21 is a utopia: "I saw the holy city, new Jerusalem, coming down out of heaven from God, prepared as a bride adorned for her husband" (v. 2). But it is not like the utopias envisioned by human beings. Most human utopias present either what their inventor would like to see happen (Plato's *Republic,* Thoreau's *Walden),* or they warn against what might happen (Huxley's *Brave New World,* Orwell's *1984).* The biblical utopia is something that has already happened but which is also to happen more fully when Christ returns.

In theology this unique biblical perspective has been expressed as the "already" and the "not yet." Already the kingdom of God is in our midst (Lk. 17:21). Nevertheless we pray, "Thy kingdom come" (Mt. 6:10).

The Revelation vision of the new Jerusalem has this perspective. As John wrote, he was thinking of the city that would be. It is characterized by God's presence. "And I heard a loud voice from the throne saying, 'Behold, the dwelling of God is with men. He will dwell with them, and they shall be his people, and God himself will be with them' " (Rev. 21:3). It is marked by holiness. "Nothing unclean shall enter it, nor any one who practices abomination or falsehood, but only those who are written in the Lamb's book of life" (v. 27). Death, sorrow and pain will be eliminated. "Death shall be no more, neither shall there be mourning nor crying nor pain any more, for the former things have passed away" (v. 4). It is a place of constant delight and satisfaction.

Those things are already present in some measure in the Christian community. God already dwells with his people in the person of his Holy Spirit (Jn. 14:16-18). Christians are marked by a discernible measure of holiness (Jn. 17:17; 15:3). They sorrow but not as those who have no hope (1 Thess. 4:13). The value for Christians of the portrait of the ideal city of God in Revelation is that it tells us what we already are, what we increasingly can be even in this life and what we will inevitably be as God brings to completion that work already begun.

Evangelical Secularism

The place to begin in a discussion of any present realization of the city of God is not with the perfection to come but with the realization that genuinely believing people are also themselves sometimes quite secular.

When we speak of the secularization of the church we mean in part that the large denominations have capitulated to the world's system. That is, they have capitulated in the areas of biblical authority, theology, program and methods with the result that in place of the old standards of the church there have come new standards marked by the same dependence on politics and money that is characteristic of secular organizations. But there is also an *evangelical* secularism which must be faced and dealt with if true Christians are to be any use in the world. To be sure, the evangelical church has not capitulated in the same ways that the larger denominations have. Nevertheless, the values of the world have increasingly forced themselves upon us so that we have become secular in at least some areas almost without knowing it. The gospel is present, or we would not be able to speak of "evangelical" churches. To a degree even theology is present. But the world's values have begun to take effect anyway. So we see evangelical secularism in materialism, faddism, Madison Avenue techniques, and indifference to spiritual realities and concerns.

Many persons point to our materialism. *World Vision* magazine, in its issue of January 1976, quoted a number of evangelical leaders who had been asked to write about Western civilization and the mission of the church. Most of them in one way or another criticized our materialism. J. D. Douglas, editor of the *New International Dictionary of the Christian Church* and editor-at-large for *Christianity Today*, wrote: "Pervading our society is an even more insidious materialism which makes Christians short of breath through prosperity and ill-equipped to run the race that is set before them." Horace L. Fenton, Jr., general director of Latin America Mission, wrote: "In the Western Church we ought to cut back immediately on all unnecessary expenditures—including the elaborate building programs which have obsessed us far too long. It is just as much a sin for a Church to lay up treasure on earth as it is for an individual Christian." Frank E. Gaebelein, headmaster emeritus of the Stony Brook School and general editor of *The Expositor's Bible Commentary*, wrote, "Negatively the growing materialism in the more affluent western nations is detrimental to the total Christian discipleship essential to the faithful mission of the Church."[1] Each of these men puts his finger on something that is not just a characteristic of our country or of the liberal church but characteristic of evangelicals as well.

This is not a philosophical materialism. A philosophical materialism would be a materialism similar to that of communism. Evangelicals are not adopting materialism in that sense. There is a negative argument which says that, because we are not communists, and communists are materialists, we are not materialists. But that does not necessarily follow. True, we do not have a philosophical materialism, but if we are honest we must admit that nevertheless we have a very practical materialism which is detrimental to the advance of the gospel in our age.

Second, we become secularized in that we so easily follow the fads of this world. I once had a conversation with Dr. Hudson Armerding, president of Wheaton College, in which we talked about the situation on the campuses, particularly Christian ones. I asked Armerding what it was that bothered him most about the culture on our Christian campuses. He said, "It's the fact that the Christian campuses always seem to be following along behind the world; they have the same concerns, but it's always a year or two later." Then he spelled it out, noting that when the Viet Nam war became a concern in the secular schools, it became a concern in the Christian schools too, but several years later. When ecology became the burning issue on the secular campuses, it also became a burning issue on the Christian campuses, but a year or two later. When women's liberation became the issue elsewhere, it also became the issue in the Christian world, but again some time later. What he was saying is that we have here a case of the world leading the church rather than the church leading the world. And what is that, if that is not the secularization of the evangelical community?

The third area in which we see secularism in our evangelical churches is our Madison Avenue approach to Christian commitment. We see this in certain stylized forms of evangelism. I want to be very careful here, because obviously the greater problem in evangelism is not doing it at all. If through a method we are able to rally people to the cause of presenting the gospel of Jesus Christ to those who have not heard it, it is

missionaries and support for missionaries. He says there
short-term projects which are well received; but the num-
of those who would commit themselves to a lifetime of
ssionary endeavor for the sake of Christ and who would
pport such persons is dwindling. It is due to the indiffer-
ce of God's people.

There is indifference to the *suffering of the world's poor*. We
e often so isolated in North America from the very poor that
seldom really see deep suffering face to face. We do not
ow what it is to see someone who is so hungry that he or she
n hardly think of anything but food. So we are indifferent to
ese things.

There is indifference to the *needs of our fellow believers*. If
here is anything you hear in the evangelical church today, it
s that evangelicals do not want to listen to the hurts in the
earts and lives of other Christians. They do not want to be
othered. They do not want to hear these things because they
are demanding; they require a response, and we are not prepared to make it. Instead we want to rest in our own personal
peace and affluence.

There is indifference to the *leadership vacuum in the churches*.
There is work to be done, but the hardest thing in Christian
work is to find men and women who recognize the need and
who will step into it and do what is necessary by the grace of
God, faithfully, if necessary year after year and at great personal hardship. We do not have much of this commitment.
Somebody once handed me a little poem on the role of the
pastor which concluded:

Ashes to ashes, dust to dust;
If the people won't do it, the pastor must.

But the pastor cannot do it all. Moreover, if he is trying to do it
all, a number of things, including the preaching of the Word
of God, will be buried by the wayside. If people in the church
are indifferent to obvious need and the pastor responds in
their place, then the whole church suffers. Each one has a

not altogether bad to do that, even if the m
But at the same time we have to recognize that
enter in even here.

For example, sometimes Christians are requ
rize a certain stylized presentation of Christian
something which in the hands of a person who
the gospel well can be useful. Certainly it h
thought through the kind of questions you mi
and the answers that seem most helpful to most
to present the gospel in a rigid way, where th
carefully chosen by a kind of popular opinion poll
is secularism.

We see the same thing in the way in which the
Christian concerns are sold to our constituenc
through advertisements in our magazines, direct m
on. It should be said, in defense of this, that it is ofte
that this is the only way in which evangelical leader
be able to awaken the concerns of Christian people
proper stance from the perspective of the individua
ahead of the appeal in one's own commitment as to he
she is going to use money. In other words, before the
comes, when you are before the Lord on your knees, a
the resources that he has given you should be used an
determine to do that on the basis of the Lord's leading a
necessarily on the basis of the sentimental pictures tha
pen to be on the front of the brochure that comes in the
about three weeks before Christmas.

Finally, we see secularism in the evangelical church in
great indifference. Indifference to what? The answer i
practically anything and everything worthwhile. We are
different to the *state of the lost*. Francis R. Steele, home di
tor of the North American Council of the North Africa M
sion, has written an article for one of the publications of th
mission entitled, "Indifference—Involvement."[2] In it
points to indifference as the number one problem in recru

gift. Each one must be willing to use it to the glory of God.

The following question was asked of a number of officials in church circles: What is the number one problem in the evangelical church today? "Apathy," said an official of the National Association of Evangelicals. "Lack of discipline," said another. "Not caring enough," said somebody who was involved in the Watergate scandal.

The evangelical church must be different. It will be in the world and, in some areas, will identify with the world's interests. But it will not be of the world. Its values will not be the world's values, nor will its priorities be the world's priorities. The true church must always strive to be increasingly what it essentially is, namely, God's city.

Distinctly Different

Let me suggest some areas in which our difference must be evident. First, the city of God must be clear as to what its *authority* is. One evidence of the secularism of the large denominations is that biblical authority, the authority of the Scriptures, has been thrown out, and the authority of consensus has replaced it. Things are done in the denominations today, not because the Bible says they should be done or even because the creeds say so, but because fifty-one percent of our people say so. If the true church is to be distinct in this area, it must let it be known that it does what it does because the Bible says so. We must be men and women of "the Book." In theory we are. We say we are. We acknowledge that our standards come from the Bible. But much of the time, in practice, evangelical churches operate exactly the way other churches do.

We have to recover the biblical standard. We cannot say, as evangelicals have often said on important issues, "Well, that particular thing just does not bother me." That kind of response is not good enough. Instead, we have to get to what the Word of God says. We have to study it, do our homework, and then we must ask: On the basis of this Word, what does God want for the church in this age?

We are going to have to do that sooner or later anyway, or else we are going to have to go the world's way entirely. History does not allow us to stand long in an ambiguous position. In the Nazi period in Germany the church went in one of two ways: either it capitulated to the Nazi point of view (and most of the established church did), or it became increasingly a church of the Book. Those who lived by the Book eventually established a communion of their own. They signed documents identifying themselves as the "Confessing Church." They did that because, when the whole drift of the society and the culture is contrary to biblical standards, it is impossible to appeal to any external norms. You cannot say, "This is backed up in the area of psychology or science or social relations," because it is not. Much of the material being written in those areas is contrary to biblical truth. So the church must increasingly fall back upon the divine revelation. Has God spoken in this Book? Does he speak? Those are the important questions. If God does speak, then we must be clear and say, "Let God be true and every man a liar." Evangelical churches are increasingly going to have to recapture that outlook.

Second, we need to be distinct in our *theology*. When we are, those who hunger for the truth of the Word of God will come to it. We see the evidence in our seminaries. I received a report of a meeting of the Council of Theological Seminaries of the United Presbyterian Church in which the needs of the United Presbyterian seminaries—Dubuque, Louisville, McCormick, Pittsburgh, Princeton, San Francisco and J. C. Smith—were discussed, and at which representatives from two leading evangelical seminaries, Fuller and Gordon-Conwell, were present. This report showed that enrollment at the denominational seminaries, where there is often no clear theology and most certainly not an evangelical theology, is declining. The lowest of the seven was Dubuque; it had only 111 students. The highest was Princeton. At the time it had 581, though that figure has since risen. But to put those figures in perspective one must recognize that enrollment at the five leading evangelical seminaries in this country is growing and already exceeds them all, Fuller alone having 1,200 students.

Where are the young men and women from Presbyterian churches going for seminary training? At that time 38.4 percent of them were being trained outside Presbyterian seminaries, at schools like Trinity, Gordon-Conwell, Fuller and others. Today it is 45 percent and rising. Why? Because those seminaries are distinct in their theology. The thesis of Dean Kelley's book is that the conservative churches are growing because they know where they stand and, therefore, people know where they stand and turn to them. The same thesis applies to seminaries. Seminaries grow for that reason too. They are an illustration of what we need in theology.

We need to articulate the great biblical doctrines, not just adopt the theology of our culture. We need to speak of human depravity, of men and women in rebellion against God, so much so that there is no hope for them apart from God's grace. We need to speak of God's electing love, showing that God enters the life of the individual in grace by his Holy Spirit to quicken understanding and draw the rebellious will to himself. We must speak of perseverance, that God is able to keep and does keep those whom he so draws. All those doctrines and all the supporting doctrines that go with them need to be proclaimed. We have to say, "This is where we stand. We do not adopt your theology. We do not agree with what we hear coming from denominational headquarters." Some of us have begun to do that and the effects are already observable.

Third, we have to be different in our *priorities*. The denominations set their agenda, the world's agenda. We must say that our priorities are not going to be the world's priorities but the priorities of the Word of God. That determination does not mean that we will neglect social concerns. They are part of the priority of the Christian life. But it does mean that we will not reject the gospel of salvation through faith in the vicarious atonement of Christ either. We will make proclamation of the gospel our number-one priority.

At the end of *The Invaded Church,* Donald G. Bloesch asks what evangelicals must do to change the world. He answers that what is needed is "a new kind of man." He gives examples. When he gets into the area of racism he analyzes the problem like this:

> *For modern secular humanism, including Marxism, the poison of racism can be removed through social reform and education. Biblical Christianity sees this problem in a different light. The real enemy is racial and cultural pride, not ignorance. And behind this pride is unbelief, hardness of heart, what the Bible calls original sin. . . . Laws are necessary to protect the defenseless, but they can only hold the dike against sin. It is the gospel alone that takes away sin, and this means that the final solution to racism and other social ills is biblical evangelism.*[3]

When we set our priorities we must be clear that this is where our emphasis goes—in time, money and in the choice of what we do and say.

New Lifestyle

Fourth, we need to be distinctly different in the area of *lifestyle.* Evangelicals have not been too conscious of this need until fairly recent times; we have lived in a culture which, although it is not Christian, nevertheless held on in part to the vestiges of an earlier Christianity. We have laws on our books because Christians of an earlier age said this is what we should do. We follow certain norms of behavior because of the influence of this earlier Christianity. All that is disappearing. Laws are changing, and there is going to be more agitation to change in future days. When those changes take place, Christians must be distinct. They must say that they do not go along with the trends of the times, the increasing secularization.

One of the priorities we must have concerns time. Sports take an enormous amount of time in people's lives, through television as well as our own participation. Sport has almost become the religion of America. It is what many people do on weekends. Even some evangelicals find their time so taken up with sports that Christian activities are crowded out. Isn't this an area in which we have to say that the drift of our day is not in the direction we want to go? Dr. Anthony Campolo, a professor at Eastern College in Pennsylvania, calls a commitment to sports the most serious threat to America today.

Much time is also spent watching television, and most of it is not edifying. At best it is diverting. Statistics say that the average American watches television for over four hours every day, and those figures are probably true of Christian people also. Is the tube worth that time? The Bible says, "[Make] the most of the time, because the days are evil" (Eph. 5:16). It means, make your life count. I wonder if many Christians are not missing out here and if the challenge of the age is not going to require us to sharpen up in such areas.

How about the use of Sunday? Personally, I do not believe that we should have blue laws. I do not believe in prescribing what is proper and improper Sunday activity for everybody. But how do *we* use Sunday? Do we go to church? Do we want to worship God? Is sixty minutes, seventy or eighty minutes, on Sunday morning the whole of our Sunday commitment? Is it the total time we want to be with Christian people? Is it all the time we can spare to receive religious instruction?

I have noticed recently that public schools are increasingly scheduling school events for Sunday, which is having its effect on our children. Our schools have the rest of the week filled up. So what do they do when they want to establish a new activity? There is a glee club, and they need people to sing. There are sports, and someone wants to get in an extra practice. There is an orchestra, and they need time to rehearse. When do they do it? They set it for Sunday morning. Christian people are going to be confronted with that again and again. Are those activities more important than having our children in church? We must ask that question. We cannot avoid it. Even if it means not getting ahead as much as we would like, even if it means not being as popular as we would like, even if it means that our children are not going to be as popular as we would like them to be—we must say, "But as for me and my house, we will serve the LORD" (Josh. 24:15).

When we do that we will have an influence on the world. I know cases where Christian parents have said to their children, "You are not allowed to do that on Sunday morning; we go to church at that hour." The children have gone to their teachers and have said, "We are sorry but we can't participate; our family goes to church at that hour." And the teachers have said, "Oh, we didn't know anybody did that. All right, we'll change the hour." Victories can be won, but we have to stand by our convictions.

Perhaps the most pressing area in which we have to be distinct is sexual ethics, particularly in our conception of marriage and the way we conduct our marriages. It is not easy to have a Christian marriage today. Everything in the world works against it. The overriding concern of our time is for personal satisfaction, and there are always things in marriage that do not seem personally satisfying. We wish it could be different. But the question is: What are we in the marriage for? Are we in it for personal satisfaction above all? Or are we there because we believe that God has brought us together with our spouse to establish a Christian home in which the truth of his Word can be raised high, Christian values demonstrated and children raised to know the Bible and live a Christian lifestyle? It must be the latter. Further, in our speaking we must make a distinction between marriages that are Christian marriages and marriages that are marriages only in the world's sense.

I recall a fictitious marriage service I once saw on television. I was curious about how the writers were going to handle the vows. The vows are Christian, as everyone knows. I wondered: Will they use them because they are the traditional vows and they cannot avoid them, or will they doctor them up to make them more secular? In this particular service the couple promised to "live with one another and cherish one another, as long as . . ." I thought they were going to say "as long as life shall last." But they said, ". . . as long as *love* shall last." In other words, "As long as I love her I'll live with her; but if I stop loving her, that's the end of the marriage." It could be a year, a month, a week. That is the viewpoint of secular men and women, and it is being openly expressed today. When Christians stand to take vows, they must make it known that their vows are for life—"until death us do part" —because that is what God wants. And they must live as Christians within the marriage bond.

Finally, the city of God must be distinct in its use of money and other resources. How do we use our money? All of us are hit by inflation. But if we compare our standard of living with that of the rest of the world, we are all millionaires. All of us have money we could use in the Lord's work. Are we faithful in that area? Some of us do not even give the Old Testament tithe, let alone our life and soul and all that we have to be used in the Lord's way.

Dependence on God

I have listed four areas in which we need to be distinctly different. Those areas correspond to the areas of secularization delineated in the last chapter. But we need to add a fifth point. We need to be distinctly different in our *visible dependence on God*. Nothing less will capture the attention of a secular world.

When I was at the Moderator's Conferences I mentioned, something happened that was very revealing. When I spoke about human lostness I got a terrible reaction on the part of those present. Nobody wanted to hear that men and women were lost apart from the grace of God. But everybody seemed to agree with one doctrine. It startled me. I had stressed the grace of God in calling some to salvation. I said, "We cannot move men; we cannot change the world. If the world is to be changed it must be by God's doing, and for that we must pray and ask him." They agreed with that just as much as they had disagreed with total depravity. I began to analyze this, and after I had done so I began to understand the reaction. It was because the people to whom I was talking were people engaged in the very things I had been talking about. They were working in the social arena—trying to help alcoholics, serving those in the ghetto, looking for improvement. And what had happened? They had looked for improvement, but it had not come. So when I said that change had to be by the grace of God, the echo of their hearts said "Amen." They did not like biblical theology, but they knew that the power of God is necessary if change is to come.

How can Christians change the world? The Lord Jesus Christ gave the answer in the Sermon on the Mount. He did not say that we are to maneuver the world. He did not say "Get elected to high positions in the Roman empire. See if you can get an evangelical promoted to emperor." It could happen, of course. He did not forbid it. But that is not the option he gave. He said, "You are the salt of the earth. You are the light of the world."

Salt does no good at all if it has lost its saltiness. Only when it is salty is it effective. So, if we are those in whom the Spirit of God has worked to call us to faith in Jesus Christ, we must really be Christ's people. It must be evident that by his grace we are not what we were previously. Our values must not be the world's values. Our commitments must not be secular commitments. Our theology must not be a decimated theology. Rather, there must be a new element in us and, because of us, in the world.

We are also "light." The purpose of light is to shine, to shine out. So the Lord said, "Look, nobody lights a candle and puts it under a bushel. It is to be set up on a candlestick where everyone will see it." We are to be lighthouses in the midst of a dark world. Being a lighthouse will not change the rocky contours of the coast. Sin is still there. The perils of destruction still threaten men and women. But by God's grace the light can be a beacon to bring ships into a safe harbor.

16 CHURCH AND STATE

Two major ambiguities exist in the relationship of the city of God to the secular city. One is the secular church, which we have already considered. It is an obvious ambiguity because, although it should be sacred in the sense of being totally devoted to God and his kingdom, it is nevertheless motivated by the authority, theology, agenda and methods of the world. It is Christian in name only. The other ambiguity is the state. It presents a problem because, although it is secular and clearly expresses the mind-set of the secular city, it nevertheless has been established by God for good ends and therefore deserves the support and prayers of Christian people.

The second ambiguity is founded in Scripture. On the one hand, the state is described as directed by demonic powers. Paul tells us we are to strive against them. "For we are not contending against flesh and blood, but against the principalities, against the powers, against the world rulers of this present darkness, against the spiritual hosts of wickedness in the heavenly places" (Eph. 6:12). In its extreme form the state is portrayed as godless Babylon destined for destruction (Rev. 18). It is a beast from the pit (Rev. 17). We are told that Christ triumphed over the powers that stand behind the state by his victory on the cross (Col. 2:15). On the other hand, the Bible also views the state in a positive light, telling us that "there is no authority except from God, and those that exist have been instituted by God" (Rom. 13:1). We are to obey such authority and pray for those who exercise it (1 Tim. 2:1-2).

The state sometimes functions as it should. At other times it functions in a demonic way. Under normal circumstances the church is to be thankful for the state and obey it. It may even regard the state as one of "the external means or aids by which God invited us into the society of Christ and holds us therein," as Calvin did. (That is the title of the fourth book of the *Institutes* in which the proper role of the state is discussed.) On the other hand, the church must also be ready to challenge the state in the name of God and his righteousness and even disobey the state whenever its laws conflict with the laws of God.

It is not always easy to determine which of the two situations one is in, however, if only because the dilemmas confronting a Christian citizen are often not clear-cut. That is the case even with the classic text concerning a Christian's responsibility to government: "Render therefore to Caesar the things that are Caesar's, and to God the things that are God's" (Mt. 22:21).

The background for that guideline was a question about taxes. "Is it lawful to pay taxes to Caesar, or not?" (v. 17). Christ's answer was affirmative, an answer echoed by Paul. "Pay all of them their dues, taxes to whom taxes are due, revenue to whom revenue is due, respect to whom respect is due, honor to whom honor is due" (Rom. 13:7). But suppose the commands of Caesar and the commands of God disagree? Do we obey Caesar, arguing that God has set him over us and that God will take care of the consequences of our act? Or do we obey God? Even the matter of taxes is not entirely clear.

What if our taxes are being used for immoral ends: to support a gestapo, an unjust war, oppression of the disenfranchised by the rich and privileged, or other evils? Clearly there are puzzling dimensions to this relationship.

One thing Christ's words about taxes do say is that the state has its legitimate sphere. Christians should be respectful of that legitimacy even more than others because they know that God has established it. Christians can never be entirely pragmatic at this point, still less opportunistic. They can never knowingly try to overthrow a legitimate government simply because they would prefer a different type of government or different people in government, still less because they want to rule themselves. Within a democracy there are legitimate procedures for changing rulers, and these are open to Christians. Revolution for its own sake or the sake of the revolutionaries themselves is excluded.

What is the legitimate sphere of government? Calvin regarded it as "the establishment of civil justice and outward morality."[1] He argued that Christ's spiritual kingdom and the civil jurisdiction are distinct. Yet the distinction does not mean that the whole of government is polluted; it exists "to cherish and protect the outward worship of God, to defend sound doctrine of piety and the position of the church, to adjust our life to the society of men, to form our social behavior to civil righteousness, to reconcile us to one another, and to promote general peace and tranquility."[2]

John Murray, in a study of "The Relation of Church and State," says that the sphere of civil government "is that of guarding, maintaining, and promoting justice, order, and peace."[3] On the other hand, "to the church is committed the task of proclaiming the whole counsel of God and, therefore, the counsel of God as it bears upon the responsibility of all persons and institutions. . . . When the civil magistrate trespasses the limits of his authority, it is incumbent upon the church to expose and condemn such a violation of his authority."[4]

What those men are saying, and what Scripture also says, is not merely that church and state represent two separate spheres of authority: God's and Caesar's. That is true, though it is not the best way of representing it. Rather, they are saying that church and state stand in relationship to one another in that both are established by God, share certain areas of concern and are responsible ultimately to the same divine Sovereign.

Four Options

Light is thrown on this relationship by the appearance of the Lord Jesus Christ before Pilate at the time of his crucifixion. The situation itself is significant. Jesus, the head of the church, was appearing before the chief representative of human government in Palestine. The issue of the trial was whether Jesus, a "king," stood in a right or wrong relationship to Caesar.

In the early part of the trial the matter of Christ's kingship came up and was quickly dismissed by Pilate. He understood rightly that Christ's kingdom was "not of this world" (Jn. 18:36) and therefore was no threat to legitimate government. But the matter did not stop there. The accusers of Christ persisted, arguing that Christ should die because he made himself "the Son of God" (Jn. 19:7). Pilate, intrigued and perhaps even slightly alarmed by this new line of accusation, reopened the examination. "Where are you from?" he asked. When Jesus gave no answer (Pilate being unqualified to examine him on what was clearly a spiritual matter), the Roman judge demanded, "You will not speak to me? Do you not know that I have power to release you, and power to crucify you?" (vv. 9-10).

Jesus replied, "You would have no power over me unless it had been given you from above; therefore he who delivered me to you has the greater sin" (v. 11). The authority of human government does not come from anything intrinsic to itself but from God. It is a delegated authority. Consequently, there are always the matters of the government's responsibility and sin.

To get the full measure of this we need to combine it with Christ's words about God and Caesar, considered earlier. They suggest four possible options regarding legitimate authority: (1) God alone as an authority with the authority of Caesar denied, (2) Caesar alone as an authority with the authority of God denied, (3) the authority of both God and Caesar but with Caesar in the dominant position, and (4) the authority of God and Caesar but with God in the dominant position.

The first position, God alone, is one some Christians have adopted at some periods of history. In the early church there were persons called anchorites who went off into the desert, separating themselves from all social contacts and living solely for God. From that early movement monasticism was born. In our time we see a somewhat similar response among some evangelical Protestants. They believe that the Christian community should be so separated from the secular sphere that individual Christians should not go into politics or vote in elections, that they should withdraw from the culture, live in distinct communities, have Christian friends exclusively, work for Christian companies or in general have nothing to do with this world. It is a way of saying that the authority of the state is illegitimate.

But Christ did not so regard it. When he told Pilate that his authority (the word *exousia,* rather than *dynamis* or *kratos,* means authority) came from God, he legitimated that authority and showed by his conduct at the trial that his disciples should also acknowledge it. Jesus respected Pilate's rule. He answered Pilate courteously and never once suggested that Pilate did not have authority to pronounce a judgment over him. Pilate pronounced wrongly, as we know. But he had authority to make the pronouncement. His authority was from God. Jesus did not suggest that it be wrested from him even though he was about to make the great error of condemning the Son of God.

Here we must again emphasize that Christians are to be subject to the higher authorities. There are some limits, as we will see. But we must begin with the fact that Christians should be model citizens. Regrettably, it is often the case that Christians disrespect authority—elected officials, police and others—and this quite naturally leads to a light attitude in regard to obeying them. That ought not to be. Rather we should be scrupulous in obeying the speed limits and other civil laws. John Calvin had a justified fear of anarchy because of the troubles of his own time. Warning against it, he wrote that obedience must be given even to wicked rulers. "We are not only subject to the authority of princes who perform their office toward us uprightly and faithfully as they ought, but also to the authority of all who, by whatever means, have got control of affairs, even though they perform not a whit of the princes' office."[5]

Are there limits? What if the king is a very wicked king, or the president a very wicked president? Yes, there are limits. Therefore, although we must be careful to render every possible measure of obedience to those in authority (usually much more than we wish), we must still do nothing contrary to the express command of God in Scripture or to that standard of morality arising from it, even though a contrary act is commanded.

Here the second part of Christ's statement comes in. After instructing Pilate in regard to the ultimate source of his authority, Jesus went on to speak of sin. "Therefore he who delivered me to you has the greater sin" (Jn. 19:11). If it were only power that Pilate had been given, it would be impossible to speak of sin as intrinsic in the exercise of the power—just as it is impossible to speak of sin in the case of the cat who kills a mouse or the germ that kills another germ. But since it was authority that Pilate was given, that is another matter entirely. Authority, being granted by another, necessarily involves responsibility to that other one; and responsibility, if it is not properly exercised, involves sin against that one. In other words, authority enhances human government, but it also limits it. It is an authority bound by the moral nature of the God from whom it comes.

One biblical limit on obedience to human authority is in regard to the _preaching of the gospel._ This is a Christian duty based on the explicit command of Jesus Christ (Mt. 28:18-20). What should happen when authorities demand differently is illustrated in the fourth and fifth chapters of Acts. The disciples had been preaching and doing miracles, which had created such a stir that they were called before a council of elders in Jerusalem. The authorities examined the disciples, in this case Peter and John. Then, since the miracle they had done in healing a lame man was so evident and the rulers could not deny it, they settled on the expedient of merely commanding the disciples to keep silence. Peter and John replied, "Whether it is right in the sight of God to listen to you rather than to God, you must judge; for we cannot but speak of what we have seen and heard" (Acts 4:19-20).

The apostles were threatened, but they went back to their preaching and were soon rearrested. The authorities again questioned them and said, "We strictly charged you not to teach in this name, yet here you have filled Jerusalem with your teaching and you intend to bring this man's blood upon us" (Acts 5:28).

Peter answered, "We must obey God rather than men. The God of our fathers raised Jesus whom you killed by hanging him on a tree. God exalted him at his right hand as Leader and Savior, to give repentance to Israel and forgiveness of sin. And we are witnesses to these things, and so is the Holy Spirit whom God has given to those who obey him" (Acts 5:29-32).

The incident indicates that Christians are to give precedence to the preaching of the gospel and are not to cease from it even though commanded to do so by the civil authorities.

A second biblical limit on obedience to human authorities is in *Christian conduct and morals*. No government has the right to command Christians to perform immoral or non-Christian acts. During the Nazi era Christians in Germany were faced with a devilish state and its openly anti-Christian and even antihuman practices. German citizens were commanded to have no dealings with Jews. They were not to trade with them, help them, have friendships with them or acknowledge them in any way. Although many German Christians obeyed the government in that regard, they did not need to obey and should not have.

Some stood up against these monstrosities. One who did so was Martin Niemoeller who, for preaching the truth, was eventually thrown into prison. We are told that another minister then visited him in prison and argued that if he would only keep silent about certain subjects and respect the government he would be set free. "And so," he concluded, "why are you in jail?"

"Why aren't *you* in jail?" Niemoeller answered.[6]

Niemoeller's course was the right one. By his silence the visiting minister was upholding a lie and indirectly encouraging a demonic regime.

In this country Christians must speak out against racism, government and corporate corruption, sex and age discrimination and other evils. They must staunchly refuse to participate in them in any way even if they are commanded to do so by their government or a business superior.

Caesar Alone

The second of the four options is the one chosen by most secularists and sometimes even by so-called Christians: the choice of Caesar alone. It is the most dangerous option. We find an expression of it at the trial of Jesus when the chief priests told Pilate, "We have no king but Caesar" (Jn. 19:15).

In this option God, who is the ultimate check on godless rulers, is forced out of the picture and therefore cannot be appealed to. Even under the worst of tyrants, if God is in the picture, he can at least be appealed to for help, and the injustices may be corrected. But if God is gone, there is nothing left but human whims and cruelty.

Without God in the picture there is no rein on Caesar, and Caesar needs a rein. In America we recognize this secularly. We have developed a system of checks and balances according to which one branch of government has control on another. Congress makes laws which govern all citizens; but the judicial branch can declare them unconstitutional. The president appoints Supreme Court judges; but Congress has authority to impeach the president. The president may initiate programs; but the Congress must fund them. We recognize the need of checks and balances on the secular level because we know by experience that persons in power are untrustworthy. If that is true on the human level, how much truer it is on the cosmic level. The united voices of rulers cannot be ultimate. God is ultimate. If we forsake God, we are at the mercy of our governors.

Second, without God in the picture we have no sure means of guiding government properly. We need checks to keep government from becoming a law unto itself and therefore abusing and tyrannizing the governed. But suppose the government is not tyrannous. Suppose it operates well. Even then it needs God. Only from God do we receive a system of morality and a wisdom beyond our own.

Today in America some persons are attempting to remove every vestige of religion from national life. It is argued that government is not in business to legislate morality. But what does the state do if it does not legislate morality? When the state develops and enforces laws against homicide, what is that but the legislation of morality? It is the state's way of saying, "We agree that life is precious and that it is wrong to take it

238 *God and History*

away." In this the state supports the sixth of the Ten Commandments. When the state makes laws against larceny and burglary, it is enforcing the eighth commandment. The same is true in its requirement of legal marriages, contracts, labor negotiations and so on for hundreds of different areas. In each of those areas the state is dealing with morality. The only point in dispute is the kind of morality to be followed. Christians must be strong to remind the state that its own sense of morality is not adequate and that it must seek God's wisdom in this matter.

Caesar Dominant

The third option is one in which God and Caesar both properly exercise authority but Caesar is dominant. It is the option of cowards. If God's authority is recognized at all, it is evident almost by definition that he must be supreme. Those who favor Caesar do so generally only because they fear him.

That was the case with Pilate. Pilate did not want to condemn Jesus. First, he pronounced him innocent. Next he tried expedients by which he might be freed: sending him to Herod, suggesting his release rather than the release of Barabbas, causing him to be beaten and then suddenly exhibited to evoke sympathy from the mob. Even after Pilate had failed in those expedients he still tried to get Christ acquitted. "Upon this Pilate sought to release him, but the Jews cried out, 'If you release this man, you are not Caesar's friend; every one who makes himself a king sets himself against Caesar' " (Jn. 19:12).

If Pilate was unwilling to pass the death sentence on Jesus, why was he eventually prevailed on to do so? The answer is in that verse. The Jewish leaders threatened to denounce him to Caesar with the result that Pilate, who feared such a denunciation more than anything else, capitulated.

Pilate is seen here in his most contemptible stance, yet he is also pitiable. Pilate was the governor. He spoke for Caesar and had the legions of Caesar at his call to enforce his bidding.

Yet this individual who should have been above fear was rid-
dled by it and thus was made weak-kneed in the greatest moral
encounter of his career. Of what was the governor afraid?
He was afraid of three things. He was afraid of _Christ_. We are
told that after Pilate had heard that Jesus made himself out to
be the Son of God "he was the more afraid" (Jn. 19:8) and
determined anew to release him. It was certainly not the kind
of holy reverence for Christ that a true follower of the Lord
might have. But it was a true fear. Pilate thought that Jesus
might actually be more than a man, perhaps one of the half-
human, half-divine gods of Greek and Roman antiquity, and
so might move fate against him if he judged unfairly.

Pilate was afraid of the _people_. He did not like them, of
course. His many dealings with the Jews showed his consummate disdain and even hatred for them. Yet he knew their
power and feared to have them united in opposition to him. If
he had not feared the people, he would have released Jesus
and have shown no concern to pacify them.

Most significant, Pilate feared _Caesar_. With cause. The sus-
picious nature of Caesar Tiberius was well known, and Pilate
had already had other confrontations with the Jews which
had worked to his disfavor. What if Caesar should disapprove
of his handling of this matter? What if the Jewish leaders
should send a delegation to Caesar saying that Pilate had refused to deal forcefully with one who was guilty of high trea-
son? If Pilate had possessed a clean record, he could perhaps
have overlooked a threat based on false charges. But his
record was not clean, and it was possible that Pilate could lose
his position and even his life if such an accusation was made.
(Several years later Pilate was removed from office by the
proconsul of Syria and banished to France.)

Pilate's failure suggests the answer to the questions raised
earlier. Pilate feared man. Consequently, he was unable to do
the just thing and even fell so low as to pronounce sentence
on the Son of God.

God Is Sovereign

The fourth option is the right one: the authority of God and Caesar but with God in the dominant position. This position is basic to Christ's words, "You would have no power over me unless it had been given you from above; therefore he who delivered me to you has the greater sin." From this position the Christian can in a sense demythologize the state, reminding it of the obvious limitations of its power and even the absurdity of some of its claims. Jacques Ellul does this in *The Political Illusion.*[7] He regards contemporary appeals to the state to solve our most basic problems as the height of folly and calls upon individuals to resist its ever-expanding encroachment on their lives. Christians can also remind the state of its divinely given responsibilities and of the fact that it is accountable to God.

In short, Christians must fear God more than man and must let it be known that they do. To do this effectively there must be three requirements. First, individual Christians must have it firmly fixed in their minds that God is truly sovereign in human affairs, including affairs of state. Most Christians know this, of course, because the Bible teaches it. But they must also have it planted in their minds so firmly that they can actually trust God when the crunch comes.

Daniel was one person who was able to exercise that kind of trust. He knew that God was sovereign. When God revealed Nebuchadnezzar's dream of the statue of gold, silver, bronze and iron to him he responded by praising God in these terms: "Blessed be the name of God for ever and ever, to whom belong wisdom and might. He changes times and seasons; he removes kings and sets up kings; he gives wisdom to the wise and knowledge to those who have understanding" (Dan. 2:20-21). But in addition to knowing this intellectually, Daniel also knew it experientially and was not afraid to stand by his convictions. When he was tempted to abandon his worship of God for a period of thirty days under threat of being thrown into a den of lions, he resisted the state in its encroachment on his religious obligations. He spurned its decrees.

We know that God delivered Daniel from the lions, just as he had earlier delivered his three companions from the fiery furnace. But the fact that God would deliver him and the others was not known to Daniel at the time his moral stand was taken. What gave him the ability to do this, particularly when so many plausible arguments might have been raised in favor of compliance, was trust in a sovereign God to whom even the powerful Nebuchadnezzar was responsible. Daniel believed that in the ultimate analysis it was God and not Nebuchadnezzar who would control the outcome.

A second requirement for an effective Christian stance against the state is a deep knowledge of Scripture on the part of individual Christians and church bodies. The reason for this is that situations are not always black and white. They may be gray. Awareness of God's sovereignty and willingness to trust him are not always sufficient. A person may be willing to do the right thing and trust God for the outcome but still not know what the right thing is. The only way the right will be known at such times is by the teaching of God's Spirit through Scripture.

Even then some areas may remain ambiguous. The matter of fighting in wartime is one, and Christians have been divided on that issue. Answers in the areas of abortion on demand, artificial prolongation of life, legal defense of criminals, the death penalty, covert government activities and so on are not always so evident as we might wish. But without the Bible there are no sure answers at all. That is the point. Consequently, no substitute exists (even for the busiest Christian) for studying the Bible and conscientiously striving to submit one's life and thoughts completely to it.

If we do not do this we are in much danger. When Jesus spoke to Pilate reminding him of his sin, he used the word "greater." Although Pilate's sin was great—he was sinning against his conscience in that he had already pronounced Jesus to be entirely innocent—the sin of the religious leaders was greater. They were sinning out of hate-filled hearts and against their own laws, which should have protected Jesus. It may even be that the sin of Judas was greatest, since he was closest to Christ and therefore sinned out of a background of the greatest knowledge. The comparison teaches that the greater danger lies, not with the state, but with those who are closest to spiritual things. Others may sin out of ignorance or neglect or cowardice. But religious people are inclined to sin out of arrogance or pride or actual hatred of God and God's truth—even when they think they are most moral.

Christians must look to the truth they affirm. It is not enough to have the name of Christian. That in itself does not give us any superior insight into morality or any point of leverage from which to speak against or disobey the government which God has set up. We can do that only as we respond, painfully at times, to God's voice which comes to us in Scripture. Then we are gripped, not by a lesser authority than that of the state (that is, our own), but by a greater one, the overriding and only infallible authority of God.

There is a third need if we are to know what is right and actually do it, even when confronted with a contrary claim by some strong social pressure. We need to be willing to surrender everything. It is quite possible to have followed the first two steps suggested—to believe and trust that God is sovereign in human affairs and to study the Bible to such a degree that we know what is right—and yet fail at the crucial moment simply because the proper course would be too costly.

This is what was wrong with Pilate after all. We cannot say that Pilate really believed in the sovereignty of God, but he believed in something like it—the power of the gods, or some form of ultimate retribution. Otherwise he would not have been afraid when told that Jesus claimed to be God's Son. We cannot say that he knew the moral standards of the true God as revealed in the Bible, because he had undoubtedly never read the Bible. Still, he knew what was right in this situation, but he went against it. Why? If it was not from fear of God and not from failure to know what was right, it can only have been from unwillingness to lose his official position. Clearly, he valued his job above all else. Pilate had to choose between what was right and what the world wanted. And when the issue was clearly defined, he did not hesitate to choose the world and its rewards.

In contrast, I think of Aleksandr Solzhenitsyn, the Russian writer who was unjustly confined in the Soviet Union's notorious prison system for eleven years and lived to tell about it in *The Gulag Archipelago.* He saw suffering such as few free people have ever seen. He saw the dehumanizing practice of the Soviet guards and the equally dehumanizing practices of some of the prisoners. He saw some break down and others grow strong. He asks, "So what is the answer? How can you stand your ground when you are weak and sensitive to pain, when people you love are still alive, when you are unprepared? What do you need to make you stronger than the interrogator and the whole trap?"

Solzhenitsyn answers,

From the moment you go to prison you must put your cozy past firmly behind you. At the very threshold, you must say to yourself: "My life is over, a little early to be sure, but there's nothing to be done about it. I shall never return to freedom. I am condemned to die—now or a little later. But later on, in truth, it will be even harder, and so the sooner the better. I no longer have any property whatsoever. For me those I love have died, and for them I have died. From today on, my body is useless and alien to me. Only my spirit and my conscience remain precious to me."

Confronted by such a prisoner, the interrogation will tremble.

Only the man who has renounced everything can win that victory.[8]

Solzhenitsyn has enunciated a great Christian principle. We must be willing to renounce everything if we are Christ's disciples. In the thick of the battle we must be willing to cast all material rewards aside.[9]

PART IV
THE END OF HISTORY

For the Lord himself will descend from heaven with a cry of command, with the archangel's call, and with the sound of the trumpet of God. And the dead in Christ will rise first; then we who are alive, who are left, shall be caught up together with them in the clouds to meet the Lord in the air; and so we shall always be with the Lord. Therefore comfort one another with these words. (1 Thess. 4:16-18)

"And when I go and prepare a place for you, I will come again and will take you to myself, that where I am you may be also." (Jn. 14:3)

17 HOW WILL IT ALL END?

Christianity is a historical religion. That point has been made in earlier pages, but it needs to be reiterated as we draw to the end of this volume (and the end of this series of books on Christian doctrine). Christianity is historical not merely in the sense that as a religion it is a phenomenon of history—that would be true of every other religion as well. Rather, it is historical in the sense that according to its teaching God has acted decisively in history, revealing himself in specific external events attested in the Old and New Testament Scriptures and he will yet act to bring history to its predestined conclusion.

That teaching sets Christianity off from the modern form of Gnosticism known as existentialism. To existentialists, even the so-called existential theologians, historical considerations are irrelevant for faith. It makes no difference whether God actually created the world, or whether the Fall of the race actually took place in history. It makes no difference whether Jesus actually died for sin or rose from the dead. Historical disproof of the resurrection of Christ, or even his existence, means nothing to such theologians.

Existential theology has two separate realms of truth, one historical and verifiable, the other above or beyond history and nonverifiable. True Christianity knows nothing of that dichotomy. It insists that the events of its history are as real as any other events and as equally subject to historical verification. They differ from other events only in that God has acted in them in a special way and has thereby filled them with meaning.

There is also a sense in which Christianity gave rise to the very idea of history. The idea of movement in history leading to a meaningful goal simply did not exist before the full impact of the biblical faith. Theologian Carl F. H. Henry has written of this impact:

> *The ancient world perceived human events in relation to cosmic or astral processes which it often divinized, or it viewed these events in the context of repetitive cycles or as significant only within a given culture or civilization, if indeed it regarded what happens in time as significant at all. Contemporary extensions of such theories may be seen in current notions of dialectical materialism, cultural relativity, and astrological influence upon human affairs. In contrast to the Greeks to whom the idea of history was fundamentally foreign, and who sought nothing of perpetual and abiding significance in history, the Hebrew prophets knew that history is the realm in which God decisively acts and works out his purposes. The Bible throughout insists that God the Creator holds mankind eternally accountable for every thought, word and deed, and that each successive generation moves toward a final future in which the God not only of creation but also of redemption and judgment will consummate human history in the light of his divine offer of salvation.*[1]

God, who has acted *in history* in past events, is also to act *in history* to consummate this age. So when we ask "How will it all end?" we do not suddenly pass out of the realm of history into a never-never-land of utopian speculation. We merely pass to that which has not yet occurred but which is nevertheless certain of occurring for the simple reason that God is behind it and is himself the one who tells us it will.

Our Blessed Hope

When we speak of certainty we must acknowledge that Christians are not in full agreement about the details of these future events. They disagree about the millennium, a period of one thousand years during which Jesus is to reign upon earth; some see this as a specific future period, some as symbolic of the age of the church in which we are now living. Even among those who accept the millennium as a specific future period there are differences as to where it fits in with other events. How do the millennium and the return of Christ relate to the period of great tribulation spoken of in Daniel 9:27 and other texts, assuming that these do in fact speak of a specific tribulation period? What about the role of Israel in prophetic events? Armageddon? Antichrist? The diversity among evangelicals in handling these themes may be readily seen by comparing the final sections of most books of theology.

What tends to be lost in the awareness of such differences, however, is the large *agreement* that exists, plus the fact that the areas in which Christians are agreed (at least all evangelical Christians) are the most important. Regardless of the way the millennium, the great tribulation and other problems of prophecy are handled, most writers focus on the return of Christ, the resurrection of the body, and the final judgment as the essential and dominant elements of eschatology. Wherever the other events fit in (assuming there are other events), they at least have to fit in around those more important elements.

Agreement is particularly evident about Christ's return. Arnold T. Olson has written,

> *Ever since the first days of the Christian church, evangelicals have been "looking for that blessed hope, and the glorious appearing of*

*the great God and our Saviour Jesus Christ." They may have
disagreed as to its timing and to the events on the eschatological
calendar. They may have differed as to a pre-tribulation or post-
tribulation rapture—the pre- or post- or non-millennial coming.
They may have been divided as to a literal rebirth of Israel. However, all are agreed that the final solution to the problems of this
world is in the hands of the King of kings who will someday make
the kingdoms of this world his very own.*[2]

The reason for their agreement is the overwhelming evidence
in the Bible as to the certainty and importance of Christ's
return.

In the New Testament one verse in twenty-five deals with
the Lord's return. It is mentioned 318 times in the 260 chapters. It occupies a prominent place in the Old Testament in
that most of the Old Testament prophecies concerning the
coming of Christ deal, not with his first advent in which he
died as our sin-bearer, but with his Second Advent in which he
is to rule as king.

The return of Jesus Christ is mentioned in every one of the
New Testament books except Galatians (which was written
with a particular and quite different problem in view) and the
very short books such as 2 and 3 John and Philemon. Jesus
spoke of his return quite often. Mark records him as saying,
"Whoever is ashamed of me and of my words in this adulter-
ous and sinful generation, of him will the Son of man also be
ashamed, when he comes in the glory of his Father with the
holy angels" (Mk. 8:38). "Then they will see the Son of man
coming in clouds with great power and glory. And then he
will send out the angels, and gather his elect from the four
winds, from the ends of the earth to the ends of heaven"
(Mk. 13:26-27). John tells us that Christ's last words to his
disciples included the promise, "When I go and prepare a
place for you, I will come again and will take you to myself,
that where I am you may be also" (Jn. 14:3).

In the last chapter of John the author records a statement

of Jesus to Peter in which a reference to his return is incidental but is, nevertheless, all the more impressive on that account. Jesus had been encouraging Peter to faithfulness in discipleship, but Peter with his usual impetuousness had turned and seen the beloved disciple. He asked, "Lord, what about this man?" (Jn. 21:21). Jesus replied, "If it is my will that he remain until I come, what is that to you? Follow me!" (v. 22). John pointed out that although many Christians of his day had interpreted this to mean that John would not die until Christ came back, that was not what Jesus had said. He said only that even if that were the case, it should not affect Peter's call to faithful service.

Paul's letters are also full of the doctrine of Christ's return. To the Christians at Thessalonica he wrote, "For the Lord himself will descend from heaven with a cry of command, with the archangel's call, and with the sound of the trumpet of God. And the dead in Christ will rise first; then we who are alive, who are left, shall be caught up together with them in the clouds to meet the Lord in the air; and so we shall always be with the Lord" (1 Thess. 4:16-17). To the Philippians Paul wrote, "But our commonwealth is in heaven, and from it we await a Savior, the Lord Jesus Christ, who will change our lowly body to be like his glorious body, by the power which enables him even to subject all things to himself" (Phil. 3:20-21).

Peter called the return of Jesus Christ our "living hope" (1 Pet. 1:3). Paul called it "our blessed hope" (Tit. 2:13). John declared with conviction, "Behold, he is coming with the clouds, and every eye will see him, every one who pierced him; and all tribes of the earth will wail on account of him" (Rev. 1:7). He ended the Revelation with "He who testifies to these things says, 'Surely I am coming soon.' Amen. Come, Lord Jesus!" (Rev. 22:20).

In these verses and many others the early Christians expressed their belief in Jesus' personal return, a return that was to be closely associated with a period of great wicked-ness on earth, the resurrection and transformation of their own bodies, an earthly rule of the glorified Jesus and a final judgment of individuals and nations. They acknowl-edged that their lives should be lived on a higher plane be-cause of it.

This is the first reason why the return of Christ is a practical doctrine and not merely an escape valve for wishful thoughts. Lord Shaftesbury, a great English social reformer, said near the end of his life, "I do not think that in the last forty years I have lived one conscious hour that was not influenced by the thought of our Lord's return." That conviction was obviously one of the strongest motives behind his social programs.

If we are expecting the Lord's return, that conviction ought to alter our concern for social issues. At the height of the race crisis in the United States in the early 1960s two signs hung on the wall of a restaurant in Decatur, Georgia. The first sign was biblical. It read "Jesus is com-ing again!" The second sign, directly below it, said "We re-serve the right to refuse service to anybody!" The signs were humorous because they implied that the owner of the restaurant, who apparently was looking for the return of Jesus, might refuse him service, and because racial or any other form of discrimination is incongruous in the light of Christ's coming. If we are motivated by prejudice, con-templating some sin, tearing down or criticizing other people, wasting our gifts or in any other way failing to live as Christ's faithful disciples—then the return of Jesus has not made its proper impression on our thinking.

A second reason why the return of Jesus is a practical doctrine is that it comforts those who are suffering. It helped the early Christians. We may imagine that as they lay in prison, suffering and tormented, often near death, they looked for Christ's coming and thought that perhaps in an instant and without warning Jesus would appear and call them home. As they entered the arena to face the lions or looked up in their cell to face their executioner, many would have thought "Perhaps this is the moment Jesus will return; even now, before the beasts can spring or the ax can fall, I shall be caught up to meet him."

Believers in Christ have lost children, parents and close friends. Belief in the return of Jesus is comforting to them. The people of Paul's day had lost friends through death, and he wrote to them reminding them of this blessed hope. "Therefore comfort one another with these words" (1 Thess. 4:18). Reuben A. Torrey, a former president of the Bible Institute of Los Angeles, once wrote, "Time and again in writing to those who have lost for a time those whom they love, I have obeyed God's commandment and used the truth of our Lord's return to comfort them, and many have told me afterwards how full of comfort this truth has proven when everything else had failed."[3] The return of Jesus is a practical doctrine because it is an encouragement to godly living and, at times, even to go on living—which means that it has bearing upon present history as well as upon history's end.

Resurrection of the Body

The second doctrine of the "end things" upon which Christians are widely agreed is the resurrection, specifically the resurrection of the bodies of believers at Christ's Second Coming. This doctrine is of tremendous importance for several reasons.

First, the Christian doctrine of the resurrection recognizes that death is an enemy (1 Cor. 15:26) and is therefore something unnatural, something evil that was not God's original intention for humanity. It is important to stress this because some forms of Christianity encourage a false optimism that denies the reality of the three great evils: sin, suffering and death. Christian Science (which is not Christianity at all even though it uses the name *Christian*) carries this outlook to an extreme, but the tendency is often present in Christian circles too.

We sometimes see it in relation to a person who is dying. I read the story of a Christian who was in the last stages of cancer and who described what had been happening. She said, "I can see the people who come to visit me because there is a mirror in the hall and they are reflected there as they come by. Many pause to put on a pleasant expression. Then they come into the room and talk about what is going to be taking place at church next week or the week after that. They speak of the time when I am going to be better and be with them again. But they know I won't be. They know I'm dying. I know I'm dying, but they don't want to talk about it. So they put on a pleasant face and pretend that the evil isn't there." In the case of the person whose testimony I was reading, there was a triumphant faith in Jesus who rose from the dead and gives eternal life to all who believe in him—in addition to an awareness of the evil. Death in that room was transformed. But it is not always so, and frequently, as in the case of the friends, there is denial that death is an enemy.

Do we deny because we think that somehow it is more spiritual to pretend that death is not real? I do not know. But I do know that such attempts are unsuccessful. Try doing that with sin. Say, "Sin is not sin." See if that is more spiritual. Pretend that homosexuality is all right, that pornographic films are not bad, that economic injustice and racial oppression do not exist. If you do that, you lose the cutting edge of Christian social concern and reformation, and evil soon becomes tolerable. If you cannot operate that way in the area of social evil, you cannot operate that way in regard to death. Because, although in one sense denial might satisfy *us* if we are not now facing death—at least to the extent that we are not thinking about it—it does not satisfy anybody who is face to face with it. False optimism does no good.

On the other hand, the Christian doctrine of the resurrection speaks of victory over death provided for us by the Lord Jesus. After writing about death as an enemy, Paul went on to speak of the ultimate victory to come. "When the perishable puts on the imperishable, and the mortal puts on immortality, then shall come to pass the saying that is written: 'Death is swallowed up in victory' " (1 Cor. 15:54). He concluded, "But thanks be to God, who gives us the victory through our Lord Jesus Christ" (v. 57).

What a victory that is! It is an entrance of the soul and spirit into the presence of God, to be followed in God's own time by a physical resurrection.

Death involves every part of our being. When God said to Adam and Eve in the garden, "Of the tree of the knowledge of good and evil you shall not eat, for in the day that you eat of it you shall die" (Gen. 2:17), they ate of it and died. They died in every part of their being. They had a spirit, soul and body, and died in each one. They died in spirit and showed it by hiding from God. They died in soul; all the anger, lust, hate, jealousy, pride and other sins we know so well began to enter the experience of the race. Eventually their bodies died also.

When God saves us he saves us in spirit, soul and body. He gives us a new spirit in the moment of the new birth. He creates a new soul through the process of sanctification. At the resurrection he gives us a new body. The salvation he provides is a _whole_ salvation.

Assurance of these things is ours because of Christ's resurrection. Without this, our hope of a resurrection would be no more than wishful thinking. It might be true, but it would not have the certainty that it has for Christian people. Jesus' own resurrection provides powerful assurance of the

Christian's resurrection.

We begin by noting that Christ's death was a real death; unless it was a real death we are not talking about a real resurrection. Jesus really died. Unbelievers usually try to deny either that there was a real resurrection or that there was a real death. Elaborate theories have been worked out, particularly in the nineteenth century, to deny Christ's death. Some suggested that Jesus only swooned and then revived in the tomb or that the authorities crucified the wrong person. Theories like that were developed seriously.

Today not even the most liberal scholars would take such an approach. They know that Jesus really died. The death of Jesus Christ under Pontius Pilate is a fact of history. Rather, these scholars "spiritualize" the resurrection.

When Hollywood tries to portray these things in movies it at best spiritualizes Christ's resurrection. I saw one such movie on television. There was the death. It was real enough. When the Roman soldier took his hammer and drove the nail through the hand, there was no doubt that it was real metal and flesh and wood. The death was real. But when the resurrection came all you could hear was music. You could not even see the Lord. People rushed about joyfully. But where was Jesus? I looked for him. At last there was a ghostly view of him floating off into the clouds. If the resurrection had been like that, I guarantee that Thomas for one would not have believed in it, and I do not think Peter and John would have either. The resurrection was not like that. It was a real flesh-and-blood resurrection, and those men knew it when they touched Christ's body. Because it had taken place, they were willing to go out from that obscure corner of the Roman Empire into their world proclaiming the Lord's death and resurrection. They were willing to be crucified themselves rather than deny their Lord. That is how real it was.

A poem by John Updike says this in contemporary language. It is called "Seven Stanzas at Easter."

Make no mistake: if He rose at all
it was as his body;
if the cells' dissolution did not reverse, the
_   molecules reknit,_
the amino acids rekindle,
the Church will fall.

It was not as the flowers,
each soft Spring recurrent;
it was not as His Spirit in the mouths and fuddled
_   eyes of the eleven apostles;_
it was as His flesh: ours.

The same hinged thumbs and toes,
the same valved heart
that–pierced–dies, withered, paused, and then
_   regathered out of His Father's might_
new strength to enclose.

Let us not mock God with metaphor,
analogy, sidestepping transcendence;
making of the event a parable, a sign painted
_   in the faked credulity of earlier ages:_
let us walk through the door.

The stone is rolled back, not papier-mâché,
not a stone in a story,
but the vast rock of materiality that in the slow
_   grinding of time will eclipse for each of us_
the wide light of day.

And if we will have an angel at the tomb,
make it a real angel,

weighty with Max Planck's quanta, vivid with hair,
  opaque in the dawn light, robed in real linen
spun on a definite loom.

Let us not seek to make it less monstrous,
for our own convenience, our own sense of beauty,
lest, awakened in one unthinkable hour, we are
  embarrassed by the miracle,
and crushed by remonstrance.[4]

A mythical resurrection does not give birth to conviction. A real resurrection does.

Day of Judgment

Most of what has been said up to this point has been encouraging, particularly for Christians, but there is a sober side too. Christ is coming. His coming will be a joy for Christians, who will be raised to meet him. But it will also mean the beginning of Christ's judgments for those who have spurned the gospel.

Christians acknowledge this truth every time they recite the Apostles' Creed. They say Jesus will come again from heaven "to judge the living and the dead." The Victorian poet Robert Browning wrote, "God's in his heaven; all's right with the world." But although God is in his heaven, all is not right with the world, and a day is coming when God will speak out against the world in judgment. Paul told the Athenians that God "has fixed a day on which he will judge the world in righteousness by a man whom he has appointed, and of this he has given assurance to all men by raising him from the dead" (Acts 17:31).

That is a sobering fact. It tells us that history has an end, and its end involves accountability. We shall answer for what we have done, and we shall all be judged either on the basis of our own righteousness (which will condemn us) or on the basis of the perfect righteousness of him who is our Savior. Some people refuse to face this reality and go on ignoring the day of reckoning.

In a sermon given on the Mount of Olives in the middle of his last week in Jerusalem, Jesus used three parables to teach what the final judgment would be like for such people. One parable was about ten maidens who had been invited to a wedding banquet. Five were wise and five were foolish. The five wise maidens prepared for the banquet by buying oil for their lamps. The five foolish maidens did not. As they waited in the long evening hours they all fell asleep. Suddenly a cry went forth, "Behold, the bridegroom! Come out to meet him." They arose, but the five foolish maidens had no oil for their lamps. On the advice of the wise they set out to buy some. But while they were getting their oil the bridegroom came and the wedding party followed him into the house and the door was shut. Later the five foolish maidens returned and called at the door, "Lord, lord, open to us."

But he answered, "Truly, . . . I do not know you."

Jesus concluded, "Watch therefore, for you know neither the day nor the hour" (Mt. 25:13).

The second parable was about three servants. Their master was to go on a journey. He called the servants to him and gave each money: to the first, five talents; to the second, two talents; to the third, one talent—each according to his ability. Then he departed, and the servants who had received five talents and two talents respectively invested the money while the third servant hid his talent in the ground. After a long time the master returned and asked for an accounting. The man who had received five talents produced those talents plus five more. The servant who had received two talents produced two talents plus two more. But the one who had been given only one talent returned only that one to the Lord saying, "Master, I knew you to be a hard man, reaping where you did not sow, and gathering where you did not winnow; so I was afraid, and I went and hid your talent in the ground. Here you have what is yours" (Mt. 25:24-25). The master condemned that servant, taking away his talent and casting him forth into "the outer darkness" (v. 30).

Finally, the Lord told the parable of the separation of the sheep from the goats. The goats are the lost, and they were condemned because they neglected to feed the Lord when he was hungry, give him drink when he was thirsty, welcome him when he was a stranger, clothe him when he was naked, visit him when he was sick and comfort him when he was cast in prison. They said, "Lord, when did we see thee hungry or thirsty or a stranger or naked or sick or in prison, and did not minister to thee?"

He replied, "Truly, I say to you, as you did it not to one of the least of these, you did it not to me" (vv. 44-45). On the other hand, he welcomed those who did these things.

Each of those parables, though different from the others in detail, contains the same essential features. In each case, there is a sudden return of the Lord. In each case, some are prepared for his coming and others are not. In each case there are rewards and judgments. In each case, those who are lost are no doubt amazed at that outcome.

Thus it will be with our generation. We have more opportunities to learn about Christ in our day than ever before in history. Books and magazines and radio programs and movies and television have all told about him. The call has gone forth, "Behold the man! Look to this one for salvation. He loves you. He died for you. He rose again. Turn from your sin and place your trust in him as your Savior!" But many go blithely on and will be overwhelmed in the day of God's reckoning.

Today is the day of God's grace. Wisdom consists in knowing "Jesus Christ and him crucified" (1 Cor. 2:2).

18 HOME AT LAST

The first few verses of John 14 are among the most popular in the Bible. They speak about heaven, but the reason for their popularity is not that they reveal details about heaven or even about life beyond the grave. They do not. Nor is it that other, more extensive passages on the subject of heaven are lacking. The book of Revelation describes heaven as a glorious city, a country, God's kingdom, paradise. It abounds in walls, thrones, precious jewels, choirs, angels. Why is John 14 so popular? The answer is probably because of the warm image that is found there: heaven is a home. We need a home. We long for a home. Jesus calmly told his troubled disciples that we have one.

"Let not your hearts be troubled; believe in God, believe also in me. In my Father's house are many rooms; if it were not so, would I have told you that I go to prepare a place for you? And when I go and prepare a place for you, I will come again and will take you to myself, that where I am you may be also" (Jn. 14:1-3).

Our need for a home arises from the fact that we have lost one. We had a home once, in Eden. But sin caused the loss of that home and, ever since, the history of the human race has been one of wandering. We think of Cain, who killed his brother and was condemned to a life of drifting. He had no home. In Genesis 11 we find men trying to create a city in which homes would be established. But the men of Babel were in opposition to God, and God scattered them. They were made homeless.

With the coming of Abraham we find a new, heartening element. To be sure, God's first dealings with Abraham were to take him from his home—it was a sinful place filled with idols and idol worshipers. But in place of the home he lost, God promised Abraham a new place: "the land that I will show you" (Gen. 12:1). What is more, God gave the boundaries and indicated the specific territory. It was "from the river of Egypt to the great river, the river Euphrates, the land of the Kenites, the Kenizzites, the Kadmonites, the Hittites, the Perizzites, the Rephaim, the Amorites, the Canaanites, the Girgashites and the Jebusites" (Gen. 15:18-21). But even though Abraham was brought into the land and even though his descendants were later settled there in large numbers, even as great a land as the Promised Land was ultimately inadequate. Abraham is praised in the New Testament not because he fixed his hope on some earthly home (important as that may be), but because he looked for a heavenly home. "He looked forward to the city which has foundations, whose builder and maker is God" (Heb. 11:10).

Although our earthly homes are necessary and significant, they are not permanent. Our basic need for a home is fully met only when the Lord Jesus Christ himself prepares a home for us in heaven. Now we are in a strange land, even in an enemy's country. In that day we shall be in the Father's house and shall be home. That is a Christian's destiny.

Where Is Heaven?

We do not know much about heaven except that it is where we shall be and where we shall be with Jesus. One day my six-year-old daughter's first-grade science class was discussing the universe—how big it is and what it is composed of. The conversation drifted around to heaven, and the children began to ask where heaven fit in. Was it between the stars? Was it beyond them? The only valid answer (the one we gave our daughter when she came home) was that heaven is where God is and where Jesus has gone to prepare that place which he has promised us.

This is the focal point of Revelation 5. It speaks of the four and twenty elders, the angels and a vast host of other creatures from everywhere in the universe. These beings were mentioned, not for descriptive purposes, but because each bore testimony to Christ and thus served to show how he is prominent. The four and twenty elders praised him with this song: "Worthy art thou to take the scroll and to open its seals, for thou wast slain and by thy blood didst ransom men for God from every tribe and tongue and people and nation, and hast made them a kingdom and priests to our God, and they shall reign on earth" (vv. 9-10). Then the angels gave their testimony: "Worthy is the Lamb who was slain, to receive power and wealth and wisdom and might and honor and glory and blessing!" (v. 12). At last the remaining creatures joined in: "To him who sits upon the throne and to the Lamb be blessing and honor and glory and might for ever and ever!" (v. 13). Heaven is where God is. It is his presence (and not some high concentration of golden streets or jewels) that makes it heaven.

The words of Jesus were a comfort to the disciples and

are precious to us. The disciples were going to lose the physical presence of Jesus for a time, but he told them that one day they would be reunited with him in his Father's home. Heaven would be a home for them because they would be with Jesus.

Dwight L. Moody used to illustrate this point by the story of a young child whose mother became very sick. While the mother was sick one of the neighbors took the child away to stay with her until the mother got well again. But the mother grew worse and died. The neighbors thought they would not take the child home until the funeral was over and would never tell her about her mother being dead. After a while they simply brought the little girl home. At once she went to find her mother. First she went into the sitting room to find her mother; then she went into the parlor. She went from one end of the house to the other, but she could not find her. At last she asked, "Where is my mama?" When they told her that her mother was gone, the little girl wanted to go back to the neighbor's house again. Home had lost its attraction for her since her mother was not there any longer. Moody says, "No, it is not the jaspar walls and the pearly gates that are going to make heaven attractive. It is the being with God."[1]

Reunion

In heaven we will also be with one another, and that too makes heaven attractive. Many Christian people are anxious about whether they will recognize their friends in heaven. They have no doubt that they will *be* in heaven; "to be absent from the body [is] to be present with the Lord" (2 Cor. 5:8 KJV). Still, they are confused about what is to happen in the life to come. "Do you think I will know my Bill?" "Will I recognize Sally?" If we could not recognize our friends and family, then heaven inevitably would lose much of its attractiveness. It is hard to see how we could really be happy there in that case, regardless of how dazzling the streets or how beautiful the music of the angels.

But the Word of God is explicit about our mutual recognition. We _will_ know each other. Bill will know Sally. Sally will know Bill. We will know parents and children, friends and relatives, and those who have died in the Lord before us.

One very encouraging indication that comes from the Old Testament is a phrase often used in connection with the death of the patriarchs. It is the phrase "and he was gathered to his people." It occurs in texts like these: "Abraham breathed his last and died in a good old age, an old man and full of years, and _was gathered to his people_" (Gen. 25:8); "These are the years of the life of Ishmael, a hundred and thirty-seven years; he breathed his last and died, and _was gathered to his kindred_" (Gen. 25:17); "Isaac breathed his last; and he died and _was gathered to his people,_ old and full of days; and his sons Esau and Jacob buried him" (Gen. 35:29); "When Jacob finished charging his sons, he drew up his feet into the bed, and breathed his last, and _was gathered to his people_" (Gen. 49:33); "Aaron _shall be gathered to his people;_ for he shall not enter the land which I have given to the people of Israel" (Num. 20:24); and "The LORD said to Moses, 'Go up into this mountain of Abarim, and see the land which I have given to the people of Israel. And when you have seen it, you also _shall be gathered to your people,_ as your brother Aaron was gathered' " (Num. 27:12-13).

Many Old Testament scholars regard this phrase as being nothing more than a conventional way of saying that he died. It is to be explained, so they say, by the thought that the individual was being placed in the same graveyard as those who had died before him. But that is hardly satisfactory in the case of the Bible stories involved. When Abraham died he was buried in a cave at Machpelah in the land that was to become Israel; it was not the burial place of his ancestors. They had been buried back in Ur of the Chaldees, and his father had been buried at Haran. Further, in reading the account of his death, it is hard to overlook the fact that Abraham is said to have been gathered to his ancestors in verse 8 of Genesis 25, but to have actually been buried only in verse 9. Consequently, the phrase "gathered to his people" cannot refer to the burial but must refer to the death itself, as a result of which Abraham joined those who had gone before him. The same thing is true of Moses, who died by himself in the mountain. The book of Deuteronomy tells us that "no man knows the place of his burial to this day" (Deut. 34:6).

David's comment on being told of the death of Bathsheba's child is also important; it shows that David believed in a personal reunion with departed loved ones in the life to come. The Bible tells us that God struck the child so that it became sick and died. While it was languishing, David (who understood that he was to blame) prayed for the child and fasted, lying all night upon the earth. His grief and concern were so great that later, after the child had died, those who were close to him were afraid to tell him lest his grief should then know no bounds. But David detected the change in their attitude. He asked, "Is the child dead?" When they told him that the child had died, David surprised them by rising from his place of mourning, washing himself and dressing and resuming his duties as leader of the nation.

The servants asked about his change of attitude; they could not understand it. David explained, "While the child was still alive, I fasted and wept; for I said, 'Who knows whether the LORD will be gracious to me, that the child may live?' But now he is dead; why should I fast? Can I bring him back again? I shall go to him, but he will not return to me" (2 Sam. 12: 22-23). The last comment does not mean merely that David would eventually die himself. The point of the story is that David comforted himself (and Bathsheba) after the child's death, and there would be no comfort unless David believed that, although he could not bring the child back, nevertheless, one day they would see the child again in heaven.

In the New Testament we find additional indication of these truths in the events that took place on the Mount of Transfiguration. On that occasion the Lord took three of his disciples, Peter, James and John, with him to the mountain and there was transformed to show forth his celestial glory. Moses and Elijah, two other glorified saints, appeared beside him. Luke called them "men" (that is, not disembodied spirits), and reported that Peter and presumably also the others recognized them. Peter said, "Master, it is well that we are here; let us make three booths, one for you and one for Moses and one for Elijah" (Lk. 9:33). Here both Moses and Elijah had retained their identities and were recognized by the three disciples.

Christ's story about the rich man and Lazarus makes a similar point. The Lord told how the rich man went to hell and, being in torment, lifted up his eyes and "saw Abraham far off and Lazarus in his bosom" (Lk. 16:23). Here is a case that involves recognition of the departed, not only as they appear in this life, but as they appear to each other in the life to come.

Finally, there are the words of Jesus in which he speaks of Gentiles joining with believing Jews in a great reunion in heaven. "I tell you, many will come from east and west and sit at table with Abraham, Isaac, and Jacob in the kingdom of heaven" (Mt. 8:11). That is a great promise. But it is not possible unless there is to be a full recognition of all who have died when they come together in the life to come. The patriarchs are to know each other at that reunion, and so will all those who have died in Christ and who will be gathered to him from the far corners of the earth. In that day we may well be surprised at who is in heaven, for many will be there whom we do not expect to be there. And we will probably be surprised to find that many whom we thought would be there are not present.

Many have lost loved ones. If we live long enough, we will all lose loved ones. Yet we have not lost them ultimately. They are with Jesus, and we will be reunited with them.

All We Are Meant to Be

We have seen that, first, we will see Jesus and, second, we will see and recognize each other. A third point is that we will see each other not as we are now or have been but as we are meant to be. "Beloved, we are God's children now; it does not yet appear what we shall be, but we know that when he appears we shall be like him, for we shall see him as he is" (1 Jn. 3:2).

For many years, every time I read that verse I read the word *we* as if it said *I*. I read "I will be like him," and I took comfort in that. I reasoned that I will be like him in *holiness,* and that was wonderful. Now I am unholy. I constantly sin and must constantly ask for forgiveness. In that day I will no longer have to pray "Father, forgive me. . . ." Then I shall be without sin, like Jesus. I also reasoned that I will be like Christ in *knowledge,* not exhaustive knowledge, to be sure (I will not be omniscient), but accurate knowledge. Now, by contrast, so much of what I know is mixed with error. Finally, I reasoned that I will be like him in *love.* It is true that by his grace I do love now. But that love is imperfect. It vacillates. It is selective. In that day I will be able to love as Jesus loves, perfectly and without wavering.

Those truths were a great comfort to me, and I was right to be comforted. Now I am impressed with something else that is also true. Not only will *I* be made like Jesus. *We* will *all* be like him. As a result, the sin, ignorance, anger, hate, weariness and perversity that so often mar our relationships with each other will be eliminated.

There will be no disappointments in that day. In that day we will have a fresh view of each other. We will see each other, not as we have come to know each other here below, in sin, but in perfection.

Moreover, we will see each other rewarded for faithful service in this life, since the Bible speaks of crowns given to those who have been faithful. The Lord said, "Behold, I am coming soon, bringing my recompense, to repay every one for what he has done" (Rev. 22:12). There is a wrong way of thinking of rewards. If we are serving only for what we get out of the arrangement, we are no more than hirelings. If we are working for rewards in this life—for money or the praise others may (or may not) give us—we are not fit to be Christ's servants. Still, there is a right way to think about rewards. They are set before us as one reason why the patriarchs and other biblical characters were faithful. They had much to discourage them. Often they experienced trials, hardships, beatings, pain, ridicule, but they endured because they "looked to the reward" (Heb. 11:26). Rewards can strengthen our perseverance, too.

Like Jesus Now

For some people these words are already quite meaningful. They are old or sick, some close to dying. The thought of being with Jesus forever and being like him is a great blessing. On the other hand, others are not in that position and for them this study does not seem timely. I could point out that we are all dying, some nearer to that point than others. I could point out that no one knows the moment of his or her death. It could be thirty years from now; it could be tomorrow or tonight. Instead, let me make an application in two other areas.

First, if you are a Christian and if it is true that you will eventually be with Jesus, spend time with him now. Do this through your own personal Bible study and prayer. What would we think of a couple who are about to be married but who do not feel the need to spend time together before the marriage? They say, "Oh, we will be together a lot after we are married; we have other things we want to do now." Such a marriage would not seem promising. We should want to get to know Jesus better if we are looking forward to being with him in heaven.

A second application is to our moral conduct. If we are going to be like Jesus one day, we must strive to be like him now. Having said that we will be like him in glory, John added, "And every one who thus hopes in him purifies himself as he is pure" (1 Jn. 3:3).

Each winter, after the pressures of the Christmas and New Year's services at Tenth Presbyterian Church in Philadelphia, my family and I take a four-day vacation to the Pocono mountains in eastern Pennsylvania. We vacation at an immense lodge, beautifully situated on a large mountain estate. We look forward to this greatly as the vacation days approach. Thinking of it helps us do our work better. When the time eventually comes, we drive for about three hours and arrive in the evening as dusk is settling over the mountain landscape. We park. We approach the door. The doormen, who have been there in some cases for twenty or thirty years, come up to greet us and take our bags. Then they say, "Welcome home! Welcome home!" It is not home (regrettably). It is only a clever device on the part of the lodge to make its guests welcome. But one day we are going to glory where those words will be spoken by our own blessed Lord, the One who has prepared our home for us. "Welcome home!" he will say. And we really will be home. Forever.[2]

NOTES

Chapter 1

[1]*Newsweek,* 17 Apr. 1978, p. 25.

[2]*Harper's,* May 1978, pp. 23-24.

[3]These steps correspond to the doctrines developed in the first three volumes of this series: I: the knowledge of God and the corresponding knowledge of ourselves as rebels in need of a Savior; II: the knowledge of Christ as Savior; and III: the knowledge of the Holy Spirit and his work of applying the salvation provided by Christ to us in the initial moment of our belief in Christ and throughout our lives as Christians.

[4]James Bannerman, *The Church of Christ: A Treatise on the Nature, Powers, Ordinances, Discipline and Government of the Christian Church,* Vol. I (1869; rpt. London: Banner of Truth Trust, 1974), pp. 91-92.

[5]Herbert Butterfield, *Christianity and History* (New York: Charles Scribner's Sons, 1950), p. 121.

Chapter 2

[1]R. G. Collingwood, *The Idea of History* (London: Oxford Univ. Press, 1976), pp. 28-31. "The Greek mind tended to harden and narrow itself in its anti-historical tendency. The genius of Herodotus triumphed over that tendency, but after him the search for unchangeable and eternal objects of knowledge gradually stifled the historical consciousness" (p. 29).

[2]Epicurus, *Fragments*, 55, Whitney J. Oates, ed., *The Stoic and Epicurean Philosophers* (New York: Random House, 1940), p. 50.

[3]Marcus Aurelius, *Meditations*, xi, 1. *The Stoic and Epicurean Philosophers*, p. 571.

[4]Plato, *Phaedo*, B. Jowett, trans., *The Works of Plato* (New York: Tudor Pub. Co., n.d.), III, 217-18.

[5]Gordon H. Clark, *A Christian View of Men and Things* (Grand Rapids, Mich.: Eerdmans, 1967), pp. 46-49.

[6]Ibid., p. 53.

[7]Oswald Spengler, *The Decline of the West*, 2 vols., trans. Charles Francis Atkinson (New York: Alfred A. Knopf, 1926, 1928).

[8]Arnold J. Toynbee, *A Study of History*, 12 vols. (London: Oxford Univ. Press, 1934-61).

[9]James Montgomery Boice, *God the Redeemer*, Vol. II in Foundations of the Christian Faith (Downers Grove, Ill.: InterVarsity Press, 1978), pp. 174-80.

[10]*Time*, 5 Dec. 1969, p. 27.

[11]Robert F. Lucid, "People's Religion," *Pennsylvania Gazette*, Mar. 1974, p. 7.

[12]Butterfield, p. 67.

Chapter 3

[1]Oscar Cullmann, *Christ and Time: The Primitive Christian Conception of Time and History*, trans. Floyd V. Filson (Philadelphia: Westminster Press, 1950), p. 19.

[2]Emil Brunner, *Dogmatics*, Vol. 2: *The Christian Doctrine of Creation and Redemption*, trans. Olive Wyon (Philadelphia: Westminster Press, 1952), pp. 237-38.

[3]J. Gresham Machen, *The Virgin Birth of Christ* (New York: Harper, 1932).

[4]Rousas J. Rushdoony, *The Biblical Philosophy of History* (Nutley, N.J.: Presbyterian and Reformed Pub. Co., 1969), p. 110.

[5]James Montgomery Boice, *Philippians: An Expositional Commentary* (Grand Rapids, Mich.: Zondervan, 1971), p. 144. For a full discussion of the nature of Christ's work on the cross, see *God the Redeemer*, Vol. II of this series.

[6]Boice, *God the Redeemer*, pp. 223-31.

[7]Cullmann, pp. 108-9.

Chapter 4

[1]Ralph L. Keiper, "The Problem of Knowledge in the World of Men," *Tenth: An Evangelical Quarterly*, July 1975, p. 10.

[2]I have borrowed a portion of the material on Christ as Shepherd and the church as his flock from my own lengthier study of this passage in *The Gospel of John*, Vol. III (Grand Rapids, Mich.: Zondervan, 1977). See "One Flock, One Shepherd," pp. 113-20. The full treatment of the passage is on pp. 76-120.

[3]Francis A. Schaeffer, *True Spirituality* (Wheaton, Ill.: Tyndale, 1971), pp. 172, 174.

[4]Bannerman, Vol. I, pp. 42-43.

[5]William Barclay, *The Gospel of John,* Vol. II (Philadelphia: Westminster Press, 1956), pp. 74-75.

[6]D. Martyn Lloyd-Jones, *God's Way of Reconciliation* (Grand Rapids: Baker Book House, 1972), pp. 282-88.

Chapter 5

[1]William Barclay, *Flesh and Spirit: An Examination of Galatians 5:19-23* (Nashville: Abingdon Press, 1962), pp. 77-78.

[2]Ray C. Stedman, *Secrets of the Spirit* (Old Tappan, N.J.: Revell, 1975), pp. 147-48.

[3]Charles Haddon Spurgeon, "Unity in Christ," *Metropolitan Tabernacle Pulpit,* Vol. XII (Pasadena, Tex.: Pilgrim Pub., 1970), p. 2.

[4]For a fuller treatment of these six marks of the church see the author's *The Gospel of John,* Vol. IV (1978), pp. 395-445, 463-71, from which the material in this chapter has been condensed.

Chapter 6

[1]John R. W. Stott, *Christ the Controversialist: A Study in Some Essentials of Evangelical Religion* (London: Tyndale Press, 1970), p. 160.

[2]A. W. Tozer, *The Pursuit of God* (Harrisburg: Christian Pub., 1948), p. 9.

[3]Barclay, *The Gospel of John,* Vol. 1, p. 154.

[4]C. S. Lewis, *Letters to Malcolm: Chiefly on Prayer* (New York: Harcourt, Brace & World, 1964), p. 4.

[5]Parts of this chapter have already appeared in print as part of the author's commentary on *The Gospel of John,* Vol. I (1975), pp. 363-69.

Chapter 7

[1]Peter Lombard, *The Four Books of Sentences,* Book IV, I, 2, in Eugene R. Fairweather, ed., *A Scholastic Miscellany: Anselm to Ockham,* The Library of Christian Classics, Vol. X (Philadelphia: Westminster Press, 1956), p. 338.

[2]John Calvin, *Institutes of the Christian Religion,* Vol. II, ed., John T. Mc-neill, trans. Ford Lewis Battles (Philadelphia: Westminster Press, 1960), p. 1172.

[3]John Murray, *Collected Writings,* Vol. II: *Select Lectures in Systematic Theology* (Edinburgh: Banner of Truth Trust, 1977), pp. 367-68.

[4]Not all these difficulties are dealt with in this chapter. Many of them concern other areas of theology: for example, the validity of infant baptism, which is actually a question of covenant theology rather than of the significance of baptism itself. Those who wish to pursue the subject further can refer to the substantial literature available.

..ny of the Re-
..ant baptism. Shortly
...mann, Barth's colleague at
...ook disagreeing with Barth. It is
... *Testament*, trans. J. K. S. Reid (London:
... Joachim Jeremias wrote a masterful volume en-
... *Baptism in the First Four Centuries* (London: SCM Press,
1960). He was contradicted by Kurt Aland in *Did the Early Church
Baptize Infants?* trans. G. R. Beasley-Murray (London: SCM Press,
1962). Jeremias's reply to Aland is *The Origins of Infant Baptism*, trans.
G. M. Barton (London: SCM Press, 1963). Two other works are:
Dwight Hervey Small, *The Biblical Basis for Infant Baptism* (Westwood,
N.J.: Revell, 1959); and G. R. Beasley-Murray, *Baptism in the New
Testament* (London: Macmillan, 1963). The last volume has a bibli-
ography of 234 items.

[5]See the article on *"Baptō, Baptizō"* by Oepke in Gerhard Kittel, ed.,
Theological Dictionary of the New Testament, trans. Geoffrey W. Brom-
iley (Grand Rapids, Mich.: Eerdmans, 1964), I, 529ff., for the early
history of these words.

[6]For a similar discussion of these and other passages see Jay E. Adams,
Meaning & Mode of Baptism (Nutley, N.J.: Presbyterian and Reformed
Pub. Co., 1975).

[7]Gen. 41:26; Dan. 2:38; Mt. 13:38; 1 Cor. 10:4; Rev. 1:20; Jn. 10:7;
15:1. For a discussion of these and other texts, see Bannerman, Vol.
II, pp. 147-52.

[8]Bannerman, Vol. II, pp. 158-59. The texts are Mt. 28:20; 18:20 and
Rev. 3:20.

Chapter 8

[1]Ray C. Stedman, *Body Life* (Glendale, Calif.: Regal Books, G/L Publications, 1972), p. 39.

[2]Quoted in John R. W. Stott, *One People* (London: Falcon Books, 1969),
p. 9.

[3]Ibid., p. 47.

[4]Stedman, *Body Life,* p. 43.

[5]C. Everett Koop, "Faith Healing and the Sovereignty of God," *Tenth:
An Evangelical Quarterly,* July 1976, p. 61.

[6]A supposed textual basis for the ceasing of tongues is 1 Corinthians
13:8. "Love never ends; as for prophecies, they will pass away; as for
tongues, they will cease; as for knowledge, it will pass away." But to
read this verse as saying that tongues are to cease after the apostolic
age is to misuse it. If the verse means that, then knowledge must
cease too, which is not the case. Actually, the verse is looking ahead

to the time of Christ's return and is warning that the limited experiences of this present day shall pass when we are made like Jesus. "When the perfect comes, the imperfect will pass away" (v. 10).

[7]Francis A. Schaeffer, *The New Super-Spirituality* (Downers Grove, Ill.: InterVarsity Press, 1972), p. 24.

[8]John R. W. Stott, *Your Mind Matters* (Downers Grove, Ill.: Inter-Varsity Press, 1972), p. 10.

[9]Some of the material on tongues has been adapted from Boice, *The Gospel of John*, Vol. 4, pp. 195-200.

[10]Stedman, *Body Life*, p. 54.

Chapter 9

[1]Stott, *One People*, pp. 28-42. Stott discusses the proper pattern on pp. 42-47.

[2]Elton Trueblood, *The Incendiary Fellowship* (New York: Harper & Row, 1967), p. 39.

[3]Stott, *One People*, p. 30.

[4]Trueblood, p. 40.

[5]Stedman, *Body Life*, p. 105. The full discussion of Luke 4:18-19 is on pp. 95-105.

[6]I have borrowed a section of this word to preachers from a chapter of my own in *The Foundation of Biblical Authority* (Grand Rapids, Mich.: Zondervan, 1978).

Chapter 10

[1]Stott, *One People*, p. 43.

[2]George C. Fuller, "Deacons, the Neglected Ministry," *The Presbyterian Journal*, 8 Nov. 1978, p. 9.

[3]Ibid., p. 10.

[4]Ibid., p. 19.

[5]This is not to say that the existence of bishops as a special office within certain branches of the Christian church is necessarily wrong but only that their existence is not supported by the use of the word in the New Testament. A denomination will want to look very carefully and critically at any aspect of its structure that does not arise out of the specific instructions of the apostles as recorded in the New Testament. It will want to ask whether its practice is a proper extension of what is found there and is compatible with it. But the fact that a church adds structures not found in the New Testament is not in itself wrong since different situations in different periods of church history sometimes call for different and even highly innovative programs. It can be argued that the office of bishop fills the administrative role formerly filled by the apostles and thus serves properly to tie the local churches together.

[6]Lawrence R. Eyres, *The Elders of the Church* (Philadelphia: Presbyterian and Reformed Pub. Co., 1975), p. 14.
[7]Gene A. Getz, *Sharpening the Focus of the Church* (Chicago: Moody Press, 1974), p. 124.
[8]Eyres, p. 30.
[9]Gene A. Getz, *The Measure of a Man* (Glendale, Calif.: Regal Books, G/L Publications, 1974), p. 210.

Chapter 11
[1]Stedman, *Body Life*, p. 107.
[2]Stott, *One People*, p. 70.
[3]Ibid., pp. 70, 73.
[4]Francis A. Schaeffer, *The Church at the End of the 20th Century* (Downers Grove, Ill.: InterVarsity Press, 1970), p. 140.
[5]Stott, *One ple*, p. 87.
[6]Stedman, *Body Life*, pp. 110-11.
[7]Trueblood, *The Incendiary Fellowship*, p. 105. The full discussion is on pp. 100-121.

Chapter 12
[1]Getz, *Sharpening the Focus of the Church*, p. 80.
[2]Tertullian, *Apology*, chap. 37. *The Ante-Nicene Fathers*, Vol. III, eds. Alexander Roberts and James Donaldson (Grand Rapids, Mich.: Eerdmans, 1963), p. 45.
[3]Edward Gibbon, *The Decline and Fall of the Roman Empire*, Vol. I (New York: Random House, n.d.), p. 388.
[4]Adolf Harnack, *The Mission and Expansion of Christianity in the First Three Centuries* (New York: Harper, 1961), pp. 366-68.
[5]R. C. Sproul, "Prayer and God's Sovereignty" in *Our Sovereign God*, addresses presented to the Philadelphia Conference on Reformed Theology (1974-76), ed. James M. Boice (Grand Rapids, Mich.: Baker Book House, 1977), pp. 127-28.

Chapter 13
[1]Augustine, *The City of God*, Book 14, Chapter 28, in *A Select Library of the Nicene and Post-Nicene Fathers of the Christian Church*, Vol. II, ed. Philip Schaff (Grand Rapids, Mich.: Eerdmans, 1977), pp. 282-83.
[2]Francis A. Schaeffer, *Genesis in Space and Time: The Flow of Biblical History* (Downers Grove, Ill.: InterVarsity Press, 1972), p. 114.
[3]Not all evolutionists are motivated by each of those three desires. Since there are Christian scientists who accept a theistic evolutionary hypothesis, obviously *they* are not. Still, I would maintain that the appeal of the evolutionary outlook, and the general hold it has on contemporary life, have to do with its elimination of God as a factor in human affairs.

[4]See Philip Edgcumbe Hughes, *Christianity and the Problem of Origins* (Philadelphia: Presbyterian and Reformed Pub. Co., 1974), p. 11.

Chapter 14
[1]Harvey Cox, *The Secular City: Secularization and Urbanization in Theological Perspective* (New York: Macmillan, 1965), p. 23. The entire discussion is on pages 21-24.
[2]Ibid., p. 26.
[3]Ibid., p. 36.
[4]Robin Scroggs, "Tradition, Freedom and the Abyss" in *The Chicago Theological Seminary Register,* Vol. LX, No. 4 (May 1970), pp. 12-13. Quoted by Donald G. Bloesch, *The Invaded Church* (Waco, Tex.: Word Books, 1975), p. 75.
[5]John Macquarrie, *God and Secularity,* Vol. 3 of the "New Directions in Theology Today" series (Philadelphia: Westminster Press, 1967), pp. 30, 52.
[6]Peter L. Berger, "Needed: Authority," *The Presbyterian Journal,* 20 Oct. 1971, p. 10.

Chapter 15
[1]*World Vision,* Jan. 1976, pp. 8-10.
[2]*The Cross,* Fall 1975, pp. 8-9.
[3]Bloesch, p. 99.

Chapter 16
[1]Calvin, *Institutes,* Vol. II, p. 1485.
[2]Ibid., p. 1487.
[3]John Murray, "The Relation of Church and State" in *Collected Writings,* Vol. I: *The Claims of Truth* (Edinburgh: Banner of Truth Trust, 1976), p. 253.
[4]Ibid., p. 255.
[5]Calvin, p. 1512.
[6]Donald Grey Barnhouse, *God's Discipline,* "The Epistle to the Romans," Vol. 9 (Grand Rapids, Mich.: Eerdmans, 1958), pp. 106-7.
[7]Jacques Ellul, *The Political Illusion,* trans. Konrad Kellen (New York: Vintage Books, 1967).
[8]Aleksandr I. Solzhenitsyn, *The Gulag Archipelago, 1918-1956: An Experiment in Literary Investigation,* I-II (New York: Harper & Row, 1973), p. 130.
[9]Large portions of this chapter are based on studies of Christ's appearance before Pilate already published in Boice, *The Gospel of John,* Vol. 5.

Chapter 17
[1]Carl F. H. Henry, *God, Revelation and Authority,* Vol. 2: *God Who Speaks and*

Shows (Waco, Tex.: Word Books, 1976), p. 312.

[2]Arnold T. Olson, "The Second Coming of Christ" in *Prophecy in the Making: Messages Prepared for the Jerusalem Conference on Biblical Authority*, ed. Carl F. H. Henry (Carol Stream, Ill.: Creation House, 1971), p. 115. The diversity of views among evangelicals and others is well represented in the essays appearing in this volume. My own views can be found in *The Last and Future World* (Grand Rapids, Mich.: Zondervan, 1974).

[3]R. A. Torrey, *The Return of the Lord Jesus* (Grand Rapids, Mich.: Baker Book House, 1966), p. 15.

[4]John Updike, "Seven Stanzas at Easter," *Telephone Poles and Other Poems* (New York: Alfred A. Knopf, 1961).

Chapter 18

[1]*Dwight L. Moody* in the "Great Pulpit Masters" series, Vol. 1 (New York: Revell, 1949), pp. 210-11.

[2]Parts of this chapter are drawn from a fuller treatment of heaven in chapters 12, 13 and 57 of Boice, *The Gospel of John*, Vol. 4.

SUBJECT INDEX

Abel, and Cain, 192
Abortion, 241
Abraham, 37, 262, 265, 267; called by God, 21-22; covenant with, 51, 61-62; faith of, 124, 200
Absolution, 172
Adam, 18; and Eve, 34, 109, 110, 191-92, 255
Administrators, 128-29
Agenda, the world's, 209
Alaric, 189
Alcoholism, 209
Alexander the Great, 48
Altizer, Thomas J. J., 201-2
Anchorites, 233
Antichrist, 249
Anticlericalism, 140-41
Apathy, 219
Apostles and prophets, 121
Apostles' Creed, 42, 258
Aristotelianism, 30
Armageddon, 249
Armerding, Hudson, 216
Arrogance, 162
Assurance, 255-56
Atonement, 54
Attributes of God, 43-44
Augustine, 189-90, 194
Aurelius, Marcus, 29
Authority, 219-20
Babel, 262
Babylon, 194-99
Babylonian captivity, 62

Bacon, Francis, 30
Bannerman, James, 10, 19, 70, 112
Baptism, 103-8, 181; identification with Christ, 106-8
Barclay, Robert, 139
Barclay, William, 71
Barth, Karl, 206
Bathsheba, 266
Benedictus, 51-52
Berger, Peter, 207
Bezalel, 118
Bible, knowledge of the, 241-42; study of the, 270. See also Word of God
Biblical religion, 21
Bishops. See Elders
Blameless, elders to be, 160
Bloesch, Donald G., 222
Body life, 165-75
Body of Christ, 143-44
Bonhoeffer, Dietrich, 202
Brotherhood, 71
Browning, Robert, 258
Brunner, Emil, 48
Burdens, bearing one another's, 171
Buren, Paul van, 202
Butterfield, Herbert, 11, 24, 42
Caesar, Augustus, 48; check on, 237; God and, 229-44; Julius, 47-48
Cain, 193; and Abel, 192
Calvin, John, 10, 95, 100-111, 190, 231
Canterbury, Archbishop of, 203
Catholicism, Roman, 10, 18
Character, of Christ, 69
Chaucer, Geoffrey, 91
Christ Jesus, crucifixion of, 52-54; death of, 109-10; door, the, 23;

example, our, 147; focal point of history, 45-56; follower of, 164; foundation stone, the, 64-65; incarnation of, 49-52; life of, 23; like him now, 269-70; Lord of history, 55-56; love of, 183-85; Mediator, the, 55-56; resurrection of, 54-55; Second Coming of, 249-53; suffering of, 53; will be like him, 268-69; work of, 65
Christian Science, 254
Christianity, historical religion, 21, 247; social, 20
Christians, equipping, 137-47; need one another, 67; needs of, 218
Church, 10, 17, 59-185; Christ's, 59-72; empowered by the Holy Spirit, 68-70; essential elements of the, 63-72; focal point of history, a, 59-60; invisible, 70; marks of the, 73-86; must be different, 219-27; office, 137-64; Old Testament background of the, 60-62; secular, 201-11; unity of the, 65-67, 70-72
Church and state, 196-97, 229-44; separation of, 196-97
Church office, elected, 153; principles governing, 150-53
Churches, problems of large, 167-69
Cicero, 48
Cities, tale of two, 189-244
City, of God, 199-200, 213-27; secular, the,

189-200
City of God, 190
Clark, Gordon H., 31-32
Clergy, 119
Clericalism, 138-40
Collingwood, R. G., 10, 29
Comfort, 69; in suffering, 252-53; mutual, 174
Communion, 108-14. *See also* Lord's Supper
Conduct, Christian, 236; moral, 270
Confessing Church, the, 220
Confession of sin, 172-74
Conformity, 83
Consensus, 206
Constantine, 82
Covenant, 22, 110
Cox, Harvey, 41, 202-4, 207
Creation, doctrine of, 33-36; Greek view of, 34
Cross, demonstrates God's love, 86; importance of the, 52-54
Crucifixion, 54; Christ's, 52-54
Cullmann, Oscar, 10, 45-46, 55
Daniel, 194-95, 240-41
Darwin, Charles, 31
David, King, 22, 90; death of his child, 266-67
Day of judgment, 258-60
Deacons, choice of the first, 150-51; office of, 150-56; work of, 153-56
Death, an enemy, 253-55; real, 256; victory over, 255
"Death of God" theologians, 201-2
Death penalty, 241
Dependence on God, 225-27
Descartes, René, 30

Determinism, 37
Diotrephes, 139
Discernment, 127
Disciples, making, 181
Discrimination, 252
Diversity, 116
Doctrine, biblical, 221
Douglas, J. D., 215
Drunkard, 162
Dualism, 209; of clergy and laity, 141
Easter, poem about, 257-58
Ecology, 209
Eden, 262
Edification, 130-31
Elders, 156-64; men only to be, 160-61; qualifications of, 159-64; to be teachers, 158-59; work of, 156-59
Elements, material, 100-101
Elijah, 267
Ellul, Jacques, 240
Emmaus disciples, 54
End of history, 247-70
Energy crisis, 209
Enoch, 124, 193
Epicurus, 29
Escapism, 41
Evangelism, 142, 155; redefined, 209; stylized, 216-17
Evangelists, 121-22
Eve. *See* Adam and Eve
Evolution, 31-32, 197
Examination, self, 110-11
Exhortation, 123
Exiguus, Dionysius, 45
Existentialism, 247-48
Exodus, the, 22, 203
Eyres, Lawrence, R., 158
Fads, 216
Faith, 124-25; heroes of the, 125; redefined, 208-9; worship a mark of, 89
Fall of the race, 41

Fear, Pilate's, 238-39
Fellowship, 10, 165-75; sentimental, 24; with God and man, 18-19
Fenton, Horace L., 215
Feuerbach, Ludwig, 36
Fire, of God, 174-75
Followers of Christ, 164
Forgiveness, mutual, 172
Frustration, 9, 16
Fuller, George C., 149-50; 154, 156
Gaebelein, Frank E., 215
Gerstner, John H., 180-81
Getz, Gene A., 10, 177
Gibbon, Edward, 178
Gifts, spiritual, 115-35. *See* spiritual gifts
Glory, God's, 43-44; man's, 198
Gnosticism, 247
Goal of history, 33
God the Father, and Caesar, 232-44; attributes of, 43-44; Christian view of, 30; city of, 213-27; controls history, 33; dependence on, 225-27; glory of, 43-44; Most High, 198-99; sovereign, 39, 240-44; wrath of, 182-83
Goodness, 163
Gospel, preaching the, 235
Government, church, 149-64; legitimate sphere of, 231-32
Graham, Billy, 122
Great Commission, 177-85; every Christian's job, 178-79; motivation for the, 179-85
Guilt, 54
Halsey, Margaret, 15-17
Hamilton, William, 202
Harper's magazine, 16
Healings and miracles,

125-27
Heart, wicked, 17
Heaven, 261-70; reunion in, 264-69; where God is, 263-64
Hegel, 36
Helgesen, Sally, 16
Helpers, 128
Henry, Carl F. H., 248
Herod, King, 48
Herodotus, 28-29
History, Christian view of, 15-56; circular view of, 28-30; end of, 247-70; God of, 21; God's purpose in, 37-38; Greek view of, 28-30; interpretation of, 35; Lord of, 55-56; progressive view of, 27-28; 30-33; universal scope of, 34-36
Holiness, 163; mark of the church, 75-78
Holy Spirit, 10; empowers the church, 68-70
Home, heavenly, 261-70
Hope, our blessed, 249-53
Hospitality, 161
Humanism, secular, 194
Humility, 200
Huxley, Thomas, 213
"Hymn of Man," 198
Hymns, singing of, 100; "Am I a Soldier of the Cross?" 125
Identification with Christ, 106-8
Identity, human, 17; loss of, 19; need for, 23
Illustrations, cancer patient, 254; child whose mother died, 264; church in Cabrican, 80-81; "God's Work in God's World," 210-11; _Major Barbara,_ 210; moderator's confer-

ences, 205, 225-26; "no one ever cried for me before," 184-85; _Resurrection_ (movie) 256-57; Sheila, 184; sign in Georgia restaurant, 252; spending time together, 270; told to evangelize, 180-81; true life pageant, 60; two Pilgrims, 210; "Welcome home," 270; "Why aren't you in jail?" 236; "You and I are brothers," 71-72
Image of God in man, 9
Immersion, 104
Incarnation, 54; Christ's 49-52
Indifference, 217
Individualism, 24
Industrial Revolution, 31
Inerrancy, 146
Insecurity in church leaders, 205
Instruction, mutual, 174
Intervention in history, God's, 22
Isaac, 62, 124, 267
Isaiah, 90
Isolation, 18
Jacob, 267
James, 267
Jerusalem, new, 213
Jesus Christ, redefined, 208. _See also_ Christ Jesus
Jews, dispersion of, 47-48
John the Baptist, 51
John the evangelist, 267
Joseph, 37
Joy, mark of the church, a, 73-75
Judgment, day of, 258-60; doctrine of the final, 42-43
Justice of God, 43
Keiper, Ralph, 60
Kenyon, Wynne, 206
Kingdom of God, 38-40

Kingdoms, doctrine of the two, 190
Knowledge, 123-24
Koop, C. Everett, 126-27
Laity, 119
Lamech, 193
Language, figurative, 112
Lawrence, Sir John, 140
Lazarus, rich man and, 267
Leader, a good, 164
Leadership, plurality of, 151-52; vacuum, 218
Lewis, C. S., 94
Life of Christ, historic, 23
Lifestyle, Christian, 222-25
Light of the world, 226-27
Ligonier Valley Study Center, 180
Liturgy, 94
Lloyd-Jones, D. Martyn, 72
Lombard, Peter, 100
Lord of history, 55-56
Lord's Prayer, 33
Lord's Supper, 108-14; future significance of the, 113-14; past significance of the, 108-10; present significance of the, 110-13; views of the, 111-13
Love, 68; Christ's, 183-85; of God, 43; mark of the church, a, 84-86; mutual, 169-70; nebulous, 24
Luther, Martin, 95, 190
Machen, J. Gresham, 49-50
Macquarrie, John, 206
Magnificat, 50
March of Time, The, 27
Marks of the church, 73-86

Marriage, 18, 224-25
Marx, Karl, 36
Marxism, 209, 222
Mary, mother of Christ, 50
Materialism, 215; practical, 216
Meaning, need for, 23
Meaninglessness, 18
Means of grace, 102
Mediator, 55-56
"Me" generation, 15
Mercy, 128, 143; ministry of, 153-55
Methods, the world's, 209-11
Millennium, 249
Miller, Keith, 10
"Mindless" Christianity, 132
Miracles and healings, 125-27
Mission, mark of the church, a, 79-82; motivations for, 179-85
Missionaries, informal, 178-79
Money, use of, 225
Moody, Dwight L., 264
Morality, 237-38
Morals, Christian, 236
Moses, 38, 62, 96, 106, 267
Mount of Olives, 259
Murray, John, 102, 231
Narcissism, 15
Nature, disenchantment of, 202
Nature religions, 21
Nebuchadnezzar, 194-98, 200, 240
Newsweek magazine, 15
Niebuhr, Reinhold, 10
Nicander, 104
Niemoeller, Martin, 236
Noah, 124, 193
Novice, elder not to be a, 162
Obedience, 44
Office, church, 137-64

Olson, Arnold T., 249
Optimism, 31
Oratory, distrust of, 146
Ordination of women, 206-7
Organizational unity, 82
Orwell, 213
Oversight, Christian, 122-23, 157-58
Parables of judgment, 259-60
Pastors, 122-23
Paul, 251, 258
Pax Romana, 47
Pentecost, 129
People, gathered to his, 265-66
People of God, 18-20, 60; challenge to the, 211. *See also* Christians *and* Church
Pessimism, 40
Peter, 235, 251, 267; at Pentecost, 68-69; confession of Christ, his, 63-65
Philip, 155
Philosophy, failure of, 48
Pilate, 232-44
Planning, social, 31-32
Plato, 29, 48, 213
Platonism, 30
Playboy philosophy, 16
Poor, the, 218
Prayer, 100, 133, 270
Preaching, decline of, 145-47
Priorities, 221-22
Progress, inevitable, 30-33; modern view of, 27-28
Prophets and apostles, 121
Providence, doctrine of, 36-38
Puritans, 145
Qualifications, spiritual, 152
Quarrelsome, 162
Quick-tempered, 162

Racism, 209
Rambo, Victor, 142
Red Sea, crossing of the, 106
Redemption, doctrine of, 40-42
Reformation, Protestant, 95
Remembrance, 108-10
Reproach, above, 160
Reputation, 162-63
Responsibility, division of, 151; human, 33
Resurrection, Christ's, 54-55; historical, 54; importance of the, 55; of Christ real, 256-57; of the body, 253-58
Reunion in heaven, 264-69
Revelation, doctrine of, 38-40
Rewards, 269
Righteousness of God, 43
Robinson, John A. T., 202
Rushdoony, Rousas J., 52
Sacraments, 99-114; elements of the, 100-103; number of the, 100
Sacred and secular, the, 201
Saint, a, 77
Saints, equipping the, 137-47
Salt of the earth, 226
Salvation, Greek view of, 29-30; redefined, 208; signs and seals of, 99-114
Sanctification, 77
Satan, 65, 191
Schaeffer, Francis A., 70, 132, 170
Science, faith in, 31-32
Scriptures. *See* Word of God
Seals and signs, 99-114
Second Coming, 249-53
Secularism, 189-200;

evangelical, 214-19
Self, cult of, 15-18; pre-
occupation with, 9
Self-control, 163
Seminaries, evangelical,
220-21
Service, 142; mutual,
170-71
Session, Presbyterian, a,
158
Seth, godly line of, 193
Shaftesbury, Lord, 252
Shakespeare, William, 91
Shaw, George Bernard,
210
Sheep, and goats, 260;
feeding Christ's, 144-47
Signs and seals, 99-114
Sin, confession of, 172-
74; original, 40;
problem of, 53-54; un-
confessed, 167
Sinai covenant, 203
Social concern, 252
Solzhenitsyn, Aleksandr,
243-44
Soul, rational, 29
Sovereignty of God, 43
Spengler, Oswald, 34-36
Spinoza, Baruch, 31
Spirit, and truth, 92-97;
soul and body, 255. See
Holy Spirit
Spirits, ability to dis-
tinguish, 127
Spiritual gifts, 115-35;
chart of, 120; defined,
117-19; discussed, 119-
33; finding your,
133-35
Sports, 223
Sproul, R. C., 180-81
State, 229-44; check on
the, 237; legitimate
sphere of the, 231-32;
limits of the, 234-36
Stedman, Ray, 10, 78-79,
117-19, 134, 142, 173
Stephen, 61
Stott, John R. W., 10, 87,

119, 132, 138-41, 149,
167, 169
Struggle in history, 33
Substitution, 110
Suffering, comfort in,
252-53
Sunday, use of, 223-24
Surrender, 242-44
Swinburne, Algernon
Charles, 198
Taxes, 230-31
Teach, apt to, 161
Teachers, 123
Teaching, 158-59,
181-82
Television, 223
Temperance, 161
Temple, Jewish, 96-97
Temptation, satanic, 65
Ten maidens, parable of
the, 259
Tenth Presbyterian
Church, 10, 168-69, 270
Tertullian, 178
Theology, 220-21;
world's, the, 207-9
Thoreau, Henry David,
213
Three servants, parable
of the, 259-60
Thucydides, 28
Tiberius Caesar, 239
Time, fullness of, 46-48;
Greek words for, 22-23;
important, 24-25;
location in, 20; made
full, 49-55; march of,
27-28; use of, 223-24
Time magazine, 40
Tongues, counterfeit
forms of, 129-30;
speaking in, 129-33
Torrey, Reuben A., 253
Toynbee, Arnold J.,
34-35
Tozer, A. W., 87
Training others, 155-56
Transfiguration, Mount
of, 267
Trueblood, Elton, 10,

139, 175
Truth, mark of the
church, a, 78-79
Undershepherds, 145
Unity, 115; church, 165-
75; mark of the church,
82-84
Updike, John, 257
Utopias, 213
Vahanian, Gabriel, 202
Values, desacralization
of, 203; turning to the
world's, 206
Vangioni, Fernando,
184-85
Violence, 162
Virgin birth, 49-50
Wall, the broken, 70-72
War, 241
Warp and woof, 20
Westminster Confession
of Faith, 95, 99
Wisdom, 123-24; of God,
43; of other Christians,
134-35; world's, 204-7
Women's liberation
movement, 16
Word of God, authority
of the, 204-7; holding
firm the, 163; knowl-
edge of the, 240-41
Word studies, baptō and
baptizō, 103-6; chairein,
74; charisma, 117; dokeō,
91-92; ekklēsia, 60-61;
episcopos, 157; "flock"
and "fold," 66; koinonia,
166; petros, 64; "wor-
ship," 91-92
Work of the ministry,
141-43
Worship, and feelings,
93; Christocentric, 96-
97; how to, 87-97;
principles of, 88-91;
truthful, 95-97;
unacceptable, 90; with
the body, 93
Wrath, God's, 182-83
Zechariah, 51

SCRIPTURE INDEX

Genesis
1—*34*
2:16-17—*109*
2:17—*255*
2:18—*18*
3:15—*191-92*
4:20-22—*193*
4:23-24—*193*
4:26—*89*
4 and 5—*192*
5—*193*
5:8-9—*266*
11—*262*
12:1—*262*
12:1-2—*61*
12:1-3—*21*
12:8—*62*
15:6—*62*
15:13-14, 18—*62*
15:18-21—*262*
17:4, 7-8—*62*
25:8, 17—*265*
35:29—*265*
49:33—*265*

Exodus
3:7-8—*62*
5:1—*22*
20:1-17—*22*
20:3-4—*89*
31:3-5—*118*
40—*77*

Numbers
20:24—*265*
27:12-13—*265*

Deuteronomy
6:13—*88*
9:10—*61*
10:4—*61*
11, 27, 28—*22*
18:16—*61*
34:6—*266*

2 Samuel
7:12-16—*22*
12:22-23—*266*

Psalms
22:22, 25—*61*
24:8, 10—*91-92*
33:10-11—*39*
51:16-17—*91*
77:20—*144*

Isaiah
1:11-17—*90*
21:4—*104*
45:7—*39*
61:1-2—*142*

Jeremiah
16:14-15—*62*
50:6—*182*

Ezekiel
9:4, 6—*107*
18:4—*109*

Daniel
1:2—*195*
2:20-21—*240*
2:47—*200*
4:30—*198*
4:31-33—*199*
4:34-35—*39, 200*
4:37—*200*
5:21—*39*
9:27—*249*

Amos
5:21-24—*90*

Matthew
1:21—*52*
1:23—*182*
4:10—*88*
6:6—*89*
6:9-10—*33*
6:10—*213*
8:11—*267*
13:15—*17*
14:13-21—*154*
15:8, 18-19—*17*
15:32-39—*154*
16:13-21—*63*
16:18—*63*
16:21-23—*65*
22:17, 21—*230*
25:13—*259*
25:24-25, 30, 45—*260*
25:34-40—*156*
26:17-30—*108*
26:18—*23*
28:18—*56*
28:18-20—*103, 180, 235*
28:19-20—*123*
28:20—*69*

Mark
7:6-7—*90, 95*
7:24-30—*154*
8:31—*52*
8:38—*250*
9:31—*52*
9:49—*175*
10:45—*141*
13:26-27—*250*
14:12-26—*108*
14:22—*112*

14:24—*110*
14:26—*100*
16:15-16—*179*
16:16—*105*

Luke
1:46-55—*50*
1:51—*17*
1:67-80—*51*
2:10-11—*74*
3:16—*175*
4:18-19—*142*
6:21-22—*25*
8:26-39—*154*
9:33—*267*
15—*183*
16:15—*78*
16:23—*267*
17:21—*213*
22:7-23—*108*
24:21—*54*
24:25-27—*53*
24:45-48—*179*

John
1:1—*55*
1:12—*105*
2:4—*23, 53*
3:3—*200*
3:16—*43, 86*
3:18—*183*
4:23—*88*
4:24—*92*
5:30—*43*
6:38—*43, 164*
7:30—*23, 53*
8:20—*23, 53*
8:29—*164*
8:32—*142*
9—*142-43*
10:4—*147*
10:7-10—*23*
10:11—*122, 145*
10:16—*66*
12:23—*23, 53*
12:27—*53*
12:32—*52*
13:1—*23, 53*
13:15—*171*
13:34-35—*84,*

169
13:35—*68*
14:1-3—*261-62*
14:3—*250*
14:6—*96*
14:16-17—*69*
14:16-18—*214*
14:27—*69*
15:3—*214*
15:11—*74, 78*
15:12, 17—*169*
16:32—*23*
17—*73, 77, 79,
84, 86, 89*
17:1—*23, 53*
17:4—*43*
17:13—*74, 78*
17:15-17—*75*
17:17—*78, 95,
214*
17:18-19—*80, 82*
17:19—*77*
17:20-23—*82*
17:21, 23—*84*
17:24—*55*
17:26—*84*
19:7—*232*
19:8—*239*
19:10—*232*
19:11—*232, 234*
19:12—*238*
19:15—*236*
20:21—*179*
21:15-17—*144*
21:21—*251*

Acts
1:8—*68, 179*
2:1-11—*129*
2:3—*175*
2:9-11—*165*
2:42—*68*
4:4—*68*
4:11-12—*64*
4:19-20—*235*
5:3, 9—*127*
5:28-32—*235*
6:1-6—*151*
6:7—*124*
7:38—*61*

8:5, 26-40—*155*
13:8—*124*
14:22—*124*
14:23—*140*
17:31—*258*
20:28—*157-59*
21:8—*155*
23:26—*74*
24:25—*23*

Romans
1:7—*77*
1:18—*183*
1:24—*17*
2:5—*17*
3:10-12—*109*
4:21—*125*
6—*107*
6:3-4—*106*
6:5, 11—*107*
6:23—*109*
8:28—*39*
10:3—*76*
10:8—*124*
12:4-5—*116*
12:6-8—*121, 123*
12:7-8—*128*
12:13—*161*
13:7—*230*
13:8—*169*
15:14—*174*
16:1—*160*

1 Corinthians
1:2—*77*
2:2—*260*
8:6—*56*
10:1-2—*106*
10:31-33—*163*
11:23-28—*108*
11:25—*110*
11:28-29—*111*
12—*129*
12:3-11—*130*
12:4-6—*84, 116*
12:7—*119*
12:8-9—*123*
12:8-10—*121,
124, 126*
12:8-11—*130*

12:10—*127*
12:11—*116, 118*
12:12-27—
130-31
12:27—*23*
12:28—*128,
131*
12:28-30—*121,
123, 126*
12:28—14:12—
131
13—*131*
13:12—*79*
13:13—*84*
14—*121, 129*
14:1—*131*
14:13-38—*131*
14:19—*131*
14:39—*126, 132*
15:22—*107*
15:26—*253*
15:28—*56*
15:54, 57—*255`*

2 Corinthians
1:1—*77*
3:18—*69*
5:8—*264*
5:13, 20—*185*
5:14-15—*183*
5:18—*71*
5:19—*42*
6:2—*25*

Galatians
3:27—*105*
4:4-5—*47*
5—*89*
5:13—*170*
5:22—*124*
5:22-23—*162*
6:2—*171*
6:10—*154*

Ephesians
1:1—*77*
1:23—*23*
2:8—*124*
2:12—*182*
2:13—*54*

2:14—*71*
2:14-15—*166*
2:19—*116, 166*
3:8-10—*59*
4:1-3—*172*
4:4-6—*116*
4:7, 11-12—*116*
4:11—*121-22*
4:11-13—*138*
4:12—*118*
4:13—*144*
4:15-16—*166*
4:30—*107*
4:31-32—*172*
5:16—*223*
6:12—*229*
6:16—*124*

Philippians
1:1—*77*
2:9ff.—*56*
2:15—*191*
3:3—*89*
3:10—*107*
3:20-21—*251*
4:4—*74*

Colossians
1:16—*56*
1:18—*23*
2:15—*230*
3:12-13—*172*
4:5-6—*163*

1 Thessalonians
3:12—*170*

4:9—*170*
4:11-12—*163*
4:13—*214*
4:16-17—*251*
4:18—*174, 253*

1 Timothy
2:1-2—*230*
2:12—*161*
3:1—*157, 164*
3:1-7—*152, 160, 163*
3:1-13—*141*
3:2—*152, 160-61*
3:3—*162*
3:4—*160*
3:6-7—*162*
3:8-13—*152*

2 Timothy
2:19—*108*
3:1-5—*163, 211*

Titus
1:5—*141*
1:5-9—*141, 152, 160*
1:6-7—*160*
1:7—*157, 162*
1:8—*161, 163*
1:9—*152, 163*
2:13—*251*

Hebrews
1:2, 10ff.—*55*

10:4—*110*
11:1—*124*
11:4—*192*
11:5—*193-94*
11:7—*194*
11:9-10—*200*
11:10—*262*
11:13—*125*
11:26—*269*
12:14—*75*
13:2—*161*
13:20—*122*

James
1:17—*118*
5:16—*172, 174*

1 Peter
1:3—*251*
1:11—*23*
1:20—*55*
2:4-6—*65*
2:9—*75, 177*
2:10—*24*
2:12—*163*
4:9—*161*
4:10—*119*
4:11—*121, 128*
5:1-4—*152, 158*
5:2-3—*140*
5:4—*122*

1 John
1:3—*18, 167*
1:6-7—*167*
3:2—*79, 268*

3:3—*85, 270*
3:11, 23—*170*
3:17-18—*170*
4:1-6—*127*
4:7, 11-12—*170*
4:17—*73*

2 John
5—*170*

3 John
9-10—*139*
10—*161*

Jude
11—*193*

Revelation
1:7—*251*
3:20—*105*
5:9-10, 12-13—*263*
5:13-14—*89*
7:17—*79*
17—18—*230*
18:2—*194*
19:10—*88*
20:11-15—*183*
21:2—*194, 213*
21:3—*199, 214*
21:4—*79, 214*
21:22—*199*
21:27—*214*
22:12—*269*
22:20—*251*